John Traug
1041 N Sunnys
Decatur, IL 625

10695773

101 MORE
HYMN STORIES

Books by Kenneth W. Osbeck
(published by Kregel Publications)

Amazing Grace: 366 Hymn Stories for Personal Devotions
Devotional Warm-ups for the Church Choir
52 Bible Characters Dramatized
52 Hymn Stories Dramatized
The Ministry of Music
My Music Workbook
101 Hymn Stories
101 More Hymn Stories
Pocket Guide for the Church Choir Member

101 MORE HYMN STORIES

Kenneth W. Osbeck

Foreword by
Cliff Barrows

kregel
PUBLICATIONS

Grand Rapids, MI 49501

101 More Hymn Stories by Kenneth W. Osbeck.

Copyright © 1985 and published by Kregel Publications, a division of Kregel, Inc. P.O. Box 2607 Grand Rapids, MI 49501. All rights reserved. No portion of this work may be reproduced in any form whatsoever without written permission from the publisher, except in the case of brief quotations embodied in articles or reviews.

Library of Congress Cataloging-in-Publication Data
Osbeck, Kenneth W.
   101 More Hymn Stories.
   Includes bibliography
     p. cm.
   Includes index.
   1. Hymns, English—History and criticism. I. Title.
II. Title: One Hundred One More Hymn Stories. III. Title:
One Hundred and One More Hymn Stories.
ML3186.0855   1985   783.9'09   84-27847
                                                    CIP

ISBN 0-8254-3420-3

     10 11 12 13 Printing/Year 99 98 97

Printed in the United States of America

CONTENTS

Contents

Contents

DEDICATION

Affectionately dedicated to my wife, Betty.

FOREWORD

In reviewing church history, it is clearly evident that great congregational singing has usually accompanied great preaching and the stirrings of God upon people. All major revivals and spiritual awakenings have witnessed a renewed response in sacred song. This was true of the Protestant Reformation Movement during the sixteenth century, the seventeenth century Pietistic Renewals, the evangelistic ministries of such stalwarts as the Wesleys in the eighteenth century, and the revival fires that fanned America and Europe during the nineteenth century.

What is behind the hymns that are sung in our churches and mass meetings? One noticeable feature of a church that is alive is its congregational singing. This form of worship to the Lord has lifted many a heart from a spirit of lethargy to one of jubilance and praise.

In my own experience with the Billy Graham Association during nearly four decades, I have been impressed many times with the importance of music — especially congregational singing — in the furtherance of the gospel. There can be little disagreement with the claim that next to the Bible itself, the hymnal is a book of primary importance in the Christian ministry.

It is for this reason that I heartily commend Ken Osbeck's latest book of hymn backgrounds, *101 More Hymn Stories*. A view of God's touch upon a poet or musician's life with a resultant musical expression that can often be used by multitudes for several centuries is certainly worthy of every believer's consideration. This is a book that can be used to enrich personal and family devotions. Also, I would consider it a must for every pastor and leader of congregational singing.

It is my prayer that God will use this fine book along with Ken Osbeck's other companion book, *101 Hymn Stories*, to bless and inspire the lives of individual believers, to heighten our congregational singing in corporate worship, and then to prepare us for an eternity of singing the praises of our great God.

Billy Graham Evangelistic Association
Editor of *Crusade Hymn Stories*

CLIFF BARROWS

PREFACE

"God sent His singers upon the earth
With songs of sadness and of mirth,
That they might touch the hearts of men,
And bring them back to heaven again."
"The Singers" by Longfellow

The visiting of church structures, both large and small, has always been one of my traveling delights. After observing the distinctive architectural characteristics and aesthetic features of a new sanctuary, I generally find myself browsing through the local church hymnal. I never cease to marvel at this one spiritual activity that churches of every branch of Christendom have in common around the world — voicing many of the same expressions of worship, praise and human concern. Experience has confirmed the conviction that next to the Bible, the hymnal is man's most important aid in the worship of the Almighty. Or, as another has observed, "Hymns are a rich deposit of Christian devotion, echoing the adoration of heaven and uplifting the faithful on earth who make their discovery."

The response from the first book of *101 Hymn Stories* has been rewarding. It has been gratifying to hear reports from many Christians that they have "rediscovered" their church hymnal. A short time ago, I received a call from a newly-retired Christian couple who said they were having one of the finest times of their lives by simply visiting several nursing homes each day, relating to the residents the stories from the *101 Hymn Stories*, the experiences that prompted the writing of a particular song, and getting these older folks to sing favorite hymns. Numerous pastors mention that they have found meaningful sermon illustrations from these hymn stories. There have also been comments from individuals, who have allowed themselves to become careless about church attendance, who have said that reading this book has been a reminder of the many songs they once sang as young people in Sunday School; and it has brought spiritual conviction and renewal to their lives.

It is my prayer that God will continue to use the inspiration and information behind these *101 More Hymn Stories* to deepen and broaden our worship and praise of Himself. I have tried to give a variety of hymn styles in this volume, including more twentieth century gospel hymnody as well as the enduring favorites of the past. Together let us strive to make our church services times of optimum spiritual blessing through meaningful and vital congregational singing. May we who have been entrusted with the leadership of God's people renew our concern for the "assembling of ourselves together... exhorting (encouraging) one another, and so much the more, as we see the day approaching" (Hebrews 10:25).

Allow me to offer these simple suggestions. The next time you open your church hymnal in a public service to lift your voice in praise, take a few extra moments for personal spiritual enrichment by noting thoughtfully the words you sing. When possible, make an effort to learn something further of the experiences that prompted the writing of each hymn. The hymnal can also be an excellent aid in one's own, daily, personal devotional life. Then perhaps God has given you a talent for expressing spiritual feelings and truths with words and music. May I encourage you to use and develop this gift. It is my conviction that the hymnal should be an ever-developing book, so that the spiritual experiences that prompted these expressions of the past should be occurring in our lives today, producing new statements of the ageless truths. Finally, keep a good hymnal on your home piano, so that you can enjoy informal times of singing and discussing favorite hymns with family and friends. It has often been said that a believer's practical theology may well be his hymnology.

Hymns breathe the praise of the saints, the vision of the prophets,
The prayers of the penitent and the spirit of the martyrs.

They bring solace to the sad, assurance to the perplexed,
Faith to the doubter and comfort to the oppressed.

They span the centuries of history and bridge the barriers of denominations.

Study them to be pure in heart, Sing them to be joyful in spirit,
Store them in the mind to possess a treasury of worship.

It has not been possible to determine the authorship or source of all the material used in this book. Grateful acknowledgment is hereby proffered to the various authors, publishers, and copyright owners whose cooperation and help have made this volume possible.

"Praise ye the Lord: for it is good to sing praises unto our God; for it is pleasant; and praise is comely" (Psalm 147:1).

Kenneth W. Osbeck

Note: When the author mentions a hymn number i.e. (No. _____), he refers to a song story in this volume. When he mentions *101 Hymn Stories* No. _____ or *ibid*, No. _____ , he refers to that number in the earlier volume, *101 Hymn Stories* by Kenneth W. Osbeck.

1

A Charge to Keep I Have

BOYLSTON

Charles Wesley, 1707-1788-alt.

Lowell Mason, 1792-1872

1. A charge to keep I have— A God to glo - ri - fy,
2. To serve the pres - ent age, My call - ing to ful - fill—
3. Arm me with jeal - ous care, As in Thy sight to live;
4. Help me to watch and pray, And on Thy - self re - ly;

Who gave His Son my soul to save And fit it for the sky.
O may it all my pow'rs en - gage To do my Mas - ter's will!
And O Thy serv - ant, Lord, pre - pare A strict ac - count to give!
And let me ne'er my trust be - tray, But press to realms on high.

A Charge to Keep I Have

13

Author—Charles Wesley, 1707-1788
Composer—Lowell Mason, 1792-1872
Tune Name—"Boylston"
Meter—SM (66.86)
Scripture Reference—Leviticus 8:35

> I therefore, the prisoner of the Lord, beseech you that ye walk worthy of the vocation wherewith ye are called.
> Ephesians 4:1

One of the most powerful evangelizing influences England ever experienced was the Methodist hymnody, begun by John and Charles Wesley, in the 18th century. The 6,500 hymns of Charles were written on every phase of Christian experience and Methodist theology. Both of these brothers believed strongly in the spiritual potential of music and congregational singing. They used their hymns to "arouse sinners, encourage saints, and to educate all in the mysteries of the Christian faith." In 1780, the Wesleys published a comprehensive hymnal comprising their many hymns that had been used for fifty years. This hymnal was titled *A Collection of Hymns for the Use of the People Called Methodists*. John Wesley wrote a preface in which he summed up its purpose:

> Large enough to contain all the important truths of our most holy religion. . . . In what other publication of this time have you so full and distinct an account

of Scriptural Christianity? Such a declaration of the heights and depths of religion, speculative and practical? So strong cautions against the most plausible errors? And so clear directions for making our calling and election sure: For perfecting holiness in the fear of God.

Charles Wesley is said to have been inspired to write the text for this hymn while reading Matthew Henry's commentary on the Book of Leviticus. In his thoughts on Leviticus 8:35, Henry wrote, "We shall everyone of us have a charge to keep, an eternal God to glorify, an immortal soul to provide for, one generation to serve." This hymn text first appeared in Wesley's *Short Hymns on Select Passages of Holy Scriptures,* Volume One, 1762. It was printed under the title "Keep the Charge of the Lord, That Ye Die Not." It is one of sixteen hymn texts by Charles Wesley based on the Book of Leviticus.

John and Charles Wesley often incurred much opposition and persecution in their ministry for God. Sometimes this mob opposition was inflamed by the local Anglican clergymen, who would go from house to house, charging that the Wesleys were preaching blasphemy against the established church and hence should be run out of town. In his book, *The Gospel in Hymns,* Albert Edward Bailey gives this account:

14

> If it was hard on the preachers, it was worse on the converts. They were outrageously treated — stoned, mauled, ducked, hounded with bulldogs, threatened, homes looted, businesses ruined. Anyone who walked through a town could pick out, by their ruinous condition, the homes where the Methodists lived.

This hymn text reflects the strength of these early Methodists. John Wesley once remarked upon hearing of his followers' persecution: "Our people die well." On another occasion a physician said to Charles Wesley, "Most people die for fear of dying; but I never met with such people as yours. They are none of them afraid of death, but calm and patient and resigned to the last."

Charles Wesley is also the author of the hymns "Depth of Mercy" (No. 20) and "Hark! The Herald Angels Sing" (No. 31). Other Charles Wesley hymns include: "Christ the Lord Is Risen Today" (*101 Hymn Stories,* No. 13), "Jesus, Lover of My Soul" (*ibid.,* No. 45), and "O for a Thousand Tongues" (*ibid.,* No. 65).

The tune "Boylston" was composed for this text by the American educator and musician, Lowell Mason. Boylston is the name of a street in Boston as well as a town in Massachusetts. The tune was first used with this text in the *Unison Collection of Church Music,* published in 1832. This hymn was a favorite with the campground meetings, especially popular in this country during the latter half of the nineteenth century.

Lowell Mason, often called the "Father of American Church and Public School Music", was born on January 8, 1792, in Medfield, Massachusetts. He spent his early life in Savannah, Georgia. In 1827, he moved to Boston and while residing there founded the Boston Academy of Music for the purpose of reaching and teaching the masses with music. In 1838, Mason was instrumental in formally introducing music education into the public school curriculum in Boston. Later, Lowell Mason made a trip to Europe to study teaching methods there. Upon his return to this country, he began promoting musical conventions, which had wide acceptance and influence. In 1851, Mason moved to New York City, where he began publishing hymnals and choral collections. In all, Lowell Mason is credited with composing and arranging approximately 700 hymn tunes, including such well-known hymns as: "From Greenland's Icy Mountains" (*101 Hymn Stories*, No. 25), "Nearer My God to Thee" (*ibid.*, No. 61), and "When I Survey the Wondrous Cross" (*ibid.*, No. 100). In 1855, New York University conferred upon Mason the degree of Doctor of Music, the first such degree ever granted by an American school.

Lowell Mason is also the arranger for the Christmas carol "Joy to the World" (No. 52) and the hymn "O Day of Rest and Gladness" (No. 66) and is the composer of the hymn "My Faith Looks Up to Thee" (No. 60).

* * *

"The Divine-Human Cooperative: God will never do what I can do — He only does what I cannot do."

W. W. Welch

"Awake, my soul! Stretch every nerve,
And press with vigor on;
A heavenly race demands thy zeal,
And an immortal crown."

Philip Doddridge

QUIT YOU LIKE MEN
"Quit you like men, be strong;
There's a burden to bear,
There's a grief to share,
There's a heart that breaks 'neath a load of care —
But fare ye forth with a song.

"Quit you like men, be strong;
There's work to do,
There's a world to make new;
There's a call for men who are brave and true —
On! on with the song!"

William Herbert Hudnut

2 A Shelter in the Time of Storm

Vernon J. Charlesworth, 1838-?

Ira D. Sankey, 1840-1908

1. The Lord's our Rock, in Him we hide— A shel-ter in the time of storm;
2. A shade by day, de-fense by night— A shel-ter in the time of storm;
3. The rag-ing storms may round us beat— A shel-ter in the time of storm;
4. O Rock di-vine, O Ref-uge dear— A shel-ter in the time of storm;

Se - cure what-ev - er ill be - tide— A shel-ter in the time of storm.
No fears a - larm, no foes af-fright— A shel-ter in the time of storm.
We'll nev-er leave our safe re-treat— A shel-ter in the time of storm.
Be Thou our help-er ev - er near— A shel-ter in the time of storm.

16

CHORUS

O Je-sus is a Rock in a wea-ry land, A wea-ry land, a wea-ry land;

O Je-sus is a Rock in a wea-ry land— A shel-ter in the time of storm.

A Shelter in the Time of Storm

Author—Vernon J. Charlesworth, 1838-? with Alteration
Composer—Ira D. Sankey, 1840-1908
Scripture Reference—Psalm 94:22

> Thou art my hiding place; Thou shalt preserve me from trouble; Thou shalt compass me about with songs of deliverance.   Psalm 32:7

Ira D. Sankey's influence on modern gospel hymnody is difficult to measure. It would be almost impossible to complete an evangelistic campaign or a Bible conference today without using at least one hymn written, published, or made popular by him. In all, Sankey contributed his musical talents to the writing of more than eighty gospel songs as well as compiling more than ten hymnbooks and other musical volumes. Toward the end of his life, Sankey became aware that his name was appearing on too many songs, so he began using a pseudonym. The one he chose was Rian A. Dykes, a name which appeared on a number of his hymns. The letters for this pseudonym when rearranged spell Ira D. Sankey.

Ira Sankey was born of Scotch-Irish ancestry. In 1857, his family moved to Newcastle, Pennsylvania, where he attended high school and joined the Methodist Church. Here he began his first choir work and music ministry. His strong baritone voice soon attracted such attention that crowds would come just to hear him sing.

In 1860, Sankey enlisted in the 12th Pennsylvania Regiment. While in the army, he frequently led the singing for religious services; however, the idea of devoting his life to the music ministry did not seem feasible to him. Upon his return from the service, he became a clerk with the Internal Revenue Service.

In 1870, Ira Sankey was sent as a delegate to the Y.M.C.A. convention at Indianapolis, Indiana, where he met, for the first time, the noted evangelist, Dwight L. Moody. The group singing during the meetings had been extremely poor. Finally, the suggestion was made to have Mr. Sankey lead. Immediately, there was a new spirit and enthusiasm injected into the gathering. Sankey has left the following account of this initial meeting with the evangelist:

> As I drew near Mr. Moody, he stepped forward, took me by the hand, and looked at me with that keen, piercing fashion of his, as if reading my very soul. Then he said abruptly, "Where are you from?" "Pennsylvania", I replied. "Are you married?" "I am." "How many children do you have?" "Two." "What is your business?" "I am a government officer." "Well, you'll have to give it up!" I was much too astonished to make any reply, and he went on speaking as if the matter had already been decided. "I have been

17

looking for you the last eight years. You'll have to come to Chicago and help me in my work.''

After several months of prayerful indecision, Sankey resigned his government position and moved to Chicago with his family to begin his fruitful ministry with the evangelist and later to become known as the ''Father of the Gospel Song.'' For nearly thirty years, Sankey and Moody were inseparable in the work of the gospel, both in this country and throughout Great Britain. Sankey's smooth, cultured ways complemented and compensated for Moody's rough manner, poor grammar and impulsiveness. They were often referred to as the ''David and Jonathan of the Gospel Ministry.''

Though Ira D. Sankey had little or no professional voice training, his voice was described as an exceptionally ''strong baritone of moderate compass.'' An English newspaper once wrote the following review:

> As a vocalist, Mr. Sankey has not many equals. Possessed of a voice of great volume and richness, he expresses with exquisite skill and pathos the gospel message, in words very simple but replete with love and tenderness, and always with marked effect on the audience. It is, however, altogether a mistake to suppose that the blessing which attends Mr. Sankey's efforts is attributed only or chiefly to his fine voice and artistic expression. They, no doubt, are very attractive, and go far to move the affections and gratify the taste for music; but the secret of Mr. Sankey's power lies not in his gift of song but in the spirit of which the song is only the expression.

18

Another writer commented as follows regarding Sankey's manner of singing:

> There was something about his baritone voice that was enormously affecting. He had a way of pausing between lines of the song, and in that pause the vast audience remained absolutely silent.

Generally, Sankey accompanied himself on a small reed organ, singing simply but with careful enunciation and much feeling and emotion. Often, however, there was an intense opposition to his ''human composure hymns'' and the use of an organ in a service, especially in the meetings in Scotland. Here some of the staunch, conservative Presbyterian Scots spoke of Sankey's ''kist of whistles'' and how they believed that there was a devil in each pipe of that organ. Moody often tried to relieve the tension by explaining to the audiences that Sankey's organ was only a ''very small one,'' and besides that, he would add, ''the Psalms were written under the old dispensation and really not meant for people to sing under the new dispensation.'' This argument would amuse and soothe some, but it did not always satisfy all. Though there were great numbers of individuals converted to Christ in these meetings in Scotland, many of these believers still found it difficult to accept the new type of rhythmic gospel music employed by Sankey. The story is told of one meeting in which Sankey had just started a solo when a woman's shrill voice rang from the gallery as she made her way toward the door, crying: "Let me oot! Let me oot! What would John Knox think of the like of you?" This women's abhorrence of gospel music was not hers alone. What she expressed was felt by many of the older Scottish Christians. Another story is told of a troubled Scot who visited his pastor after hearing Sankey sing and said: "I cannot do with those hymns. They are all the time in my head, and I cannot get them out. The Psalms never trouble me that way." The wise pastor replied, "Very well, then, I think you should keep the hymns."

"A Shelter in the Time of Storm" was one of the typical easily sung, rhythmical songs that Sankey used extensively in these campaigns. As the meetings progressed throughout the British Isles, Sankey and his gospel music became increasingly respected and accepted. The following paragraph appeared in one of the British papers near the close of the meetings:

> Mr. Moody is very fortunate in having such a colleague as Mr. Sankey. He has enriched evangelistic work by something approaching the discovery of a new power. He spoils the Egyptians of their finest music, and consecrates it to the service of the tabernacle. Music in his hands is, more than it has yet been, the handmaid of the gospel and the voice of the heart. We have seen many stirred and melted by his singing, before a word has been spoken. Indeed, his singing is just a powerful, distinct, and heart-toned way of speaking, that seems often to reach the heart by a short cut, when mere speaking might lose the road.

19

Not only is Ira Sankey regarded as America's most influential, evangelistic musician, but he is also noted for his publishing and promotion of gospel music. His *Sacred Songs and Solos*, published in England, sold more than eight million copies and is still in print. Also, in collaboration with Philip P. Bliss and other gospel musicians of that time, he produced such popular works as *Gospel Hymns and Sacred Songs* (1875), *Gospel Hymns No. 2* (1876), No. 3 (1878), No. 4 (1883), No. 5 (1887), No. 6 (1892), and the entire collected *Gospel Hymns, Nos. 1-6* (1894). The royalties and profits from these publications did much to finance the various campaigns conducted by Moody and Sankey.

Other popular gospel hymns by Ira D. Sankey include: "Trusting Jesus" (No. 93), "Hiding in Thee" (*101 Hymn Stories*, No. 29), and "The Ninety and Nine" (*ibid.*, No. 91). Additional popular hymns contributed by Sankey are "Under His Wings I Am Safely Abiding," "For You I Am Praying," and "Faith Is the Victory."

The text for "A Shelter in the Time of Storm" was written by an English pastor, Vernon J. Charlesworth. In 1869, Charlesworth was appointed headmaster of Charles Spurgeon's Stockwell Orphanage. In 1885, Ira Sankey copyrighted the text with his music and the refrain, which he added, and titled the new hymn "My God Is the Rock of My Refuge" based on Psalm 94:22:

> But the Lord is my defense; and my God is the rock of my refuge.

Sankey included this hymn in his publications of *Sacred Songs and Solos*, as well as in *Gospel Hymns No. 5*. In his book, *My Life and the Story of the Gospel Hymns*, Sankey has written this account regarding "A Shelter in the Time of Storm:"

> I found this hymn in a small paper published in London, called "The Postman." It was said to be a favorite song of the fishermen on the north coast of England, and they were often heard singing it, as they approached their harbors in the time of storm. As the hymn was set to a weird minor tune, I decided to compose one that could more easily be sung by the people.

20   *   *   *

"To realize the worth of the anchor, we need to feel the wrath of the storm."

Unknown

"I never met with a single instance of adversity which I have not in the end seen was for my good. I have never heard of a Christian on his deathbed complaining of his afflictions."

Alexander M. Proudfit

"As sure as God puts His children into the furnace of affliction, He will be with them in it."

Charles Haddon Spurgeon

FEAR TOMORROW?
"I do not fear tomorrow!
For I have lived today;
And though my course was stormy,
My Pilot knew the way.

"I do not fear tomorrow!
If the sails set east or west;
On sea or safe in harbor,
In Him, secure, I rest."

Phyllis Michael

3   According to Thy Gracious Word

James Montgomery, 1771-1854   From the "Greatorex Collection," 1851

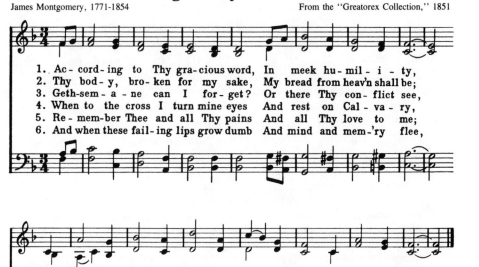

1. Ac - cord - ing to Thy gra - cious word, In meek hu - mil - i - ty,
2. Thy bod - y, bro - ken for my sake, My bread from heav'n shall be;
3. Geth-sem - a - ne can I for - get? Or there Thy con - flict see,
4. When to the cross I turn mine eyes And rest on Cal - va - ry,
5. Re - mem-ber Thee and all Thy pains And all Thy love to me;
6. And when these fail - ing lips grow dumb And mind and mem -'ry flee,

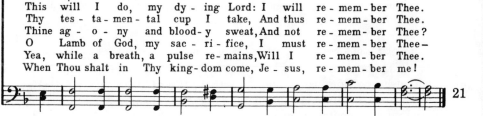

This will I do, my dy - ing Lord: I will re - mem - ber Thee.
Thy tes - ta - men - tal cup I take, And thus re - mem - ber Thee.
Thine ag - o - ny and blood - y sweat, And not re - mem - ber Thee?
O Lamb of God, my sac - ri - fice, I must re - mem - ber Thee—
Yea, while a breath, a pulse re - mains, Will I re - mem - ber Thee.
When Thou shalt in Thy king - dom come, Je - sus, re - mem - ber me!

According to Thy Gracious Word

Author—James Montgomery, 1771-1854
Music—From the "Greatorex Collection," 1851
Tune Name—"Manoah"
Meter—CM (86.86)
Scripture Reference—Luke 22:19

> For as often as ye eat this bread, and drink this cup, ye do show the Lord's death till
> He come.   1 Corinthians 11:26

Many students of hymnody feel that one of the most noteworthy communion hymns found in the church hymnal is "According to Thy Gracious Word" by James Montgomery. The text recounts vividly the sacrificial atonement of Christ and the believer's response to Christ's command in Luke 22:19—"This do in remembrance of Me."

It is generally agreed that except for Isaac Watts and Charles Wesley, no writer has made a greater contribution to English hymnody than James Montgomery. He wrote approximately 400 hymns with nearly one-fourth of these still in use today. Several other well-known hymns by Montgomery that are still widely sung include: "Angels From the Realms of Glory" (*101 Hymn Stories*, No. 7), "In the Hour of Trial," and "Prayer Is the Soul's Sincere Desire." John Julian, noted authority of hymnology, has written the following tribute to James Montgomery:

> His poetic genius was of a high order, higher than most who stand with him in the front rank of poets. His ear for rhythm was exceedingly accurate and refined. His knowledge of Holy Scripture was most extensive. His religious views were broad and charitable. His devotional spirit was of the holiest type. With the faith of a strong man, he united the beauty and simplicity of a child. Richly poetic without exuberance, dogmatic without uncharitableness, tender without sentimentality, elaborate without diffusiveness, richly musical without apparent effort, he has bequeathed to the Church of Christ wealth which could only have come from a true genius and a sanctified heart.

James Montgomery was born at Irvine, Ayrshire, Scotland, on November 4, 1771, and died on April 30, 1854, in Sheffield, York, England. His parents were Moravian missionaries to the West Indies. After a brief time in an English Moravian seminary, James was dismissed because of his preoccupation with writing poetry. Eventually, he became interested in newspaper writing and editing and soon became editor of the radical *Sheffield Register* newspaper in London: the paper's name was changed later to the *Sheffield Iris*. As editor of this paper, Montgomery championed many humanitarian causes such as the abolition of slavery. He was always ready to assist the poor and defend the down-trodden and was twice imprisoned for writing on controversial issues. In 1797, he published a volume of poems called *Prison Amusements*, so named from the fact that many of these works had been written in prison. In time, however, his integrity and worth were recognized and he was even awarded an annual pension by the British government as a reward for his contribution to society.

Other causes which James Montgomery championed were the singing of hymns in the Anglican worship service as well as a concern for foreign missions. He is said to have been one of the first English hymnists to sound the note for world evangelism. He never forgot that his own parents had given their lives in bringing the gospel to the natives of the West Indies. Montgomery was also a strong promoter of the British Bible Society.

Montgomery's hymns were published in three separate collections: *Songs of Zion* (1822), *The Christian Psalmist* (1825), and *Original Hymns for Public, Private, and Social Devotion* (1853). "According to Thy Gracious Word" was first published in the 1825 collection. James Montgomery is also the author of the Christmas carol "Angels From the Realms of Glory" (*101 Hymn Stories*, No. 7).

The tune "Manoah" first appeared in Henry W. Greatorex's *Collection of Church Music*, published in Hartford, Connecticut, in 1851. The tune name does not seem to have any special significance, although in Scripture, Manoah was the father of Samson. Greatorex was born in Derbyshire, England, December 24, 1813. He came to the United States, in 1839, and served as organist in a number of eastern city churches. His 1851 collection contained thirty-seven of his original tunes and arrangements. He is also noted for his musical setting of the well-known "Gloria Patri."

* * *

"Here, O my Lord, I see Thee face to face,
Here would I touch and handle things unseen,
Here grasp with firmer hand eternal grace,
And all my weariness upon Thee lean.

"Here would I feed upon the bread of God,
Here drink with Thee the royal wine of heav'n,
Here would I lay aside each earthly load,
Here taste afresh the calm of sin forgiv'n.

"I have no help but Thine, nor do I need
Another arm save Thine to lean upon:
It is enough, my Lord, enough indeed —
My strength is in Thy might, Thy might alone.

"Mine is the sin, but Thine the righteousness,
Mine is the guilt, but Thine the cleansing blood:
Here is my robe, my refuge, and my peace,
Thy blood, Thy righteousness, O Lord, my God."

Horatius Bonar

23

4 After

N. B. Vandall, 1896-1970

N. B. Vandall, 1896-1970

1. Aft-er the toil and the heat of the day, Aft-er my trou-bles are past,
2. Aft-er the heart-aches and sighing shall cease, Aft-er the cold win-ter's blast,
3. Aft-er the shad-ows of evening shall fall, Aft-er my an-chor is cast,

Aft-er the sor-rows are tak-en a-way, I shall see Je-sus at last.
Aft-er the con-flict comes glo-ri-ous peace— I shall see Je-sus at last.
Aft-er I list to my Sav-ior's last call, I shall see Je-sus at last.

REFRAIN

He will be wait-ing for me—   Je-sus, so kind and true;   On His
            for me—   so kind and true;

beau-ti-ful throne, He will wel-come me home— Aft-er the day is through.

© Copyright 1934. Renewal 1961 by N. B. Vandall. Assigned to Singspiration, Inc. All rights reserved. Used by permission.

24

After

Author and Composer—N. B. Vandall, 1896-1970

   . . . weeping may endure for a night, but joy cometh in the morning. Psalm 30:5

   The anticipation of eternal glory is a very real and meaningful prospect for every child of God. The Scriptures have much to say about heaven. Many of our great hymns inspire and motivate us with this truth; and, with the Apostle Paul, we would have to conclude that without this hope, we would be of all men most miserable.

N. B. Vandall, a veteran gospel evangelist and singer, has composed a number of favorite gospel songs that have been widely sung by Christians everywhere. Two other popular songs of his are "My Home, Sweet Home" and "My Sins Are Gone." Like so many gospel hymns, "After" was forged out of a deep soul experience. Mr. Vandall recalls vividly the experience that prompted the writing of this hymn, in 1934:

One evening several years ago, as I sat on the davenport reading the evening paper, my wife asked me to call our four boys to supper. Rather lazily, I laid the paper aside and went toward the front porch to give our usual signal whistle for them to come in from play. However, before I reached the porch, I heard children's voices screaming and crying. Rushing down the steps, I saw our second boy, Ted, running toward me. He was choking with hysteria. I had to shake him before he realized who I was.

"What's wrong, son? Here's Daddy. You're not hurt, are you? Come on, now, what's wrong?"

"Oh, Daddy!" he gasped. "I'm all right — but it's Paul!"

"Calm down now, son. What's it all about?"

Between sobs he gasped out the story. Paul, playing between the curb and the sidewalk, had been hit by a car, out of control by its driver. It had dragged him up the street. Paul had been covered with blood when taken from under the car, unable to speak.

"Oh, Daddy," sobbed Ted, "they have taken him away, and I don't know where he is."

I ran to the scene of the accident. A neighbor there said, "Yes, Mr. Vandall, it was your boy!"

We found Paul in a nearby doctor's office, still unconscious. The doctor had called an ambulance to take the boy to the hospital and was quite hopeless about his condition. The hospital doctor confirmed his fears. The boy had a brain concussion, a fractured skull, a broken leg, a shoulder misplaced, the left collar bone broken, and the left side of his head literally scalped and lost in the dirt of the street.

The surgeon, kind but frank, said, "The boy is badly hurt. We will do the best we can, but do not hope for too much."

I replied, "Doctor, I am sure you will do the very best you can, but you hold out so little hope. I am a World War veteran, having served with the Marines for almost two years, and I've seen some hard things — they said I was tough. But I'm a Christian minister now, and this is my boy and you offer no hope. Please let me stand by and hold his hand and pray while you do what has to be done."

The doctor looked me over for what seemed an eternity and then granted

25

my request. For one hour and fifteen minutes, I held on in prayer while they cleaned and sewed up the head wounds. Then we took Paul upstairs and set the broken bones. No opiates were given because of his heart condition. The doctor said, "His heart cannot stand any more and may stop at any time."

Wearily I made my way back to my humble home. I tried to comfort my wife by telling her that everything was all right, when, in my own heart, I had no assurance. I looked at the davenport where just a few hours before I had been resting and reading with no thought of trouble. I fell on my knees and tried to pray — words would not come. I remember saying only, "Oh, God!"

I am glad that we serve a God who knows our heart's cry. Hardly had those words been uttered when God came. It seemed to me that Jesus knelt by my side and I could feel His arms around me as He said, "Never mind, my child. Your home will be visited with tribulation and sorrow, but in the afterwards to come, these things shall not be. Your home is in heaven, where tears shall be wiped away."

Please do not think that I am a fanatic — but for the time, at least, I forgot my little boy lying at death's door, and brushing aside my tears, made my way to the piano and wrote the song "After."

Paul did recover from the accident. He is still very nervous and his eyesight is impaired, but I thank God for His goodness in giving him back to us. God in His wisdom, through heartache, gave a song that has been a comfort to a vast number of His people.

Many believers, like Mr. Vandall, can look back upon their lives and testify that often it was the occasion of some exceptionally stormy and difficult experience that made God's presence unusually precious to them. And though we would certainly never seek a repeat of those trying times, yet there is gratitude, that God in His providence allowed this to happen, in order that He might prove Himself to us personally, in a special way. Yet, while we enjoy our Lord's presence through all the experiences of life each day we live, we eagerly await that day, when we will be welcomed to our eternal home, by the Savior.

N. B. Vandall was born at Creston, West Virginia, on December 28, 1896. He was converted to Christ at a camp meeting in Sebring, Ohio in 1920. Mr. and Mrs. Vandall were the parents of four sons. Mr. Vandall went to be with the Lord on August 24, 1970 followed by Mrs. Vandall on February 27, 1973.

* * *

"This world is the land of the dying; the next is the land of the living."
Tryon Edwards

5   All Glory, Laud and Honor

ST. THEODOLPH

Theodolph of Orleans, 760-821
Trans. by John M. Neale, 1818-1866

Melchior Teschner, 1584-1635

1. All glo-ry, laud and hon - or To Thee, Re-deem - er, King,
2. The com-pa - ny of an - gels Are prais-ing Thee on high,
3. To Thee, be-fore Thy pas - sion, They sang their hymns of praise;

To whom the lips of chil - dren Made sweet ho - san - nas ring:
And mor-tal men and all things Cre - at - ed make re - ply:
To Thee, now high ex - alt - ed, Our mel - o - dy we raise:

Thou art the King of Is - rael, Thou Da - vid's roy - al Son,
The peo - ple of the He - brews With palms be - fore Thee went;
Thou didst ac - cept their prais - es— Ac - cept the praise we bring,

Who in the Lord's name com - est, The King and bless- ed One!
Our praise and prayer and an - thems Be - fore Thee we pre - sent.
Who in all good de - light - est, Thou good and gra - cious King!

27

All Glory, Laud and Honor

Author—Theodolph of Orleans, 760-821
English Translation—John M. Neale, 1818-1866
Composer—Melchior Teschner, 1584-1635
Tune Name—"St. Theodolph"
Meter—76.76 Doubled
Scripture References—Matthew 21:1-17; Mark 11:10; Luke 28:37,38

Blessed is the King of Israel that cometh in the name of the Lord.   John 12:13

This traditional, Palm Sunday processional hymn was very likely written about 820 A.D. by Bishop Theodolph of Orleans, France, while he was imprisoned at the monastery of Angers. Theodolph was well known in his day as a poet, pastor, and beloved bishop of Orleans. He was born in Spain of Ostrogothic parentage. He was known as a close friend of Charlemagne, the emperor who tried to revive the Roman Empire in the eighth century. Charlemagne called Theodolph to his court at Aachen, Germany, about 781, and later appointed him Bishop of Orleans. When Emperor Charlemagne died, in 814, the bishop was put into a monastic prison by Charlemagne's son and successor, Louis I the Pious, for allegedly plotting against him. A well-known legend has long been associated with this hymn. It is believed by many that a short time before the bishop's death, in 821, Louis was visiting in the area where the bishop was imprisoned and by chance passed under his cell. The bishop is said to have been singing and worshiping by himself: and when the emperor heard this particular hymn being sung, he was so moved by the incident, that he immediately ordered the bishop's release. Shortly thereafter, it appears that the bishop died, with some accounts alleging that he was poisoned before leaving the cloister.

The composer of this tune, Melchior Teschner, was born in Fraustadt, Silesia, in 1584. He became a cantor in the German Lutheran Church of his town and subsequently a Lutheran pastor of Oberpriestschen, near Fraustadt. This chorale tune was composed, in 1613, for another German hymn text authored by Valerius Herberger, a well-known German preacher of that day. Teschner's melody was considered by J. S. Bach, 1685-1750, to be so good, that he in turn borrowed it for use in his St. John Passion.

The translation of this Latin hymn by John M. Neale has become popular in both Catholic and Protestant, English speaking churches around the world. Neale was born in London, England, on January 24, 1818. He studied at Cambridge University, where he was noted for his prolific writing of prose and poetry. Later, he was ordained to the ministry of the Church of England. In addition to his knowledge of twenty languages, he authored

28

books on church history and church architecture as well as miscellaneous subjects. Several of his best known published works include: *Medieval Hymns and Sequences*, *Hymns for Children*, and *Hymns of the Eastern Church*. Neale translated many hymns from the Latin — e.g., "O Come, O Come, Emmanuel" — and more translations from the Greek language than any other hymnologist, totaling over two hundred in all. Though he was raised as an evangelical, he became strongly influenced by the Oxford Movement prevalent during this time. He never seceded from the Protestant to the Roman Catholic fold, however, as did many of his contemporaries.

Although the Oxford Movement in its initial phase sought to spiritually revitalize the Anglican Church, it gradually developed an obsession with making the church more liturgical and ritualistic. One of its intents was to exalt the clergy and bring the laity once again under the control of the priesthood. However, the movement did give an impetus to classical scholarship, especially the rediscovery of Greek and Latin hymnody. It broke the tyrannical rule of psalmody, which the Calvinists and Puritans had imposed on the worship of the English people. Following the first publication, in 1861, of the great Oxford Movement hymnal, *Hymns Ancient and Modern*, England for the first time had an ecumenical hymnal to take the place of the out-moded metrical psalters.

John Neale's humble conviction regarding his hymns is worthy of note. He wrote, "A hymn, whether original or translated, ought, the moment it is published, to become the common property of Christendom, the author retaining no private right in it whatsoever." Neale died in 1866, almost unnoticed in his own country, yet long-remembered as a loyal churchman and a noted literary scholar.

John Neale is also the author-translator of the hymn "Art Thou Weary?" (No. 8). In addition he has contributed to the hymnal "O Come, O Come, Emmanuel" (*101 Hymn Stories*, No. 64) and "The Day of Resurrection" (*ibid.*, No. 89).

29

*   *   *

"Ride on! ride on in majesty!
Hark! all the tribes 'Hosanna!' cry;
O Savior meek, pursue Thy road with palms
And scattered garments strowed.

"Ride on! ride on in majesty!
In lowly pomp ride on to die;
Bow Thy meek head to mortal pain,
Then take, O God, Thy power, and reign."
                                                    Henry Hart Milman

6 Am I a Soldier of the Cross?

ARLINGTON

Isaac Watts. 1674-1748

Thomas A. Arne, 1710-1778

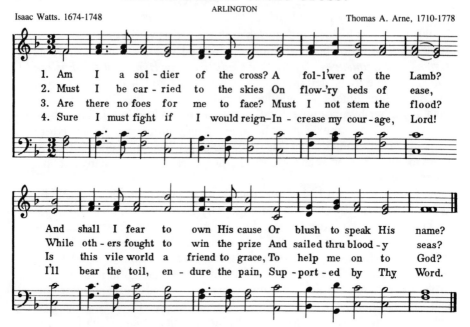

1. Am I a sol - dier of the cross? A fol-l'wer of the Lamb?
2. Must I be car - ried to the skies On flow-'ry beds of ease,
3. Are there no foes for me to face? Must I not stem the flood?
4. Sure I must fight if I would reign—In - crease my cour - age, Lord!

And shall I fear to own His cause Or blush to speak His name?
While oth - ers fought to win the prize And sailed thru blood - y seas?
Is this vile world a friend to grace, To help me on to God?
I'll bear the toil, en - dure the pain, Sup - port - ed by Thy Word.

30

Am I a Soldier of the Cross?

Author—Isaac Watts, 1674-1748
Composer—Thomas A. Arne, 1710-1778
Tune Name—"Arlington"
Meter—CM 86.86
Scripture Reference—1 Corinthians 16:13

Thou therefore endure hardness, as a good soldier of Jesus Christ.

2 Timothy 2:3

In Isaac Watts' time, much persecution was inflicted upon the English Dissenters—those who had split from the official, state Anglican Church. Such dissenting churches were known as the Free Churches. Many of these seventeenth and eighteenth-century believers were imprisoned for their convictions. Isaac Watts' father, a learned deacon in a dissenting Congregational church in Southampton, England, was in prison at the time of his son's birth, because of his non-conformist beliefs. Stalwarts such as Isaac Watts became resolute and fearless in their proclamation of the gospel. This hymn reflects these strong convictions. The hymn was written, in 1724, following a sermon by Watts entitled "Holy Fortitude or Remedies Against Fears." It was based on 1 Corinthians 16:13:

Am I a Soldier of the Cross?

Watch ye, stand fast in the faith, quit you like men, be strong.

Later Watts added another similar verse, which may be sung to this tune:

> I'm not ashamed to own my Lord,
> Or to defend His cause;
> Maintain the honor of His Word,
> The glory of His cross.

"Am I a Soldier of the Cross?" is one of the more than 600 hymns by Isaac Watts, often called the "Father of English Hymnody". In addition to being a preacher and a poet, Watts was an ardent student of theology and philosophy. His scholarly versatility is shown in such literary products as his *Treatise on Logic, Elements of Geography and Astronomy, Philosophical Essays*, and *Improvement of the Mind*. His textbook, *Logic*, was used at such universities as Oxford as well as at leading colleges in the United States.

Despite his many scholarly accomplishments, Isaac Watts is best known to posterity for his scriptural and simply-stated hymns, such as this challenging text. Dr. Samuel Johnson, noted hymnologist, has written of Watts: "Few men have left behind such purity of character or such monuments of laborious piety."

Isaac Watts was born on July 17, 1674, in Southampton, England. He was the eldest of nine children. As a boy, young Isaac displayed literary genius, writing verses at a very early age. Later, a wealthy benefactor offered to give him a university education, if he would agree to become a minister in the Established Church. This he refused to do, but he prepared instead for the Independent ministry. In 1707, he published his famous collection of 210 hymns, *Hymns and Spiritual Songs*, the first real hymnbook in the English language. Twelve years later, he published his *Psalms of David*, a metrical version of the Psalter, but, as he himself stated, rendered "in the language of the New Testament, and applied to the Christian state of worship." He died on November 25, 1748, and was buried at Bunhill Fields Cemetery, London, near the graves of other dissenting stalwarts of that day, such as John Bunyan. A monument to Watts' memory was placed in Westminster Abbey, the highest honor that can be bestowed upon an Englishman.

Isaac Watts is also the author of the advent hymn "Joy to the World" (No.52). Other contributions to the hymnal include: "I Sing the Mighty Power of God" (*101 Hymn Stories*, No. 38), "Jesus Shall Reign" (*ibid.*, No. 48), "O God, Our Help in Ages Past" (*ibid.*, No. 66), "When I Survey the Wondrous Cross" (*ibid.*, No. 100).

The tune, "Arlington" was adapted from a minuet from an overture to the opera *Artaxerxes* by Thomas A. Arne. Arne was considered to be one of the outstanding English composers of the eighteenth century. The opera was first produced in London, in 1752. The melody first appeared as a hymn tune in a hymnal, *Sacred Harmonies*, published in 1784 by Ralph Harrison.

*   *   *

"The brightest crowns that are worn in heaven have been tried, smelted, polished, and glorified through the furnace of tribulation."

Edwin Hubbell Chapin

"The Lord gets His best soldiers out of the highlands of affliction."

Charles H. Spurgeon: *Gleanings Among the Sheaves: Sorrow's Discipline*

"The blood of the martyrs is the seed of the church."

Tertullian

HIS BEST

"God has His best things for the few
Who dare to stand the test,
God has His second choice for those
Who will not take His best.
And others make the highest choice,
But when by trials pressed,
They shrink, they yield, they shun the Cross,
And so they lose His best.

"I want in this short life of mine
As much as can be pressed
Of service true for God and man—
Help me to be Thy best.
I want among the victor-throng
To have my name confessed,
And hear the Master say at last—
'Well done! you did your best.'"

Unknown

32

7 America the Beautiful

MATERNA

Katharine Lee Bates, 1859-1929

Samuel A. Ward, 1847-1903

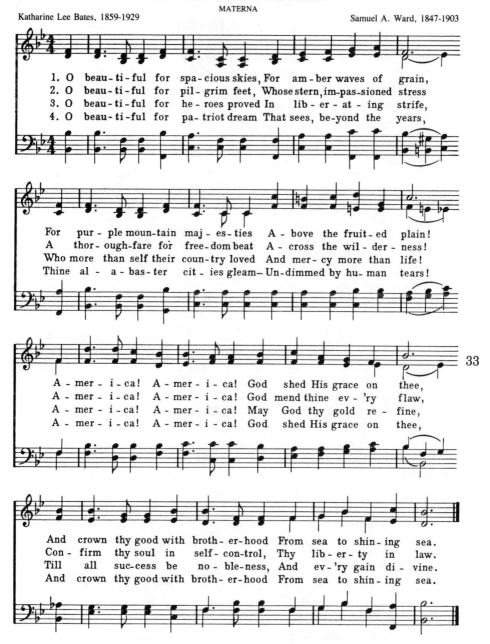

1. O beau-ti-ful for spa-cious skies, For am-ber waves of grain,
2. O beau-ti-ful for pil-grim feet, Whose stern, im-pas-sioned stress
3. O beau-ti-ful for he-roes proved In lib-er-at-ing strife,
4. O beau-ti-ful for pa-triot dream That sees, be-yond the years,

For pur-ple moun-tain maj-es-ties A-bove the fruit-ed plain!
A thor-ough-fare for free-dom beat A-cross the wil-der-ness!
Who more than self their coun-try loved And mer-cy more than life!
Thine al-a-bas-ter cit-ies gleam— Un-dimmed by hu-man tears!

A-mer-i-ca! A-mer-i-ca! God shed His grace on thee,
A-mer-i-ca! A-mer-i-ca! God mend thine ev-'ry flaw,
A-mer-i-ca! A-mer-i-ca! May God thy gold re-fine,
A-mer-i-ca! A-mer-i-ca! God shed His grace on thee,

And crown thy good with broth-er-hood From sea to shin-ing sea.
Con-firm thy soul in self-con-trol, Thy lib-er-ty in law.
Till all suc-cess be no-ble-ness, And ev-'ry gain di-vine.
And crown thy good with broth-er-hood From sea to shin-ing sea.

33

America the Beautiful

Author—Katharine Lee Bates, 1859-1929
Composer—Samuel A. Ward, 1847-1903
Tune Name—"Materna"
Meter—CM (86.86) Doubled

> Righteousness exalteth a nation; but sin is a reproach to any people.
>
> Proverbs 14:34

Katharine Lee Bates was born in Falmouth, Massachusetts, on August 12, 1859. She graduated from Wellesley College, in 1880. After teaching high school for six years, Katharine returned to Wellesley and eventually became head of the English Department. During her long professional career at Wellesley, Miss Bates became widely acclaimed for her many books, of which she authored or edited more than twenty on various subjects. Her writings included a popular textbook, *History of American Literature*, published in 1908, as well as volumes of poetry. Before her death in 1929, she was honored with literary doctorate degrees from several colleges.

Miss Bates was first inspired to write patriotic verse, in 1892, in recognition of the 400th anniversary of Columbus' discovery of America, a year every elementary school child knows so well, 1492. The following year, Miss Bates was visiting and teaching, during the summer months, in the state of Colorado. It was while viewing the countryside from the beautiful summit of Pike's Peak, a summit which towers more than 14,000 feet above sea level, that she was further inspired to write a national hymn, that would describe the majesty and vastness of our great land. She writes, "It was there, as I was looking out over the sea-like expanse of fertile country spreading away so far under the ample skies, that the opening lines of this text formed themselves in my mind."

Still later in that same year of 1893, Miss Bates visited the Columbian Exposition of the World's Fair that ran for several years in Chicago. On the site of this exposition, magnificent buildings were erected. Every structure, designed by Daniel Burnham, was a masterpiece of planning, construction, and beauty. Thousands of people came from all over the world to marvel at the splendor and to stand enraptured before the grandeur of such a spectacle. She writes, "The expression 'Alabaster Cities' was the direct result of this visit. It made such a strong appeal to my patriotic feelings that it was, in no small degree, responsible for at least the last stanza. It was my desire to compare the unusual beauties of God's nature in this country with the distinctive spectacles created by man."

Though this text sparkles with descriptive language, it is interesting to note, that each stanza is rounded off with the earnest prayer, that God

34

will always help our land to attain its real destiny. The hymn also reminds us forcibly of our noble heritage, the Pilgrims as well as the liberating heroes. In this hymn, as in her other writings, Miss Bates spoke often of the truth, that unless we crown our good with brotherhood, of what lasting value are our spacious skies, our amber waves of grain, our mountain majesties or our fruited plains? She would add, "We must match the greatness of our country with the goodness of personal godly living." Miss Bates also spoke often of the two stones that played such important roles in our nation's history: the tablets containing the Ten Commandments and Plymouth Rock. "If only we could couple the daring of the Pilgrims with the moral teachings of Moses, we would have something in this country that no one could ever take from us."

The completed poem stayed in Miss Bates' notebook for some time, until she came upon it again, in 1899, and sent it to a publisher in Boston. Several years later, Miss Bates rewrote the text, simplifying the phraseology, and this revised version was first printed in the *Boston Evening Transcript* on November 19, 1904. Slight further revision was made fourteen years later to produce the hymn as it is known today. The hymn in its present form attained wide-spread popularity for the first time, during the difficult days of World War I, and it did much to foster patriotic pride and loyalty among our people. Miss Bates once said: "That this hymn has gained, in less than twenty years, such a hold as it has upon our people, is clearly due to the fact that Americans are at heart idealists, with a fundamental faith in human brotherhood."

At least sixty tunes have been composed and tried with this text through the years. The one most commonly used today is known as the "Materna" tune, meaning "motherly." It was written nearly ten years before the text by a New Jersey music businessman named Samuel A. Ward. Mr. Ward originally composed this music for a hymn text called "O Mother Dear, Jerusalem." In 1912, permission from the composer's widow made it possible to join this tune with Katharine Lee Bates' text, a union it has enjoyed to the present.

35

*   *   *

"After what I owe to God, nothing should be more dear or more sacred to me than the love and respect I owe my country."

Jacques Auguste de Thou

"Whatever makes men good Christians makes them good citizens."

Daniel Webster

8

Art Thou Weary?

STEPHANOS

John M. Neale, 1818-1866
Stephen the Sabaite, 725-815

Henry W. Baker, 1821-1877

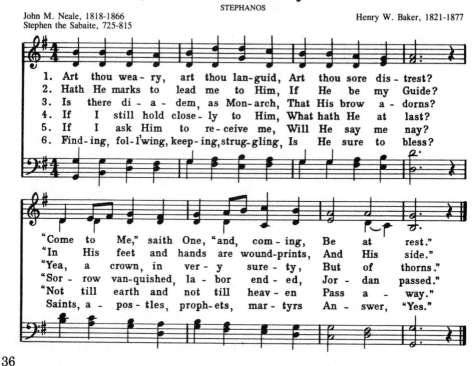

1. Art thou wea-ry, art thou lan-guid, Art thou sore dis-trest?
2. Hath He marks to lead me to Him, If He be my Guide?
3. Is there di-a-dem, as Mon-arch, That His brow a-dorns?
4. If I still hold close-ly to Him, What hath He at last?
5. If I ask Him to re-ceive me, Will He say me nay?
6. Find-ing, fol-l'wing, keep-ing, strug-gling, Is He sure to bless?

"Come to Me," saith One, "and, com-ing, Be at rest."
"In His feet and hands are wound-prints, And His side."
"Yea, a crown, in ver-y sure-ty, But of thorns."
"Sor-row van-quished, la-bor end-ed, Jor-dan passed."
"Not till earth and not till heav-en Pass a-way."
Saints, a-pos-tles, proph-ets, mar-tyrs An-swer, "Yes."

Art Thou Weary?

Author—John M. Neale, 1818-1866
Adapted from the Greek of Stephen the Sabaite, 725-815
Composer—Henry W. Baker, 1821-1877
Tune Name—"Stephanos"
Meter—85.83

> All that the Father giveth Me shall come to Me; and him that cometh to Me I will in no wise cast out.
> John 6:37

"Art Thou Weary?" is said to have been inspired by the life and writings of a Greek monk, named Stephen, who lived in the monastery of Mar Sabas, located in the wilderness of Judea, near the Dead Sea. This monastery, begun in 484 A.D., has produced some of the most important leaders for the Greek Orthodox Church. One of the greatest sons of Mar Sabas was John of Damascus, who wrote extensively in the fields of theology, philosophy, science, and the fine arts. (See "The Day of Resurrection" *101 Hymn Stories*, No. 89). This early eighth-century leader is generally considered to be most influential in shaping the beliefs and practices of the Eastern Orthodox Church. At the age of ten, Stephen was brought to the monastery by his uncle, St. John of Damascus. In 790, Stephen became the abbot of this monastery and remained so until his death at the age of ninety.

The monastery of Mar Sabas is said to stand "clinging to the face of a steep precipice, so that it is difficult to distinguish man's masonry from the natural rock." It is often visited by travelers to the Holy Land. In his book, *Anglican Hymnology*, James King gives this interesting account of his visit to the monastery. "The forty monks now there hold seven religious services daily. After being shown their gayly decorated chapel, the tomb of Saint Sabas, the tomb of Saint John of Damascus, and a cave containing thousands of skulls of martyred monks, I was led to the belfry, on the roof, where I saw the bells which send forth their beautiful chimes and gladden the hearts of pilgrims, who, 'weary and languid', pursue their journey through the desolate wilderness."

When this hymn was first published by John Neale, in his 1862 edition of *Hymns of the Eastern Church*, he credited the hymn to Stephen, but later, in his third edition of 1866, he wrote that there was so little in it of Grecian influence, that his paraphrase would better be called an original poem. Nevertheless, the hymn has a certain mystic quality that seems to reflect so well the introspective solitude of monastic life. An omitted stanza reads:

37

> If I find him, if I follow,
> What his guerdon here?
> Many a sorrow, many a labor,
> Many a tear.

During the nineteenth century, there were a number of Anglican ministers and scholars, such as John M. Neale, who developed a keen interest in rediscovering and translating into English many of the ancient Greek, Latin and German hymns. John Neale, born in London, England, on January 24, 1818, undoubtedly did more than any other person to make available the rich heritage of Greek and Latin hymns. This concern for unveiling pre-Reformation hymnody was one of the scholarly passions of the Oxford Movement. The monumental hymnal, *Hymns Ancient and Modern*, first produced by this movement, in 1861, contained 273 hymns. A large percentage of the hymns were of Latin, Greek, and German origin.

John M. Neale is the translator of the hymn "All Glory, Laud and Honor" (No. 5). He has also contributed to the hymnal "O Come, O Come, Emmanuel" (*101 Hymn Stories*, No. 64) and "The Day of Resurrection" (*ibid.*, No. 89).

The tune "Stephanos" was composed especially for this text by Henry W. Baker, general editor for twenty years of *Hymns Ancient and Modern*, for inclusion in the 1868 appendix of this collection. The harmonization of this tune is said to have been made by William H. Monk, music editor of this Anglican hymnal. Monk is also the composer of the well-known hymn text, "Abide With Me" (*101 Hymn Stories*, No. 2). In all, Monk contributed fifty original tunes for the hymnal.

It should be noted that the first line of each verse ends with a question, while the second line of the verse provides a positive answer. This type of dialogue song provides an excellent opportunity for congregational antiphonal singing—i.e., women and men, choir and congregation, one section with another, etc.

"Art Thou Weary?" has been the favorite hymn of many notable people in the past including President Franklin D. Roosevelt.

* * *

"I have read in Plato and Cicero sayings that are very wise and very beautiful; but I have never read in either of them: 'Come unto me all ye that labor and are heavy laden'."

St. Augustine

"How sweet the name of Jesus sounds in a believer's ear!
It soothes his sorrows, heals his wounds, and drives away his fear.

38

"It makes the wounded spirit whole and calms the troubled breast;
'Tis nourishment to hungry souls, and to the weary rest.

"Weak is the effort of my heart, and cold my warmest thought;
But when I see Thee as Thou art, I'll praise Thee as I ought."

John Newton

"Amidst the roaring of the sea,
My soul still hangs her hope on Thee;
Thy constant love, Thy faithful care,
Is all that saves me from despair.

"Tho' tempest-toss'd and half a wreck,
My Savior through the floods I seek;
Let neither winds nor stormy main
Force back my shatter'd bark again."

9

At Calvary

William R. Newell, 1868-1956

Daniel B. Towner, 1850-1919

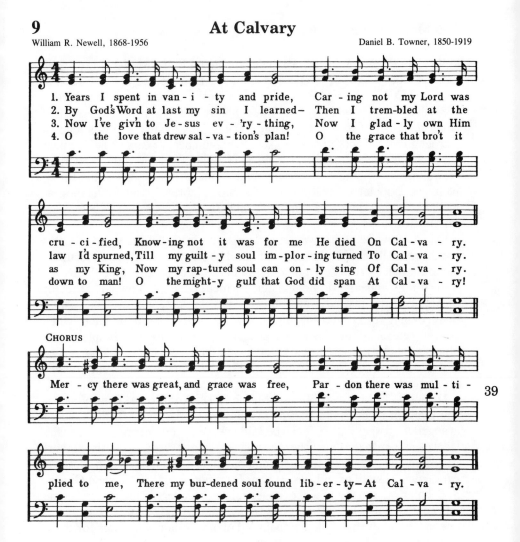

1. Years I spent in van - i - ty and pride, Car - ing not my Lord was
2. By God's Word at last my sin I learned— Then I trem-bled at the
3. Now I've giv'n to Je - sus ev - 'ry - thing, Now I glad - ly own Him
4. O the love that drew sal - va - tion's plan! O the grace that bro't it

cru - ci - fied, Know-ing not it was for me He died On Cal - va - ry.
law I'd spurned, Till my guilt - y soul im - plor - ing turned To Cal - va - ry.
as my King, Now my rap-tured soul can on - ly sing Of Cal - va - ry.
down to man! O the might - y gulf that God did span At Cal - va - ry!

CHORUS

Mer - cy there was great, and grace was free, Par - don there was mul - ti -

plied to me, There my bur-dened soul found lib - er - ty—At Cal - va - ry.

At Calvary

Author—William R. Newell, 1868-1956
Composer—Daniel B. Towner, 1850-1919

> In whom we have redemption through His blood, the forgiveness of sins, according to the riches of His grace.   Ephesians 1:7

This simple hymn text of personal testimony regarding the efficacy of God's love and grace, as expressed through Christ's suffering and death on the cross, was written by William R. Newell, a long-time associate of the Moody Bible Institute.

William R. Newell was born in Savannah, Ohio, on May 22, 1868, and died on April 1, 1956, in DeLand, Florida. He received his education at Wooster College and at Princeton and Oberlin Theological Seminaries. He later served several pastorates before being appointed assistant superintendent of the Moody Bible Institute in Chicago. He was a noted teacher and Bible conference speaker. For a number of years he held regular Bible classes in several different cities, commuting between them by train. Newell also authored many commentaries on various books of the Bible, including popular expositions on Romans, Hebrews, and Revelation as well as *Studies in the Pentateuch* and *Studies in Joshua-Job* (Kregel Publications).

One day, while on his way to a class at the Institute, the words for this hymn crystallized in Newell's mind. He stepped into an unoccupied classroom and wrote down quickly on the back of an envelope the words as they now appear. Moments later, he met Daniel B. Towner, Director of Music at the Institute, and showed him the text, with the suggestion that Towner try composing music for the words. An hour later, when Newell returned from his class, Dr. Towner had already completed the tune and with gratitude to God, they sang their new hymn together. The hymn first appeared in published form, in 1895, in the collection, *Famous Hymns*.

Daniel B. Towner was born on March 5, 1850, in Rome, Pennsylvania, and died on October 3, 1919, in Longwood, Missouri. In the field of evangelical gospel music, it can be said that D. B. Towner had few equals. He was recognized as a teacher, conductor, soloist, composer, and author. As a teacher, he trained such notable music leaders as Charles M. Alexander, Harry Dixon Loes, Homer Hammontree, H. E. Tovey, George S. Schuler, and many other evangelical song leaders. Towner first came into contact with D. L. Moody, in 1885, when Moody came to Cincinnati to conduct an evangelistic campaign. Towner trained the choir for these meetings. Mr. Moody was greatly impressed with Towner's musical abilities and spiritual sincerity and prevailed upon Towner to join him in his evangelistic endeavors. From that time until his death, Towner was associated with Moody or with one of his gospel enterprises.

During the summer of 1893, Moody asked Towner to become the first music director of the Moody Bible Institute, for the express purpose of training young people in gospel music leadership. To Moody and Towner, then, must go the credit for being the first to realize the need for evangelistic song leaders and church musicians and to undertake the systematic training. It can rightfully be said that in all he did as a teacher, composer, or public performer, D. B. Towner's constant aim was to exalt his Lord and to see others won to a personal relationship with Christ.

As a composer, Towner is credited with over 2000 published songs,

40

confining himself to gospel music and male chorus arrangements. He also compiled fourteen songbooks and hymnals as well as various textbooks for class use. The following are some of the more popular gospel hymns for which he composed the music: "Trust and Obey" (No. 92), "Grace Greater Than Our Sin," "Saved by the Blood," "Nor Silver nor Gold," "My Anchor Holds," "Anywhere With Jesus," and "Only a Sinner."

In 1900, the University of Tennessee conferred the Doctor of Music degree upon him. Another tribute to this man, who had such a profound influence on evangelical church music, was given by the choir he directed for so many years in the Moody Memorial Church of Chicago; it is a memorial tablet, which still occupies a prominent position in the auditorium of that church. All of us who have been involved with evangelical church music to the present time owe an eternal debt of gratitude to Daniel B. Towner for the foundations he has laid for our church ministries.

*   *   *

"Nothing in my hand I bring,
Simply to Thy cross I cling."
Augustus M. Toplady

41

"I must die or get somebody to die for me. If the Bible doesn't teach that, it doesn't teach anything. And that is where the atonement of Jesus Christ comes in."
Dwight L. Moody

LOVE

"O perfect God, thy love as perfect man did share
Here upon earth each form of ill thy fellow-men must bear.

"Now from the tree of scorn we hear thy voice again;
Thou who didst take our mortal flesh, has felt our mortal pain.

"Thy body suffers thirst, parched are thy lips and dry;
How poor the offering man can bring Thy thirst to satisfy!

"O Savior, by Thy thirst, borne on the cross of shame,
Grant us, in all our sufferings here, to glorify Thy name.

"That through each pain and grief our souls may onward move,
To gain more likeness to Thy life, more knowledge of Thy love."
Ada Rundall Greenaway

10   Be Thou My Vision

SLANE

Irish hymn, c. 8th century
Trans. by Mary E. Byrne, 1880-1931
Versified by Eleanor H. Hull 1860-1935

Irish Melody
Arr. by Norman Johnson, 1928-1983

42

1. Be Thou my Vi - sion, O Lord of my heart — Nought be all
2. Be Thou my Wis - dom, and Thou my true Word — I ev - er
3. Rich - es I heed not, nor man's emp - ty praise — Thou mine in -
4. High King of heav - en, my vic - to - ry won, May I reach

else to me, save that Thou art; Thou my best thought, by
with Thee and Thou with me, Lord; Thou my great Fa - ther,
her - it - ance, now and al - ways; Thou and Thou on - ly,
heav-en's joys, O bright heav'n's Sun! Heart of my own heart, what -

day or by night — Wak - ing or sleep-ing, Thy pres-ence my light.
I Thy true son — Thou in me dwell-ing, and I with Thee one.
first in my heart — High King of heav - en, my Treas-ure Thou art.
ev - er be - fall, Still be my Vi - sion, O Rul - er of all.

Words used by permission of Chatto and Windus, Ltd., London. Music © 1968 by Singspiration, Inc. All rights reserved.
Music © Copyright 1966 by Singspiration, Inc. All rights reserved. Used by permission.

Be Thou My Vision

Text—Irish hymn, c. 8th century
Translated by Mary E. Byrne, 1880-1931
Versified by Eleanor H. Hull, 1860-1935
Music—Irish Melody
Arrangement—Norman Johnson, 1928-1983
Tune name—"Slane"
Meter—10 10. 10 10

Where there is no vision, the people perish: but he that keepeth the law, happy is he.
Proverbs 29:18

"Vision is the art of seeing things invisible."
Jonathan Swift—*Thoughts on Various Subjects*

"Give us clear vision that we may know where to stand and what to stand for, because unless we stand for something, we shall fall for anything."
Peter Marshall—*Mr. Jones, Meet the Master*

"Vision is of God. A vision comes in advance of any task well done."
Katherine Logan

This eighth-century, anonymous, Irish hymn text expresses, in the quaint Celtic style, the ageless need of man to have a heavenly vision and to experience God's care and personal presence throughout this earthly pilgrimage. The author's high regard for God is evident in the various titles ascribed Him: Vision, Lord, Best Thought, Wisdom, Word, Great Father, High King, Inheritance, Treasure, Sun, Ruler, and Heart.

Another interesting verse often omitted in our hymnals is as follows:

> Be Thou my breast-plate, my sword for the fight,
> Be Thou my armour, and be Thou my might;
> Thou my soul's shelter, and Thou my high tower,
> Raise Thou me heavenward, O Power of my Power.

43

Mary Byrne's translation of this ancient Irish poem into English prose first appeared in the journal *Erin*, Volume Two, published in 1905. Later the prose was put into verse form by Eleanor H. Hull and published in her *Poem Book of the Gael*, 1912. The tune, "Slane," is a traditional Irish air from Patrick W. Joyce's collection, *Old Irish Folk Music and Songs*, published in 1909. The tune was originally used with a secular text, "With My Love on the Road." Its first association with this hymn text was in the *Irish Church Hymnal* of 1919. The tune is named for a hill, ten miles from Tara, in County Meath, where St. Patrick is said to have challenged King Loegaire and the Druid priests by lighting the Paschal fire on Easter eve. Although the melody has been harmonized by various musicians such as Norman Johnson (See "Not What These Hands Have Done," No. 64), it is generally recommended that this tune is most effective when sung in unison.

Mary Elizabeth Byrne was born in Dublin, Ireland, in 1880. She received her education at the University of Dublin and became a research worker and writer for the Board of Intermediate Education in her home town. One of her most important works was her contribution to the *Old and Mid-Irish Dictionary* and the *Dictionary of the Irish Language*.

Eleanor H. Hull was born in Manchester, England, on January 15, 1860. She was the founder and secretary of the Irish Text Society and served as president of the Irish Literary Society, in London. She authored several books on Irish history and literature.

Another anonymous writer has penned these significant thoughts about the importance of having a vision for one's life:

> A vision without a task is a dream;
> A task without a vision is drudgery;
> A vision with a task is the hope of the world.

Truly our visionary attitude throughout life is often the difference between success and mediocrity. One is reminded of the classic story of the two shoe-salesmen who were sent to a primitive island to determine business potential. The first salesman wired back, "Coming home immediately. No one here wears shoes." The second man responded, "Send a boatload of shoes immediately. The possibilities for selling shoes here are unlimited."

May we as believers be characterized as people of vision — "looking unto Jesus, the author and finisher of our faith...." Hebrews 12:2

*　　*　　*

44　　"The highest joy that can be known by those who heav'n-ward wend—
It is the Word of Life to own, and God to have as friend."

Nils Frykman

LIFE
"To the preacher, life's a sermon,
To the joker, life's a jest,
To the miser, life is money,
To the loafer, life's a rest.

"To the soldier, life's a battle,
To the teacher, life's a school.
Life's a great thing for the thinker,
But it's folly to the fool.

"Life is just one long vacation,
To the man who loves his work,
But it's constant dodging duty
To the everlasting shirk.

"To the faithful, earnest worker
Life's a story ever new;
Life is what we try to make it —
What in truth is life to you?"

Unknown

11 Because He Lives

Gloria Gaither, 1942-
William J. Gaither, 1936-

William J. Gaither, 1936-

1. God sent His Son— they called Him Je - sus, He came to love,
2. How sweet to hold a new - born ba - by, And feel the pride
3. And then one day I'll cross the riv - er, I'll fight life's fi -

heal and for - give; He lived and died to buy my
and joy he gives; But great - er still the calm as -
nal war with pain; And then, as death gives way to

_ _ par - don, An emp - ty grave is there to prove my Sav - ior lives.
sur - ance: This child can face un - cer - tain days because Christ lives.
vic - tory, I'll see the lights of glo - ry— and I'll know He lives.

CHORUS

Be - cause He lives I can face to - mor - row, Be - cause He lives

all fear is gone; Be - cause I know He holds the

45

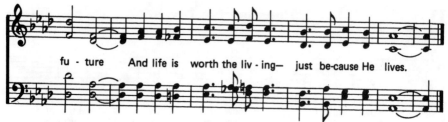

fu - ture And life is worth the liv - ing— just be-cause He lives.

Copyright 1971 by William J. Gaither. All rights reserved. Used by permission.

Because He Lives

Authors—Gloria Gaither, 1942—
            William J. Gaither, 1936—
Composer—William J. Gaither, 1936—

> Yet a little while, and the world seeth me no more; but ye see me; because I live, ye shall live also.
> John 14:19

For the past two decades the music of Gloria and Bill Gaither has greatly enriched evangelical hymnody. Such songs as "He Touched Me," "Something Beautiful," "Let's Just Praise the Lord," "The King Is Coming," "There's Something About That Name," and "I Am Loved" are just a few of the nearly four hundred songs that have flowed from the hearts and pens of this talented and godly couple.

But the one number that has especially highlighted the Gaither's ministry is a song that reflects their own philosophy of life—"the resurrection principle in the daily routines of life"—"Because He Lives." Bill Gaither recalls the circumstances that prompted the writing of this song, which was voted by the Gospel Music Association and by ASCAP as the "Gospel Song of the Year for 1974:"

We wrote "Because He Lives" after a period of time when we had had a kind of dry spell and hadn't written any songs for a while. . . . Also at the end of the 1960's, when our country was going through some great turmoil with the height of the drug culture and the whole "God Is Dead" theory which was running wild in our country and also at the peak of the Vietnam War, our little son was born,—Benjy—at least Gloria was expecting him. And I can remember at the time we thought, "Brother, this is really a poor time to bring a child into the world." At times we were even quite discouraged by the whole thing. And then Benjy did come. We had two little girls whom we love very much, but this was our first son, and so that lyric came to us, "How sweet to hold our new-born baby and feel the pride and joy he gives, but better still the calm assurance that this child can face uncertain days because Christ lives." And it gave us the courage to say "Because Christ lives we can face tomorrow" and keep our heads high, and hopefully that could be of meaning to other people.

It's rather interesting now that, although we don't consider ourselves as "old" writers, we've had many people tell us they have used that song at a funeral of a loved one; and it has been very encouraging to them, at a time when they were very discouraged. So evidently a lot of people have shared the same kind of experience of being discouraged.

Bill Gaither began his career teaching English, literature and journalism, in 1959, in his home town of Alexandria, Indiana. There he met Gloria Sickal, who taught French and English in the same high school. They began singing "Gaither music" in churches in the area and, in 1962, were united in marriage. Together they have raised three children—Suzanne, born in 1964; Amy, born in 1969; and Benjy, 1970. Gloria and Bill both left the teaching profession, in 1967, to pursue a full-time ministry of writing, recording albums, of which there are now more than thirty, and performing approximately fifty concerts each year. Today Bill also presides over several businesses, which have been a natural out-growth of the creative phenomena found in the lives and ministries of the Gaithers. These include a recording studio, a music distribution company, and a printing plant. Since 1971, Gloria has authored five books: *Make Warm Noises, Rainbows Live at Easter, Because He Lives, Decisions: A Christian's Approach to Making Right Choices*, and *Let's Make a Memory* (co-authored by Shirley Dobson). Gloria has also co-authored the nearly 400 songs published by the Gaithers as well as their popular musicals: "Alleluia—A Praise Gathering for Believers;" "His Love Reaching;" "Kids Under Construction;" and "God Has Always Had A People." In 1976, Bill and Gloria Gaither were co-creators (along with Fred Bock) of an excellent hymnal, *Hymns for the Family of God*. Regarding the title of this hymnal, Bill writes:

47

> Gloria and I have had a real concern that Christians need not be ostracized from each other because of differences in the way they worship. We are all part of the same family, and the hymnal tries to preserve the best from many theological traditions. Therefore, the broad name seems to cover exactly what we are trying to do.

When asked what he desired from the Lord for their future, Bill replied: "I hope He will help us to keep open as we grow older. I have been disappointed in the past by some of our Christian leaders who became close-minded to new ideas in presenting the gospel. I hope we can always remain open to different new ways of doing, or of preaching and singing the gospel. Hopefully, what we are doing is not only preparing people to spend eternity with the Lord, but even preparing them to enjoy it more with Him."

12 Beyond the Sunset

Virgil P. Brock, 1887-1978

Blanche Kerr Brock, 1888-1958

1. Be - yond the sun - set, O bliss-ful morn - ing, When with our
2. Be - yond the sun - set no clouds will gath - er, No storms will
3. Be - yond the sun - set a hand will guide me To God the
4. Be - yond the sun - set, O glad re - un - ion With our dear

Sav - ior heav'n is be - gun; Earth's toil-ing end - ed, O glo - rious
threat-en, no fears an - noy; O day of glad -ness, O day un -
Fa - ther, whom I a - dore; His glo - rious pres-ence, His words of
loved ones who've gone be - fore; In that fair home-land we'll know no

dawn - ing— Be - yond the sun - set when day is done.
end - ing— Be - yond the sun - set, e - ter - nal joy!
wel - come, Will be my por - tion on that fair shore.
part - ing— Be - yond the sun - set for - ev - er - more!

Copyright 1936, © Renewed 1964 The Rodeheaver Co. (A Div. of Word, Inc.) All rights reserved. International Copyright secured. Used by permission.

Beyond the Sunset

Author—Virgil P. Brock, 1887-1978
Composer—Blanche Kerr Brock, 1888-1958

For now we see through a glass, darkly; but then face to face: now I know in part; but then shall I know, even as also I am known.   1 Corinthians 13:12

One of the best-known and widely-used songs in the entire field of gospel hymnody is "Beyond the Sunset." Mr. Brock has left the following account of its writing:

This song was born during a conversation at the dinner table, one evening in 1936, after watching a very unusual sunset at Winona Lake, Indiana, with a blind guest—my cousin Horace Burr—and his wife, Grace. A large area of the water appeared ablaze with the glory of God, yet there were threatening storm clouds gathering overhead. Returning to our home, we went to the dinner table still talking about the impressive spectacle we had witnessed. Our blind guest excitedly remarked that he had never seen a more beautiful sunset.

"People are always amazed when you talk about seeing," I told him. "I can see," Horace replied. "I see through other people's eyes, and I think I often see more; I see beyond the sunset."

The phrase "beyond the sunset" and the striking inflection of his voice struck me so forcibly, I began singing the first few measures. "That's beautiful!" his wife interrupted, "Please go to the piano and sing it."

We went to the piano nearby and completed the first verse. "You should have a verse about the storm clouds," our guest urged, and the words for this verse came quickly as well. Recalling how closely our guests had walked hand in hand together for so many years due to his blindness, the third verse was soon added. Before the evening meal was finished, all four stanzas had been written and we sang the entire song together.

49

In his book of memoirs, written in 1976, Virgil Brock relates numerous incidents from his colorful life. The following are a few of these highlights:

Virgil Brock was born on January 6, 1887, in a rural community several miles southeast of Celina, Ohio. He was the sixth of eight sons born to his Quaker parents. His parents were devout and firm in their spiritual convictions. "They lived abstemiously, abhorred liquor, tobacco, and corrupt speech, and ardently practiced what they thought to be the teaching of the Bible." Virgil was converted, at the age of sixteen, at a nearby church revival meeting. Soon he felt the call for Christian service and prepared himself with studies at the Fairmount Friends Academy and Earlham College, in Indiana. During this time, he pastored several small Quaker churches. Some time later, he met and married a talented singer and pianist named Blanche Kerr, "the belle of the community." Until Blanche's death from cancer on January 3, 1958, the Brocks were continually involved in evangelism, various Christian endeavors, and song writing. A large monument was erected on May 30, 1958, in the Warsaw-Winona Lake cemetery, with the words and music of "Beyond the Sunset" fully engraved in stone as a tribute to the dedicated ministries of this talented couple.

Virgil Brock wrote more than 500 gospel songs, most of which were in collaboration with his first wife, Blanche. Several of the more popular titles include: "He's a Wonderful Savior to Me," "Sing and Smile and Pray," "Resting in His Love," "If You Could Know How Jesus Loves You," "Let God Have His Way," and many others. By his own admission, Virgil knew nothing about music theory. He needed Blanche or someone else to notate the melodies that flowed from his heart. "I'll admit that after I had written a melody I could not have read it, if I had not known the tune. To me the theory of music seems more complicated than building a spaceship." Yet in May, 1969, he was awarded an Honorary Degree of Sacred Music from Trinity College, Dunedin, Florida, in recognition of fifty years of gospel song writing.

One of Mr. Brock's delights was leading a congregation in vibrant singing. His exuberant spirit soon became contagious with any audience. Improvising choruses for a service or composing a custom song for a special occasion became effective characteristics of Virgil Brock's ministry, to the very end of his 91 years. The last few years of his life were especially fruitful. He became associated with the Sutera Twins in their campaigns in the United States and throughout Canada. His last days were spent peacefully at the Youth Haven Ranch, a mission for underprivileged children at Rives Junction, Michigan, a ministry that he also dearly loved.

*   *   *

50

"Think of stepping on shore and finding it Heaven!
Of taking hold of a hand and finding it God's,
Of breathing new air, and finding it celestial air,
Of feeling invigorated, and finding it immortality,
Of passing from storm and tempest to an unbroken calm,
Of waking up, and finding it Home!"

Anonymous

SAFELY HOME

"I am home in heaven, dear ones
All's so happy, all is bright;
There is perfect joy and beauty,
In this everlasting light.

"All the pain and grief are over,
Every restless tossing past;
I am now at peace forever,
Safely home in heaven at last.

"Then you must not grieve so sorely,
For I love you dearly still;
Try to look beyond earth's shadows,
Pray to trust our Father's will."

Selected

13

Blessed Redeemer

Avis B. Christiansen, 1895-

Harry Dixon Loes, 1892-1965

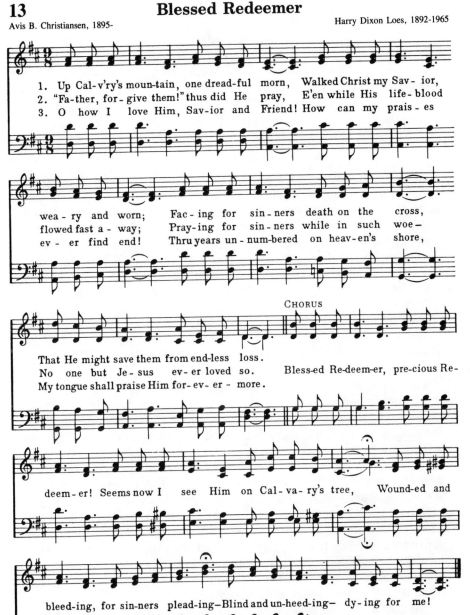

1. Up Cal-v'ry's moun-tain, one dread-ful morn, Walked Christ my Sav-ior, wea-ry and worn; Fac-ing for sin-ners death on the cross, That He might save them from end-less loss.

2. "Fa-ther, for-give them!" thus did He pray, E'en while His life-blood flowed fast a-way; Pray-ing for sin-ners while in such woe— No one but Je-sus ev-er loved so.

3. O how I love Him, Sav-ior and Friend! How can my prais-es ev-er find end! Thru years un-num-bered on heav-en's shore, My tongue shall praise Him for-ev-er-more.

CHORUS

Bless-ed Re-deem-er, pre-cious Re-deem-er! Seems now I see Him on Cal-va-ry's tree, Wound-ed and bleed-ing, for sin-ners plead-ing—Blind and un-heed-ing— dy-ing for me!

51

© Copyright 1921. Renewal 1949 by Harry Dixon Loes. Assigned to Singspiration, Inc. All rights reserved. Used by permission.

Blessed Redeemer

Author—Avis B. Christiansen, 1895-1985
Composer—Harry Dixon Loes, 1892-1965

And He bearing His cross went forth into a place of a skull, which is called in the Hebrew, Golgotha; Where they crucified Him, and two others with Him, on either side one, and Jesus in the midst.

John 19:17, 18

Mrs. Avis Christiansen is to be ranked as one of the important gospel hymn writers of the 20th century. She has written hundreds of gospel hymn texts as well as several volumes of published poems. Mrs. Christiansen states that all of her works have come out of her own Christian experience and express her heart's spiritual desires and convictions. She cannot recall any unusual experiences associated with the writing of these texts, but rather just her daily walk and intimate fellowship with the Lord. Several of her popular favorites include: "Only One Life," "In the Shadow of the Cross," "Only Jesus," "Precious Hiding Place," "Believe on the Lord Jesus Christ," "Love Found a Way," "Only Glory By and By," and many more. She has collaborated with such well-known gospel musicians as: Harry Dixon Loes, Homer Hammontree, Lance Latham, George Schuler, Wendell Loveless, Harry Clarke and Haldor Lillenas.

52

Mrs. Christiansen was born in Chicago, Illinois, in 1895, and was raised in a Christian home. She was converted to Christ in early childhood. After high school, she attended a secretarial school and later the Moody Bible Institute evening school. She was married to E. O. Christiansen, who was affiliated with the Moody Bible Institute for nearly forty years before his home-going. Together they raised two daughters. Mrs. Christiansen, was a faithful member of the Moody Memorial Church of Chicago since 1915, serving in many varied capacities in the ministry there.

Harry Dixon Loes was born in Kalamazoo, Michigan, on October 20, 1892. After serving several churches as music director and later being active for more than twelve years in evangelistic work, he joined the music faculty of the Moody Bible Institute, in 1939, where he remained as a popular music teacher until his death, in 1965. Mr. Loes was the writer of numerous gospel songs and choruses.

One day while listening to a sermon on the subject of Christ's atonement entitled "Blessed Redeemer," Mr. Loes was inspired to compose this tune. He then sent the melody with the suggested title to Mrs. Christiansen, a friend for many years, asking her to write the text. The hymn first appeared in *Songs of Redemption*, compiled by Marin and Jelks, in 1920, and published by the Baptist Home Mission Board, Atlanta, Georgia.

14 Burdens Are Lifted at Calvary

John M. Moore, 1925-

John M. Moore, 1925-

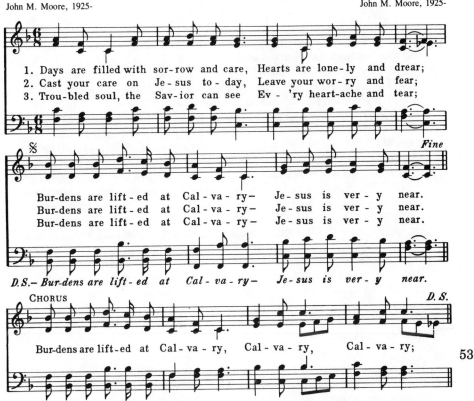

1. Days are filled with sor-row and care, Hearts are lone-ly and drear;
2. Cast your care on Je-sus to-day, Leave your wor-ry and fear;
3. Trou-bled soul, the Sav-ior can see Ev - 'ry heart-ache and tear;

Bur-dens are lift-ed at Cal-va-ry— Je-sus is ver-y near.
Bur-dens are lift-ed at Cal-va-ry— Je-sus is ver-y near.
Bur-dens are lift-ed at Cal-va-ry— Je-sus is ver-y near.

D.S.—Bur-dens are lift-ed at Cal-va-ry— Je-sus is ver-y near.

CHORUS

Bur-dens are lift-ed at Cal-va-ry, Cal-va-ry, Cal-va-ry;

© Copyright 1952. Renewal 1980 by J. M. Moore. Assigned to Singspiration (ASCAP). Division of Zondervan Corp. All rights reserved. Used by permission.

Burdens Are Lifted at Calvary

Author and Composer—John M. Moore, 1925-

And as Moses lifted up the serpent in the wilderness, even so must the Son of Man be lifted up, that whosoever believeth in Him should not perish, but have eternal life.
John 3:14, 15

John M. Moore, British Baptist minister, author and composer, relates the following incident as the basis for this beloved gospel hymn:

I wrote "Burdens Are Lifted at Calvary" after a most interesting experience. The company secretary of a large shipping firm telephoned the Seaman's Chapel and requested that I visit a young merchant seaman, who was lying critically ill in a Glasgow Hospital. After getting permission from the nursing sister,

I went in to visit the young sailor. I found him glad to have a visitor and eager to hear what I had to say. I talked about general things for a few moments and then put my hand in my case for a tract, not knowing which one I would pull out. It happened to be a tract based on "Pilgrim's Progress," with a color reproduction of "Pilgrim" coming to the cross with a great burden on his back. I showed the young seaman this picture and told him the story in brief, adding that Pilgrim's experience had been my experience, too. The more I told him, the more anxious he became. I explained that, when I came to the cross of Christ, my burden rolled away, and my sense of sin and guilt before God was removed. By this time, the tears were running down his cheeks, and he nodded his head when I asked him, "Do you feel this burden on your heart today?" We prayed together, and never shall I forget the smile of peace and assurance that lit up his face as he said that his burden was lifted! Later that night, sitting by the fireside with paper and pen, I could not get the thought out of my mind—his burden is lifted! I started writing, and the words flowed on to the paper. The tune was written at the same sitting, but never for a moment did I imagine that this little hymn would become a favorite throughout the world. Since that time, I hear of people from all over the world who are being blessed and saved, through the singing of this hymn.

The author and composer of this gospel hymn has also provided the following account of his life:

54

I was born on September 1, 1925, in the town of Kirkintilloch, Dunbartonshire, Scotland, of humble Scottish parents. I had the great advantage of a godly mother who brought me up in the truth of the gospel. At the age of sixteen, I came to a saving knowledge of Jesus Christ and later joined the local Baptist Church. There I was soon busily engaged in Sunday School work, in open air meetings, and tract distribution. I commenced my apprenticeship at sixteen years of age as an engineering draftsman, but as the call to Christian service increased, I commenced studying for the ministry at the Evangelical Baptist Fellowship Bible College in Glasgow, Scotland. Thereafter I became Assistant Superintendent in the Seamen's Chapel in Glasgow, one of the area's outstanding evangelistic centers. From there, I was called to the famous Tent Hall, Glasgow, the largest evangelistic center in Scotland, where I was pastor and superintendent for almost nine years. From there, I moved to the capitol town of the Scottish Highlands, Inverness, to become pastor of the Inverness Baptist Church for five years. Here I was married to Esther Marr, from nearby Beauly, and we now have a son, David Lawler Moore. I have travelled across the Atlantic on several occasions to tour America and Canada, preaching in churches of many denominations and participating in various Bible Conferences.

John M. Moore is currently pastor of the Willowdale Baptist Church in Willowdale, Ontario, Canada. He continues to be a prolific writer of gospel music, though none of his songs has gained such wide acceptance as has "Burdens Are Lifted at Calvary" and also the gospel song titled "Why?", both of which have been published by the Singspiration Music Company.

*   *   *

"Arise my soul, arise, shake off thy guilty fears,
The bleeding sacrifice, in my behalf appears.
Before the throne my surety stands,
My name is written on His hands.

"He ever lives above, for me to intercede,
His all redeeming love, His precious blood to plead.
His blood atoned for all our race
And sprinkles now the throne of grace.

"Five bleeding wounds He bears, received on Calvary,
They pour effectual prayers, and strongly plead for me.
'Forgive him, oh forgive,' they cry,
'Nor let that ransomed sinner die.'

"The Father hears Him pray, His dear anointed One,
He cannot turn away the presence of His Son.
His Spirit answers to the Blood,
And tells me, I am born of God."

Charles Wesley

AT THE CROSS OF JESUS

"There is love at the cross of Jesus, an everlasting love
That could leave the courts of heaven and the glory of God above,
That could come to a world of evil for the sake of the sinners lost,
That could drain the cup of anguish and never count the cost.

"There is peace at the cross of Jesus, where God was reconciled,
Where we know our sins forgiven and hear Him say, 'My child';
Where He bore the world's transgressions and all our debt was paid;
Where the weight of the Father's anger on His tender heart was laid.

"There is life at the cross of Jesus, where the victory was won,
Where sin and death were conquered by the sinless, deathless One;
O grave, where is thy triumph? O death, where is thy sting?
For the Lord of life and glory passed through thy gates a King!"

Annie Johnson Flint

15
Christ Arose

Robert Lowry, 1826-1899

Robert Lowry, 1826-1899

1. Low in the grave He lay— Je-sus, my Sav-ior! Wait-ing the com-ing day—
2. Vain-ly they watch His bed— Je-sus, my Sav-ior! Vain-ly they seal the dead—
3. Death can-not keep his prey— Je-sus, my Sav-ior! He tore the bars a-way—

CHORUS *Faster*

Je-sus, my Lord!
Je-sus, my Lord! Up from the grave He a-rose, With a
Je-sus, my Lord! He a-rose,

might-y tri-umph o'er His foes; He a-rose a Vic-tor from the
He a-rose!

dark do-main, And He lives for-ev-er with His saints to reign: He a-

rose! He a-rose! Hal-le-lu-jah! Christ a-rose!
He a-rose! He a-rose!

Christ Arose

Author and Composer—Robert Lowry, 1826-1899
Scripture Reference—Luke 24:6, 7, 8

> Now if we be dead with Christ, we believe that we shall also live with Him: Knowing that Christ being raised from the dead dieth no more; death hath no more dominion over Him.   Romans 6:8, 9

"Alleluia, He is Risen!"
"Alleluia, He is Risen Indeed!"

If you and I had been living during the early Christian era, this undoubtedly would have been our greeting to one another, as believers, on an Easter Sunday. For the past century, however, many evangelical churches have celebrated this triumphant day and have been inspired anew, with the singing of this beloved Easter hymn, written and composed by Robert Lowry in 1874.

Robert Lowry is a highly respected name among early, gospel hymn writers. He was born in Philadelphia, on March 12, 1826. At the age of seventeen, he accepted Christ as his personal Savior and later was graduated from Bucknell University with high scholastic honors, in 1854. Lowry served as a professor of literature at this university, from 1869-75, and received his doctorate degree from that institution. Lowry's first pastorate was the West Chester Baptist Church near Philadelphia, after which he served important Baptist pastorates in New Jersey, New York City, and Brooklyn. Robert Lowry continued an active, Christian ministry, until his home-going in 1899, at the age of seventy-three.

Throughout his ministry, Lowry was recognized as a most capable minister of the gospel, possessing keen insight and administrative ability. He became known as a thorough Bible scholar and a brilliant and captivating orator; few preachers of his day had greater ability to paint word pictures and to inspire a congregation. Music and a knowledge of hymnology were his favorite studies, but always as an avocation. Although Lowry wrote a number of hymns and tunes and published many songbooks, his main interest throughout life was preaching God's Word.

However, with the death of another well-known gospel musician, William Bradbury, in 1868, the Biglow Publishing Company selected Robert Lowry as its music editor. He accepted this position and soon became highly knowledgeable in the field of music publishing. Dr. Lowry was an editor or a collaborator in the preparation of more than twenty Sunday school songbooks, many of which are considered to be the finest ever published. One of his books, *Pure Gold*, sold more than one million copies. It has often been said that the quality of Lowry's publications did much to improve

57

the cause of sacred music in this country. He once stated this concern for the writing of a hymn: "It must be readily apprehended by the Christian consciousness, coming forth from the experience of the writer, and clothed in strong and inspiring words." Lowry had few equals in his day, when it came to writing gospel texts and singable tunes. In addition to "Christ Arose," he has written both the words and music for such other gospel favorites as "Shall We Gather at the River?" and "Nothing But the Blood" and has supplied just the music for such familiar hymns as: "All the Way My Savior Leads Me" (*101 Hymn Stories*, No. 5), "I Need Thee Every Hour" (No. 40), "We're Marching to Zion," "Savior, Thy Dying Love," and the plaintive song, "Where Is My Wandering Boy Tonight?"

When often asked about his method for writing songs, Lowry answered in this way:

> I have no set method. Sometimes the music comes and the words follow...I watch my moods, and when anything strikes me, whether words or music, no matter where I am, at home, or on the street, I jot it down...My brain is sort of a spinning machine, for there is music running through it all the time. The tunes of nearly all the hymns I have written have been completed on paper, before I tried them on the organ. Frequently, the words of the hymn and the music have been written at the same time.

58

And so it was with "Christ Arose." During the Easter season of 1874, while having his devotions one evening, Robert Lowry was impressed with the events associated with Christ's resurrection, especially with these words recorded in Luke 24:6-8:

> He is not here, but is risen; remember how He spoke unto you when He was in Galilee, saying, the Son of Man must be delivered into the hands of sinful men and be crucified, and the third day rise again. And they remembered His words.

Soon Robert Lowry found himself seated at the little pump organ in the parlor of his home, and, in a very spontaneous fashion, there came forth the music and the words, giving expression to the thoughts that had been uppermost in his mind. The hymn was first published, in 1875, in the collection, *Brightest and Best*, edited by William H. Doane and Robert Lowry.

The hymn's verses and refrain depict a vivid contrast between the moods of death and resurrection. Though not indicated on the page, the verses should be sung deliberately with a vigorous tempo employed for the refrain.

16

Cleanse Me

MAORI

J. Edwin Orr, 1912-

Maori Melody
Arr. by Norman Johnson, 1928-1983

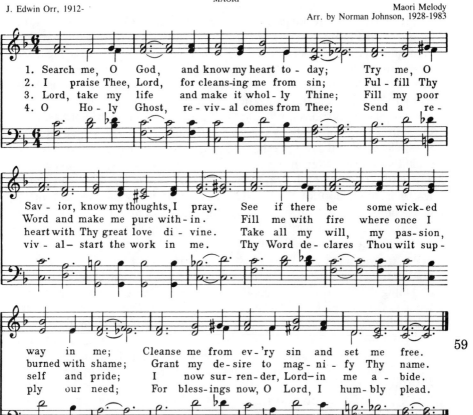

1. Search me, O God, and know my heart to-day; Try me, O Sav-ior, know my thoughts, I pray. See if there be some wick-ed way in me; Cleanse me from ev-'ry sin and set me free.

2. I praise Thee, Lord, for cleans-ing me from sin; Ful-fill Thy Word and make me pure with-in. Fill me with fire where once I burned with shame; Grant my de-sire to mag-ni-fy Thy name.

3. Lord, take my life and make it whol-ly Thine; Fill my poor heart with Thy great love di-vine. Take all my will, my pas-sion, self and pride; I now sur-ren-der, Lord-in me a-bide.

4. O Ho-ly Ghost, re-viv-al comes from Thee; Send a re-viv-al-start the work in me. Thy Word de-clares Thou wilt sup-ply our need; For bless-ings now, O Lord, I hum-bly plead.

59

Arr. © Copyright 1966 by Singspiration, Inc. All rights reserved. Used by permission.

Cleanse Me

Author—J. Edwin Orr, 1912-
Music—Maori melody
Arranger—Norman Johnson, 1928-1983
Tune Name—"Maori"
Meter—10 10. 10 10
Scripture Reference—Psalm 139:23, 24

> If we confess our sins, He is faithful and just to forgive us our sins, and to cleanse us from all unrighteousness. 1 John 1:9

The author of this hymn text, J. Edwin Orr, is widely known as an evangelist and as a noted scholar of the revival movements of history. He is presently the president of an organization known as the Oxford Association for Research in Revival or Evangelical Awakening, which is located in Los Angeles, California. This organization of church leaders from around the world is the out-growth of an annual conference begun in mid-1974 at Oxford, England, to further research and disseminate information in the field of Evangelical Awakenings. In addition to lecturing and holding workshops on this subject throughout the world, Dr. Orr is the author of a score of books, both popular and scholarly, with a circulation in English and a dozen other languages of more than a million copies, including a best-seller in the 1930's. During the 1970's, Mr. Orr wrote a new standard text each year. Since 1967, J. Edwin Orr has been a professor in the School of World Missions at Fuller Theological Seminary (presently professor emeritus), where he taught courses in the history of missions to career missionaries and evangelistic apologetics to theologues.

James Edwin Orr was born on January 12, 1912, in Belfast, Ireland, of an American father and a British mother. His education includes earned doctorates from universities in Europe, Asia, Africa, and America, including the Doctor of Philosophy from Oxford University and the Ed.D. from U.C.L.A. in 1971. He is a fellow of many learned societies. Dr. Orr also served as a chaplain in the United States Air Force in the Pacific from 1943-46. Since World War II, Mr. and Mrs. Orr have been California residents. In his many travels, Dr. Orr has visited a hundred and fifty countries, including the Soviet Union, and has been in two-thirds of the world's six hundred major cities.

Despite these numerous life-long accomplishments for God, J. Edwin Orr will no doubt be best remembered as the author of a simple, yet, one of the most challenging, revival hymn texts in all of hymnody. Dr. Orr recalls that he wrote the "Cleanse Me" text, in 1936, as a result of great inspiration during an intense movement of the Holy Spirit at the Easter, revival convention in Ngaruawahia, New Zealand. For some time prior to this Easter campaign, an attitude of unusual expectancy had been prevalent among these people. Prayer meetings spread throughout the city with much fervency, and intercession led to wide-spread confessions and reconciliations among the believers. The regular Easter Sunday tent meeting was so crowded that a midnight service had to be scheduled, and great numbers of unconverted students professed faith in Christ. The next night was given over to exultant testimony, with singing "such as one expects in heaven." The revival news soon spread throughout all of New Zealand and a similar revival spirit characterized later campaigns held in Wellington, Christchurch, Dunedin and Auckland.

Dr. Orr reports that as he was leaving New Zealand, four Aborigine girls approached and sang for him the beautiful Maori Song of Farewell:

Po atu rau, I moe a i ho ne; E haere ana, Koe ki pa ma mao;
Haere ra, Ma hara mai ano   Ki-ite tau, I tangi atu nei.

Mr. Orr was so impressed with the beauty of this Polynesian melody that soon afterward he wrote new verses to the tune on the back of an envelope in the post office at the little town of Ngaruawahia. Though the words were an out-growth of his New Zealand campaigns, the text was based on the familiar words of Scripture found in Psalm 139:23, 24:

Search me, O God, and know my heart; try me, and know my thoughts; and see if there be any wicked way in me, and lead me in the way everlasting.

Further campaigns by Dr. Orr throughout Australia in the 1930's, and later in nearly all of the English-speaking world, soon popularized this prayer hymn everywhere. During the 1952 campaign in Brazil, the Portuguese translation of the hymn was again instrumental in the spiritual awakening in that country.

The "Maori" tune has also been widely used with the secular ballad "Now Is the Hour," especially popular during the World War II years and throughout the 1950's.

Revival in Scripture, writes Dr. Orr, must be recognized as the work of God—"Wilt Thou not revive us again?" (Psalm 85:6) "Revive Thy work, O Lord!" (Habakkuk 3:2). Dr. Orr's concern for the present is stated in these words: 61

Sad to say, the study of such remarkable movements of the Spirit has been neglected, and a humanist interpretation of evangelism was applied instead. The Oxford Association for Research in Revival has been remedying this situation in the hope that the people of God may be stirred to pray for yet another, worldwide awakening.

*   *   *

"It is the genius of the gospel that it is extremely personal. It centers in a Savior, not a system; in a Master, not a message; and calls me, not to a creed, but to Christ."

Howard Crago

O BREATH OF LIFE

"O Breath of Life, come sweeping thru us,
Revive Thy Church with life and pow'r;
O Breath of Life, come cleanse, renew us,
And fit Thy Church to meet this hour.

"Revive us, Lord! Is zeal abating
While harvest fields are vast and white?
Revive us, Lord—the world is waiting!
Equip Thy Church to spread the light."

Bessie Porter Head

17 Come, Ye Disconsolate

CONSOLATOR

Thomas Moore, 1779-1852-alt.
Thomas Hastings, 1784-1872

Samuel Webbe, 1740-1816

1. Come, ye dis-con-so-late, wher-e'er ye lan-guish—
2. Joy of the des-o-late, light of the stray-ing,
3. Here see the Bread of Life, see wa-ters flow-ing

Come to the mer-cy-seat, fer-vent-ly kneel; Here bring your wounded hearts,
Hope of the pen-i-tent, fade-less and pure! Here speaks the Com-fort-er,
Forth from the throne of God, pure from a-bove; Come to the feast of love —

here tell your an-guish: Earth has no sor-row that heav'n can-not heal.
ten-der-ly say-ing, "Earth has no sor-row that heav'n can-not cure."
come ev-er know-ing Earth has no sor-row but heav'n can re-move.

Come, Ye Disconsolate

Authors—Thomas Moore, 1779-1852. Verses 1 and 2 with alterations
        Thomas Hastings, 1784-1872. Verse 3
Composer—Samuel Webbe, 1740-1816
Tune Name—"Consolator"
Meter—11 10. 11 10

Casting all your care upon Him; for He careth for you.   1 Peter 5:7

The original text for this comforting hymn was written by an Irish Roman Catholic, Thomas Moore. Although Moore is the author of thirty-two sacred songs, he is best known for his ballads and other secular poems. He wrote such sentimental favorites as "The Last Rose of Summer," "Believe Me, If All Those Endearing Young Charms," "The Minstrel Boy," and a number of other romantic ballads that have lived through the years. Following the publication of his *Irish Melodies*, 1807-1809, he became known as the "Voice of Ireland" in much the same fashion as Robert Burns represented Scotland. It is said that Moore's literary skills, both in prose and poetry, contributed much to the political emancipation of his country, for his writings revealed, to the English public, the spirit of a people, whom they had previously found distasteful. Thomas Moore was one of the few writers of his day to have made a financial success of writing poetry. He received several large sums and royalties for his works. However, because of his poor business practices, he spent the last years of his life poor, unhappy, and mentally disturbed. His death occurred on February 26, 1852, at the age of seventy-three.

Moore's father was a prosperous merchant in Dublin, where Thomas was born on May 28, 1779. Young Moore was sent to Trinity College, Dublin, but he was not allowed to graduate, because of his Roman Catholic affiliation. Thomas Moore later trained to become a lawyer but never could bring himself to begin a legal career. He also was given an Admiralty post in Bermuda, but the monotony of this life soon caused him to resign the job and devote his life exclusively to the writing of literature.

The first two stanzas of "Come, Ye Disconsolate" appeared in Moore's collection, published in 1824: A songbook entitled *Sacred Songs-Duets and Trios*. The hymn was titled "Relief in Prayer." The hymn as sung today, however, has experienced considerable revision. For example, the second line of the first stanza originally read "Come to the shrine of God, fervently kneel." This was changed to "Come to the Mercy seat, fervently kneel." The second line of the second stanza was changed from "hope when all others die" to "hope of the penitent." Moore's third stanza was completely different from the one used today. It originally read: "Go ask the infidel what boon he brings us, what charm for aching hearts he can reveal? Sweet as that heavenly promise hope sings us, earth has no sorrow that heaven cannot heal."

Thomas Hastings, American hymnist, is the one who greatly altered Moore's text. He included the hymn in the collection, *Spiritual Songs for Social Worship*, in 1831, edited by Mason and Hastings. It is generally agreed that Hastings rescued an interesting poem and made it usable for evangelical churches.

Thomas Hastings was born on October 15, 1784, at Washington, Connecticut. Though his formal musical training was meager, and, as an albino, he was afflicted with eye problems throughout his life; yet he wrote no less than fifty volumes of church music, including 1000 hymn tunes and more than 600 original hymn texts, and edited more than fifty music collections. He has supplied the music for such beloved hymns as "Rock of Ages" (*101 Hymn Stories*, No. 78), "From Every Storm Wind That

63

Blows" (*ibid.*, No. 24), and "Majestic Sweetness Sits Enthroned" (*ibid.*, No. 56). It is said, however, that Hasting's most important contribution was the effort he expended in the improvement of singing, so badly needed at that time in American churches. Thomas Hastings was regarded as the foremost choir trainer of his day, and was constantly in demand for that purpose. He was a man of strong convictions regarding sacred music. He once stated: "The homage that we owe Almighty God calls for the noblest and most reverential tribute that music can render." Along with Lowell Mason, Thomas Hastings is generally credited with being the person most influential in shaping the development of church music in the United States during the nineteenth century.

The composer, Samuel Webbe, born in London, England, in 1740, was a respected organist in several, large Roman Catholic churches in London during his lifetime. He published a number of collections of sacred music suited for Catholic services. His tune, "Consolator," which likely was adapted from an old German melody, first appeared in Webbe's *A Collection of Motets or Antiphons* in 1792. The tune reappeared with Hasting's revised text in the 1831 collection of *Spiritual Songs for Social Worship*. This meaningful text with its well-suited music has had an important place in most evangelical hymnals until the present time.

64

*   *   *

"May it always be the church's mission to provide healing for the wounded. Far too often we have spent our time wounding the healed."

Unknown

HYMN OF TRUST

"O Love divine, that stooped to share
Our sharpest pang, our bitterest
On Thee we cast each earth-born care;
We smile at pain, while Thou art near!

"Though long the weary way we tread,
And sorrow crown each lingering year,
No path we shun, no darkness dread,
Our hearts still whispering, 'Thou art near!'

"When drooping pleasure turns to grief,
And trembling faith is changed to fear,
The murmuring wind, the quivering leaf
Shall softly tell us Thou art near!

"On Thee we fling our burdening woe,
O Love divine, forever dear,
Content to suffer, while we know,
Living and dying, Thou art near!"

Oliver Wendell Holmes

18

Come, Ye Thankful People

ST. GEORGE'S, WINDSOR

Henry Alford, 1810-1871

George J. Elvey, 1816-1893

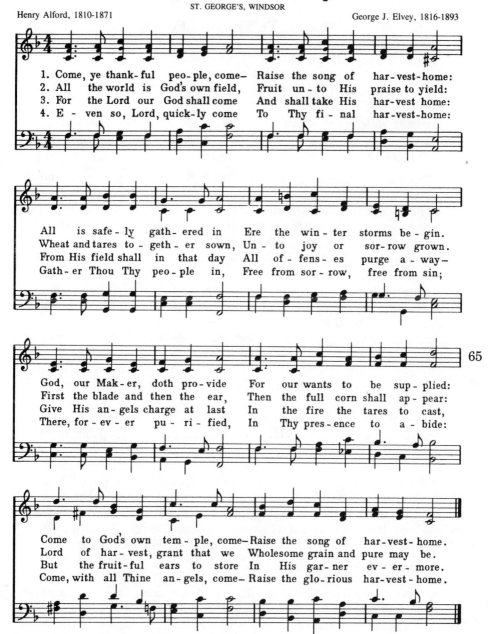

1. Come, ye thank-ful peo-ple, come— Raise the song of har-vest-home:
2. All the world is God's own field, Fruit un-to His praise to yield:
3. For the Lord our God shall come And shall take His har-vest home:
4. E - ven so, Lord, quick-ly come To Thy fi - nal har-vest-home:

All is safe-ly gath-ered in Ere the win-ter storms be-gin.
Wheat and tares to-geth-er sown, Un-to joy or sor-row grown.
From His field shall in that day All of-fens-es purge a-way—
Gath-er Thou Thy peo-ple in, Free from sor-row, free from sin;

God, our Mak-er, doth pro-vide For our wants to be sup-plied:
First the blade and then the ear, Then the full corn shall ap-pear:
Give His an-gels charge at last In the fire the tares to cast,
There, for-ev-er pu-ri-fied, In Thy pres-ence to a-bide:

65

Come to God's own tem-ple, come— Raise the song of har-vest-home.
Lord of har-vest, grant that we Wholesome grain and pure may be.
But the fruit-ful ears to store In His gar-ner ev-er-more.
Come, with all Thine an-gels, come— Raise the glo-rious har-vest-home.

Come, Ye Thankful People

Author—Henry Alford, 1810-1871
Composer—George J. Elvey, 1816-1893
Tune Name—"St. George's, Windsor"
Meter—77.77 doubled
Scripture References—Matthew 13:24-30; 36-43; Mark 4:26-29

> It is a good thing to give thanks unto the Lord, and to sing praises unto Thy name, O most high. Psalm 92:1

"Come, Ye Thankful People" is considered to be one of the most choice harvest-thanksgiving hymns in all of hymnody. It was written for the English harvest festivals, a movable feast varying with the harvest time in the various villages. Its author, Henry "Dean" Alford, is generally regarded as one of the most gifted, Christian leaders of the nineteenth century, distinguishing himself as a theologian, scholar, writer, poet, artist, and musician.

Henry Alford was born in London, October 7, 1810. His father, as well as his ancestors in several previous generations, were respected clergymen in the Anglican Church, and early in life, young Alford decided to follow their examples. At the age of sixteen, he wrote in the fly-leaf of his Bible these words which characterized his entire life: "I do this day, in the presence of God and my own soul, renew my covenant with God, and solemnly determine henceforth to become His, and to do His work as far as in me lies."

At Trinity College, Cambridge, Alford distinguished himself as a student and writer, and, upon graduation in 1832, he began his public ministry in London. He rose rapidly from one position to another, until he was named Dean of Canterbury Cathedral, the "mother-church" of all England, at the age of forty-seven, where he remained, until his death in 1871. Even in this prestigious position, Alford maintained strong relations with evangelicals and other non-conformist groups and did all he could to resist the high church movement within the Anglican Church. It was as a Greek scholar that he attained his greatest distinction. His four-volume edition of the Greek Testament, on which he labored for twenty years, became the standard critical commentary of the later nineteenth century. As a member of the New Testament Revision Committee, he made a notable contribution to biblical knowledge on both sides of the Atlantic.

Hymnology was one of Henry Alford's major interests, and he translated and composed numerous hymns, which he published in his *Psalms and Hymns* (1844), *The Year of Praise* (1867), and *Poetical Works* (1852 and 1868). Of these many works, only "Come, Ye Thankful People" is still in general use in most evangelical hymnals.

This hymn first appeared in Alford's *Psalms and Hymns*, in 1844. It was originally titled "After Harvest" and was accompanied by the text "He that goeth forth and weepeth, bearing precious seed, shall doubtless come again with rejoicing, bringing his sheaves with him" (Psalm 126:6). The hymn originally contained seven stanzas, but only four have remained in common usage.

The first stanza of this harvest hymn is an invitation and an exhortation to give thanks to God in the earthly temple—His Church—for the heavenly care and provision of our earthly needs. The following two stanzas are an interesting commentary on the Parable of the Wheat and the Tares as recorded in Matthew 13:24-30, 36-43. The final stanza is a prayer for the Lord's return—"the final harvest home"—the culminating event that Henry Alford sees as the ultimate demonstration of God's goodness in His eternal purpose of man's Redemption.

It is said that at the end of a hard day's work, as well as after every meal, it was customary practice for "Dean" Alford to stand to his feet and give thanks to God for the blessings just received or enjoyed during the day. This spirit of perpetual gratitude is clearly evidenced throughout this hymn.

Because of Alford's strenuous efforts and unlimited activities in the Christian ministry, he suffered a physical breakdown in 1870, and died on January 12, 1871. His passing was mourned throughout the entire Christian world. During his lifetime one of the "Dean's" unfulfilled, cherished dreams was to visit the Holy Land. Although this dream was never realized, it was said of him that his eyes were ever fixed upon the Heavenly Jerusalem toward which he journeyed. On his tombstone the following appropriate inscription is found: "The Inn of a Pilgrim Traveling to Jerusalem."

The composer of this tune, "St. George's, Windsor", was George J. Elvey, who served as the organist for forty-seven years at the historic, royal chapel at Windsor Castle in England. He originally composed the music for James Montgomery's text "Hark! the Song of Jubilee," published in E. H. Thorne's *Selection of Psalm and Hymn Tunes* in 1858. In 1861, this tune first appeared wedded to Henry Alford's text in the well-known Anglican Church hymnal, *Hymns Ancient and Modern.* It has found a place in nearly every published hymnal to the present time.

George Elvey was knighted by Queen Victoria, in 1871, for his many years of faithful service to the royal family as well as for his various musical publications, including several oratorios, anthems, and collections of service music. Elvey is also the composer of the familiar hymn tune "Diademata," generally used with such hymn texts as "Crown Him With Many Crowns" and "Soldiers of Christ Arise."

* * *

"The worship most acceptable to God comes from a thankful and cheerful heart."

Plutarch

19   Dear Lord and Father of Mankind

REST

John Greenleaf Whittier, 1807-1892   Frederick C. Maker, 1844-1927

1. Dear Lord and Fa-ther of man-kind, For-give our fe-v'rish
2. In sim-ple trust like theirs who heard, Be-side the Syr-ian
3. O Sab-bath rest by Gal-i-lee! O calm of hills a-
4. Drop thy still dews of qui-et-ness Till all our striv-ings
5. Breathe thru the heats of our de-sire Thy cool-ness and thy

ways! Re-clothe us in our right-ful mind; In pur-er
sea, The gra-cious call-ing of the Lord, Let us, like
bove, Where Je-sus knelt to share with thee The si-lence
cease; Take from our souls the strain and stress, And let our
balm; Let sense be dumb, let flesh re-tire; Speak thru the

68

lives Thy serv-ice find, In deep-er rev-'rence, praise.
them, with-out a word Rise up and fol-low Thee.
of e-ter-ni-ty, In-ter-pret-ed by love—
or-dered lives con-fess The beau-ty of Thy peace.
earth-quake, wind, and fire, O still small voice of calm!

Dear Lord and Father of Mankind

Author—John Greenleaf Whittier, 1807-1892
Composer—Frederick C. Maker, 1844-1927
Tune Name—"Rest"
Meter—86.886

...In quietness and in confidence shall be your strength...   Isaiah 30:15

The author of this thoughtful text has often been called "America's beloved Quaker poet." He is generally regarded as one of our nation's ablest and most distinguished poets. He was pre-eminent in writing

American ballads such as "The Swan Song of Parson Avery" and "Skipper Ireson's Ride."

Whittier wrote this hymn text, in 1872, to express his Quaker conviction that the way to God was through simplicity and sincerity. It was part of his larger seventeen-stanza poem entitled "The Brewing of Soma," published in the April, 1872, issue of the *Atlantic Monthly* magazine. "Soma" was the name of an intoxicating drink used in the religious rites of a Hindu sect in India. In this poem, Whittier describes the intoxicating effects of this drink upon those who drank it, as they imagined themselves to be in the presence of the gods, producing a "frenzy, a sacred madness, an ecstatic storm of drunken joy." He then likened the religious experiences of many in the present day churches whose practices were just as false and harmful as were the Soma rites. Whittier wrote that many churches still try to lift men up to heaven by "music, incense, vigils drear, and trance." He deplored the emotional revivals and camp meetings especially popular in his day.

> And yet the past comes round again,
> And new doth old fulfil;
> In sensual transports wild as vain
> We brew in many a Christian fane
> The heathen Soma still.

Pomp, ritual, or emotion never had a place in Whittier's view of worship. To him, the degree of man's belief in God was always reflected in the way a man made use of the life God had given him in his love relation to others. "O brother man! fold to thy breast thy brother. To worship rightly is to love each other, each smile a hymn, each kindly deed a prayer."

John Greenleaf Whittier is often grouped with his famed New England literary contemporaries, Ralph Waldo Emerson, Henry Wadsworth Longfellow, James Russell Lowell, and Oliver Wendell Holmes. However, because of the extreme poverty in which he was raised in his rural New England Quaker home, Whittier, unlike most of his noted contemporaries, did not have a formal college education. Spiritually, too, the Quaker poet stood out among his fellows, most of whom were Unitarian in their beliefs.

John Whittier began writing poetry at an early age, inspired by the works of Robert Burns. One day Whittier's sister sent one of his poems to the editor of the weekly *Free Press* in Newbury Port, William Lloyd Garrison. The editor was much impressed with the young poet's works, and the two men began a long and cherished friendship. John was encouraged by the editor to study at the Haverhill Academy for two years to prepare for a career in journalism. For some years, Whittier had an extensive journalistic career in such cities as Boston, Hartford, Philadelphia, and Washington.

69

Later, he was elected to the Massachusetts legislature and still later became editor of the *Pennsylvania Freeman*. Whittier also became closely associated with the influential magazine, *The Atlantic Monthly*, founded shortly before the outbreak of the Civil War. In all of his writings during this time, John Whittier wrote strongly for the abolition of the national curse of slavery. In 1866, with the publishing of one of his most popular works, "Snow-Bound," his national reputation as a writer was securely established. In this work, he describes beautifully the winter scenery and life style on his New England farm at Haverhill, Massachusetts. Another volume, *Poetical Works*, appeared in 1869 and his *Complete Poetical Works*, seven years later. His works included much writing in prose as well as poetry.

Whittier was thoroughly Quaker in thought, speech, and dress. He wore the quaint garb of the Society of Friends and continued to use their distinctive style of speech. The following is a conversation he is reported to have had with Ralph Waldo Emerson:

> "I suppose thee would admit that Jesus Christ is the highest development our world has ever seen."
>
> "Yes, yes," replied Emerson, "but not the highest it will see."
>
> "Dost thee think the world has yet reached the ideals He has set for mankind?"
>
> "No, no, I think not."
>
> "Then," concluded the Quaker, "is it not the part of wisdom to be content with what has been given us till we have lived up to that ideal?"

70

Whittier had little personal knowledge of hymn singing, since the Quakers did not allow singing in their services at that time. He once remarked: "Two hundred years of silence has taken all the sing out of the Quakers." Yet it was Whittier who once said, "A good hymn is the best use to which poetry can be devoted, though I do not claim to have succeeded in writing one." Though he wrote no hymns as such, hymnal editors have taken enough excerpts from his poems to make some seventy-five hymns. In this way, it can be said that Whittier has written more poems that are used as hymns than any other American poet. Another of his enduring hymns is "Immortal Love, Forever Full," which speaks so beautifully of the nearness of God in all of life's exigencies. Other Whittier hymns are "We May Not Climb the Heavenly Steeps," and "All Things Are Thine, No Gift Have We."

John Greenleaf Whittier's long and fruitful life ended on September 7, 1892 in his beloved hills of New Hampshire. He was buried at Amesbury with simple Quaker rites. The Amesbury House is now a national shrine, visited annually by many admirers of the Quaker poet. Another poet, Phoebe Cary, wrote these lines as a memorial to Whittier:

But not thy strains with courage rife,
Nor holiest hymns, shall rank above
The rhythmic beauty of thy life,
Itself a canticle of love.

It has been well said that John Greenleaf Whittier "left upon our literature the stamp of genius and upon our religion the touch of sanity."

Frederick C. Maker, the composer of this tune, "Rest," was known as an accomplished Irish musician and composer. Maker travelled extensively and lived in various parts of the world. It is said that he gave so many concerts in poor areas that he was known for accepting anything of value for his services. It is recorded that the box office receipts for one of his concerts included 100 sheep and a number of chickens. The tune "Rest" was composed for Whittier's text, in 1887, for use in the *Congregational Church Hymnal*, published in London, England.

Frederick Maker is also the composer of the hymn "Beneath the Cross of Jesus" (*101 Hymn Stories*, No. 10).

*   *   *

REAL PRAYER
"The prayer preceding all prayers is,
May it be the real I who speaks.
May it be the real Thou that I speak to."
C. S. Lewis

A PRAYER FOR CHRISTIAN LEADERS OF WORSHIP
"O God of Eternal beauty and harmony, Who has ordained that
men shall declare your glory in the joy of music—
Anoint with your Spirit all who, by voice or instrument, lead
the praises of your people,
That in sincerity and truth, we may ever magnify your name
in concert with saints and angels.
Through Jesus Christ our Lord, Amen."
Anonymous

Depth of Mercy

ALETTA

Charles Wesley, 1707-1788   William B. Bradbury, 1816-1868

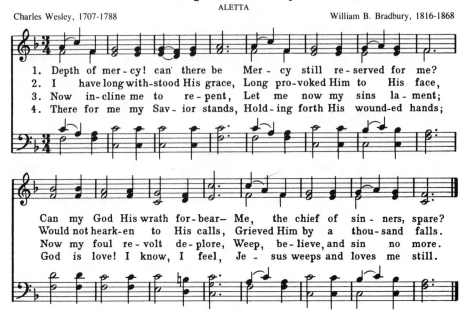

1. Depth of mer - cy! can' there be   Mer - cy still re - served for me?
2. I have long with-stood His grace,   Long pro-voked Him to His face,
3. Now in - cline me to re - pent,   Let me now my sins la - ment;
4. There for me my Sav - ior stands,   Hold - ing forth His wound-ed hands;

Can my God His wrath for - bear—   Me, the chief of sin - ners, spare?
Would not heark-en to His calls,   Grieved Him by a thou-sand falls.
Now my foul re - volt de - plore,   Weep, be - lieve, and sin no more.
God is love! I know, I feel,   Je - sus weeps and loves me still.

Depth of Mercy

*Author—*Charles Wesley, 1707-1788
*Composer—*William B. Bradbury, 1816-1868
Tune Name—"Aletta"
*Meter—*77.77

For Thou, Lord, art good, and ready to forgive; and plenteous in mercy unto all them that call upon Thee.   Psalm 86:5

Charles Wesley was born at Epworth, Lincolnshire, England, on December 18, 1707. He was next to the youngest of nineteen children born to Samuel Wesley and his remarkable wife, Susanna. The Wesley family had long been one of the distinguished families in England. Both great-grandfather and grandfather had been Oxford University graduates and Church of England clergymen. The father, Samuel Wesley, was also a clergyman in the Anglican Church. He, too, possessed more than ordinary literary gifts. He was the author of at least one hymn that has survived, entitled "Behold, the Savior of Mankind." The mother, of whom many books and articles have been written, ably assisted her husband in his ministry and also provided the academic and spiritual training for each of her nineteen children.

Charles received a thorough education both from his mother and later at the Westminster School of London, where his older brother, Samuel, was the headmaster. At the age of nineteen, he entered Oxford University. Upon graduation, Charles received holy orders from the Anglican Church and sailed for the United States with brother John, to assist Governor Oglethorpe, in Georgia, as well as to evangelize the Indians. This American experience proved to be one of the low points in both of these brothers' lives, and within a short time they returned to England, discouraged and broken in spirit.

On Pentecost Sunday, May 20, 1738, Charles attended a religious service conducted by a small group of devout, Moravian believers. The following account is found in Wesley's journal concerning that evening:

> At midnight I gave myself to Christ; assured that I was safe, whether sleeping or waking. I had the continual experience of His power to overcome all temptation, and confessed, with joy and surprise, that He was able to do exceedingly abundantly for me, above what I can ask or think.

A short time later, John had a similar Aldersgate spiritual experience. From that time on, both of these brothers became aflame for God and had a sense of missionary zeal, to confront and persuade every individual, with the need for a personal conversion experience and then to instruct believers in the great teachings of Scripture. One of the important vehicles for accomplishing these purposes was the writing and use of hymns. Charles alone wrote more than 6500 hymn texts. For music, they simply adapted any popular tune they felt was suitable in communicating effectively the message of a new text.

One of the Wesley's early concerns was for ministering the gospel to the poor prisoners in Newgate, the infamous London prison. This was the time when prisoners were cruelly treated and could be severely punished and sometimes hanged for even the slightest offense. Some of the most popular public shows of that day were the mass hangings conducted every six weeks. For lesser crimes, there were such tortures as the pillory, the stocks, the whipping post, the branding-iron, and endless time in the atrocious jail itself. John Wesley wrote in a letter to the *London Chronicle*, on January 2, 1761: "Of all the seats of woe this side of hell, few, I suppose, exceed or even equal Newgate."

Charles Wesley wrote in his diary of July 12, 1738:

> Preached at Newgate to the condemned felons, and visited one of them in his cell, sick of a fever—a poor black that had robbed his master. I told him of One who came down from heaven to save lost sinners, and him in particular; described the sufferings of the Son of God, His sorrows, agony and death. He listened with all the signs of eager astonishment; the tears trickled down

73

his cheeks while he cried, "What! was it for me? Did God suffer all this for so poor a creature as me?" I left him waiting for the salvation of God...

The Wesleys never tired of telling individuals of all social classes this simple message of God's mercy and how any life could be changed dramatically simply by accepting and believing this truth. Despite much persecution from the established church, there were countless numbers that responded wherever they preached.

"Depth of Mercy" first appeared in the Wesley hymnal, *Hymns and Sacred Poems*, published in 1740. It originally had thirteen four-line stanzas and was titled "After a Relapse Into Sin."

Charles Wesley is also the author of the hymn "A Charge to Keep I Have" (No. 1) and the Christmas carol "Hark! The Herald Angels Sing" (No. 31). Other Charles Wesley hymns include: "Christ the Lord Is Risen Today" (*101 Hymn Stories*, No. 13), "Jesus, Lover of My Soul" (*ibid.*, No.45), and "O For a Thousand Tongues" (*ibid.*, No. 65).

Dr. Belcher, in his book, *Historical Notes on Hymns and Authors*, relates the story of an English actress, who was visiting in a country town, when she heard a group of humble people in a cottage singing "Depth of Mercy." She entered and found in progress a simple service, which she followed with the deepest emotion. After she had departed, the tender words of Charles Wesley's hymn continued to haunt her, and at last she was able to secure a copy of the hymnal. Over and over she read the words with their winsome picture of Christ, wounded for her transgressions, weeping for her waywardness, but still loving her with an infinite love. Soon she surrendered her life to the Savior.

74

The actress' conscience troubled her about continuing her work on the stage, but finally she consented to do one last leading role for a new play, soon to be produced. Finally, on opening night, all was in readiness for her to make an entrance on stage singing one of the play's songs. But this she could not do, for she kept thinking of her recent conversion and of the hymn which had brought her to Christ. Finally, clasping her hands and with tears in her eyes, she sang with great impact upon the audience:

> Depth of mercy! can there be
> Mercy still reserved for me?
> Can my God His wrath forbear,
> Me, the chief of sinners, spare?

Dr. William B. Bradbury, the composer of the tune "Aletta," was one of the most important contributors to the development of early gospel hymnody in this country. He was born in York, Maine, on October 6, 1816. As a young man he moved to Boston, Massachusetts, where he became associated with Lowell Mason, often called the "Father of American Public School and Church Music." Bradbury served as choir director and organist in several, large Baptist churches in the East, where he became especially known for his work with children's choirs. He is also credited with being largely responsible for the introduction, of the teaching of music, in the New York City public schools, during this time. Several of the still popular hymns for which Bradbury contributed the music include: "Even Me" (No. 23), "The Solid Rock" (No. 87), "Sweet Hour of Prayer" (No. 82), "He Leadeth Me" (*101 Hymn Stories*, No. 28), "Jesus Loves Me" (*ibid.*, No. 47), and "Just As I Am" (*ibid.*, No. 52).

The "Aletta" tune first appeared in Bradbury's collection, *The Jubileee* (1858), where it was used for the hymn text "Weary Sinner, Keep Thine Eyes." It has been a useful tune for other 77.77 meter hymn texts such as "Holy Bible, Book Divine."

*   *   *

"Mercy signifies that essential perfection in God, whereby He pities and relieves the miseries of His creatures; and Grace flows from mercy as its fountain."

Cruden's Concordance

*   *   *

ANSWERED PRAYER

"I asked God for strength, that I might achieve,
I was made weak, that I might learn humbly to obey...
I asked for health, that I might do greater things,
I was given infirmity, that I might do better things...
I asked for riches, that I might be happy,
I was given poverty, that I might be wise....
I asked for power, that I might have the praise of men,
I was given weakness, that I might feel the need of God...
I asked for all things that I might enjoy life,
I was given life, that I might enjoy all things...
I got nothing that I asked for—but everything I had hoped for;
Almost despite myself, my unspoken prayers were answered.
I am among all men most richly blessed."

An Unknown Confederate Soldier

21 Does Jesus Care?

Frank E. Graeff, 1860-1919

J. Lincoln Hall, 1866-1930

1. Does Je-sus care when my heart is pained Too deep-ly for mirth and song; As the bur-dens press, and the cares dis-tress, And the way grows wea-ry and long?

2. Does Je-sus care when my way is dark With a name-less dread and fear? As the day-light fades in-to deep night shades, Does He care e-nough to be near?

3. Does Je-sus care when I've tried and failed To re-sist some temp-ta-tion strong; When for my deep grief I find no re-lief, Tho my tears flow all the night long?

4. Does Je-sus care when I've said good-bye To the dear-est on earth to me, And my sad heart aches till it near-ly breaks— Is it aught to Him? does He see?

CHORUS

O yes, He cares— I know He cares! His heart is touched with my grief; When the days are wea-ry, the long nights drear-y, I know my Sav-ior cares. (He cares.)

Does Jesus Care?

Author—Frank E. Graeff, 1860-1919
Composer—J. Lincoln Hall, 1866-1930
Scripture Reference—1 Peter 5:7

> . . .Lo, I am with you alway, even unto the end of the world.   Matthew 28:20

Is God really present and concerned during my times of hurt? Does He care, when the burdens weigh heavily on my every thought and activity? Does He care, when I can no longer resist some strong temptation? Does He care, when I must say a final farewell to my dearest loved one on earth?

These questions and doubts are common to nearly all of God's children at some time or other in life, just as they were to the author of this text, Frank E. Graeff. Mr. Graeff was a minister in the Methodist denomination and served some of its leading churches, in the Philadelphia Conference. Throughout the district, he was known as the "sunshine minister." C. Austin Miles, author of the popular hymn, "In the Garden," paid this tribute to Frank Graeff:

> He is a spiritual optimist, a great friend of children; his bright sun-shining disposition attracts him not only to children, but to all with whom he comes in contact. He has a holy magnetism and a child-like faith.

77

In spite of his outwardly-cheery disposition and winsome personality, Graeff was often called upon to go through severe testing experiences in his life. It was while passing through such a test and experiencing severe despondency, doubt and physical agony, that Mr. Graeff wrote this text. He turned to the Scriptures for solace and strength. First Peter 5:7 became especially meaningful to him during this particular struggle:

> "Casting all your care upon Him; for He careth for you."

The phrase, "He careth for you," spoke deeply to his need and eventually became the basis for this text.

Frank Graeff was born on December 19, 1860, in Tamaqua, Pennsylvania, and died on July 29, 1919, at Ocean Grove, New Jersey. At an early age, he felt called of God to the Christian ministry and was admitted to the Philadelphia Conference of the Methodist Church, in 1890. Graeff was always interested in the children in his churches and became well-known for his story-telling ability with the youngsters. Altogether, Mr. Graeff authored more than 200 hymns as well as a successful novel, *The Minister's Twins.*

The composer of the music, J. Lincoln Hall, born on November 4, 1866, in Philadelphia, was a prominent person in the fields of gospel and sacred music throughout his life. He graduated with high honors from the University of Pennsylvania and later received the honorary Doctor of Music degree from Harriman University. Hall was a highly respected song leader, choral conductor, composer, and music publisher. He wrote music for many cantatas, oratorios, anthems, and hundreds of gospel songs. For many years, he was associated with the Hall-Mack Publishing Company in Philadelphia, which later merged with the Rodeheaver Publishing Company in Winona Lake, Indiana.

Hall composed this music especially for Graeff's text. It was copyrighted in 1901. Mr. Hall once remarked that this musical setting was his most inspired piece of music. The first publication of the hymn seems to have been, in 1905, in the hymnal, *New Songs of the Gospel*, No. 2, published by the Hall-Mack Company.

To experience times of questions and even doubts regarding the nearness of God, as Frank Graeff did in the verses of this hymn, is only human and normal. It is only as a believer comes through such a struggle, however, with the firm conviction as Mr. Graeff did in the chorus of this hymn, "O yes He cares, I know He cares," that a child of God can be truly victorious.

78

*   *   *

CAN HE CARE?
"Among so many, can He care?
Can special love be everywhere?
A myriad homes—a myriad ways—
And God's eye over every place?
I asked: my soul bethought of this:
In just that very place of His
Where He hath put and keepeth you,
God hath no other thing to do!"
A.D.T. Whitney

22   Eternal (Almighty) Father, Strong to Save

William Whiting, 1825-1878
Robert Nelson Spencer, 1937-1961

John B. Dykes, 1823-1876

1. Al - might - y Fa - ther, strong to save, Whose arm hath bound the
2. O Christ, the Lord of hill and plain, O'er which our traf - fic
3. O Spir - it, whom the Fa - ther sent To spread a - broad the
4. O Trin - i - ty of love and pow'r, Our breth - ren shield in

rest - less wave, Who bidd'st the might - y o - cean deep
runs a - main By moun - tain pass or val - ley low:
fir - ma - ment: O Wind of heav - en, by Thy might
dan - ger's hour; From rock and tem - pest, fire and foe,

Its own ap - point - ed lim - its keep: O hear us when we
Wher - ev - er, Lord, Thy breth-ren go, Pro - tect them by Thy
Save all who dare the ea - gle's flight, And keep them by Thy
Pro - tect them where-so - e'er they go: Thus ev - er - more shall

cry to Thee For those in per - il on the sea.
guard - ing hand From ev - 'ry per - il on the land.
watch - ful care From ev - 'ry per - il in the air.
rise to Thee Glad praise from air and land and sea.*

Eternal (Almighty) Father, Strong to Save

Authors—William Whiting, 1825-1878
Robert Nelson Spencer, 1937-1961
Composer—John B. Dykes, 1823-1876
Tune Name—"Melita"
Meter—88.88.88
Scripture Reference—Psalm 107:23-32

> The Lord knoweth how to deliver the godly out of temptations, and to preserve the
> unjust unto the day of judgment to be punished.   2 Peter 2:9

"Eternal Father, Strong to Save," or known to many as the "Navy Hymn," has often been cited as the most popular hymn for travelers in the English language. It was written, in 1860, by William Whiting and has gone through numerous revisions to the present time. The hymn text was so well thought of, when it was written, that it was included in the 1861 edition of the highly regarded, Anglican Church hymnal, *Hymns Ancient and Modern*. It was set to the fine "Melita" tune, especially composed for it by one of England's highly esteemed church musicians of the nineteenth century, John B. Dykes. The present version is taken from the 1937 edition of the *Missionary Service Book*, where one of the editors, Robert Nelson Spencer, added the second and third stanzas to include a plea for God's protection for those who travel by land and air as well as those on the high seas.

William Whiting was born on November 1, 1825, in London, England. Little is known of his life except that he was an Anglican churchman and that he held the position of headmaster at the Winchester College Choristers' School, for thirty-five years. He published a book of poems, *Rural Thoughts*, in 1851 and wrote several other hymn texts no longer in use. William Whiting died at Winchester on May 3, 1878.

The composer, John Bacchus Dykes, was born on March 10, 1823, at Hull, England. Following his graduation from Cambridge University, in 1847, he became active in the ministry of the Church of England. In 1861, he was awarded the Doctorate of Music Degree from Durham University in recognition of his many musical accomplishments, including the writing of three hundred hymn tunes, many of which are still in use today. His tunes have been described as the finest examples of the Victorian times, which they represented. Several of the familiar hymns for which John B. Dykes supplied the music include: the "Nicaea" tune—"Holy, Holy, Holy" (*101 Hymn Stories*, No. 31), the "Vox Dilecti" tune—"I Heard the Voice of Jesus Say" (*ibid.*, No. 35), the "St. Agnes" tune—"Jesus, the Very Thought of Thee" (*ibid.*, No. 49), and the "Lux Benigna" tune—

"Lead, Kindly Light" (*ibid.*, No. 53). Other well-known hymns for which John B. Dykes has composed the music are the "St. Drostane" tune— "Ride On! Ride On in Majesty!," the "Dominus Regit Me" tune—"The King of Love My Shepherd Is," and the "Beatitudo" tune—"O for a Closer Walk With God."

The "Melita" tune was composed by Dr. Dykes especially for William Whiting's text and its inclusion in the *Hymns Ancient and Modern* hymnal of 1861. The tune was named for the island now called Malta, where the apostle Paul was shipwrecked, as recorded in Acts 28:1:

When they were escaped, then they knew that the island was called Melita.

It is generally believed that Whiting's text was inspired by the vivid description of the sea's dangers and God's promised deliverances as recorded in Psalm 107:23-32:

They that go down to the sea in ships, that do business in great waters; these see the works of the Lord, and His wonders in the deep.

It should be noted that the first three stanzas of this hymn are each addressed to a different member of the Godhead: Verse 1—to the Father who created and controls the sea (Job 38:10-11), Verse 2—to the Son who has power to control the elements of nature (Matthew 8:23-27), Verse 3—to the Spirit, who at the creation of the world "brooded over the face of the waters" (Genesis 1). The fourth stanza petitions the love and power of the entire Trinity and urges men everywhere to "praise the Lord for His loving-kindness, and for His wonderful works to the children of men" (Psalm 107:31).

"Eternal Father, Strong to Save" (listed in some hymnals as "Almighty Father, Strong to Save") has been widely used in naval and state ceremonial functions both in England and the United States. Many will recall its stirring use at President John F. Kennedy's funeral, November 24, 1963, as played by the Navy and Marine Bands. The fine "Melita" tune can also be used effectively with other hymn texts with comparable hymn meters (See "The Solid Rock", No. 87).

* * *

THE TASK

"Acquaint thyself with God, if thou would'st taste His works.
Admitted once to this embrace, thou shalt perceive that thou
    wast blind before:
Thine eye shall be instructed; and thine heart made pure
Shall relish with divine delight till then unfelt,
What hands divine have wrought."

William Cowper

23

Even Me

Elizabeth Codner, 1824-1919

William B. Bradbury, 1816-1868

1. Lord, I hear of show'rs of bless-ing Thou art scat-t'ring full and free;
2. Pass me not, O ten-der Sav-ior! Let me love and cling to Thee;
3. Pass me not, O might-y Spir-it! Thou canst make the blind to see;
4. Love of God so pure and changeless, Blood of Christ so rich and free,
5. Pass me not! Thy lost one bring-ing, Bind my heart, O Lord, to Thee;

Show'rs the thirst-y land re-fresh-ing— Let some drops now fall on me.
I am long-ing for Thy fa-vor— Whilst Thou'rt call-ing, O call me.
Wit-ness-er of Je-sus' mer-it, Speak the word of pow'r to me.
Grace of God so strong and bound-less: Mag-ni-fy them all in me.
While the streams of life are spring-ing, Bless-ing oth-ers, O bless me.

REFRAIN

E-ven me, e-ven me, Let Thy bless-ing fall on me.

Even Me

Author—Elizabeth Codner, 1824-1919
Composer—William B. Bradbury, 1816-1868
Scripture Reference—Ezekiel 34:26

He shall come down like rain upon the mown grass: as showers that water the earth.

Psalm 72:6

Elizabeth Harris Codner was born in 1824, at Dartmouth, Devon, England, and died on March 28, 1919, at Croydon, Surrey, England. She was the wife of an Anglican clergyman, Daniel Codner. Together they were active for many years in the ministry of the Mildmay Protestant Mission in the North end of London. As part of this ministry, Mrs. Codner edited a monthly magazine called *Woman's Work*. In addition to several small booklets, she also wrote a collection of talks to women, entitled *Mornings at Mildmay*, as well as such other works as *Brambles* and *Behind the Clouds*.

One day in 1860, while Mrs. Codner was having personal devotions at her home in Weston-super-Mare in England, she became deeply impressed with a verse of Scripture, Ezekiel 34:26:

> ...I will cause the shower to come down in the season; there shall be showers of blessing.

Mrs. Codner thought about the importance of water in the dry country of Palestine and related this to the necessity of the daily refreshment of the Holy Spirit and the Scriptures in a believer's life. While she was still contemplating this truth, a group of young people from the parish called on her and told the news of their recent trip to Ireland. They related that certain cities and areas of the Emerald Isle had experienced a spiritual awakening during the time of their visit, and the young people were thrilled to have been a witness to this event. While they were relating their experience, Mrs. Codner began to pray that these young people would not be content merely to have been spectators of the Holy Spirit's ministry, but also they would desire a genuine outpouring of His power in their individual lives. With the words of Ezekiel 34:26 in mind, she challenged them with the remark, "While the Lord is pouring out such showers of blessing upon others, pray that some drops will fall on you."

The following Sunday morning, Mrs. Codner stayed home from church because of illness, and with the impact of the young people's experience still fresh in her mind, she penned these five stanzas as we have them today. Some time later, leaflets containing this poem came to the attention of the American musician, William B. Bradbury, who composed the melody especially for the text. It was first released in Bradbury's hymnal, *Golden Shower of Sunday School Melodies*, in 1862. In its first printing, the final line ended with "Let some droppings fall on me." This was later changed to its present form "Let Thy blessing fall on me."

William Batchelder Bradbury was born on October 6, 1816, at York, Maine and died on January 7, 1868, in Montclair, New Jersey. He was recognized as one of the pioneers in music for children—in the church as well as in the public school. From 1841 to 1867, he published fifty-nine music collections, including *The Young Choir* (1841), *The Psalmodist* (1844), *The Choralist* (1847), *The Mendelssohn Collection* (1849), *Psalmasta* (1851), *The Shawm* (1853), *The Jubilee* (1858), *The Golden Chain* (1861) and *The Golden Censer* (1864).

William Bradbury is also the composer for the hymns "Depth of Mercy" (No. 20), "The Solid Rock" (No. 87), "Sweet Hour of Prayer" (No.

82), "He Leadeth Me (*101 Hymn Stories*, No. 28), "Jesus Loves Me" (*ibid.*, No. 47), and "Just As I Am" (*ibid.*, No. 52).

* * *

"The word 'Comforter' as applied to the Holy Spririt needs to be translated by some vigorous term. Literally, it means 'with strength.' Jesus promised His followers that 'The Strengthener' would be with them forever. This promise is no lullaby for the faint-hearted. It is a blood transfusion for courageous living."

E. Paul Hovey

"I should as soon attempt to raise flowers if there were no atmosphere, or produce fruits if there were neither light nor heat, as to regenerate men, if I did not believe there was a Holy Ghost."

Henry Ward Beecher

"We must not be content to be cleansed from sin; we must be filled with the Spirit."

John Fletcher

84

"Hands to work and feet to run—
God's good gifts to me and you;
Hands and feet He gave to us
To help each other the whole day through.

"Eyes to see and ears to hear—
God's good gifts to me and you;
Eyes and ears He gave to us
To help each other the whole day through.

"Minds to think and hearts to love—
God's good gifts to me and you;
Minds and hearts He gave to us
To help each other the whole day through."

Hilda Margaret Dodd

24   # Face to Face

Carrie E. Breck, 1855-1934   Grant C. Tullar, 1869-1950

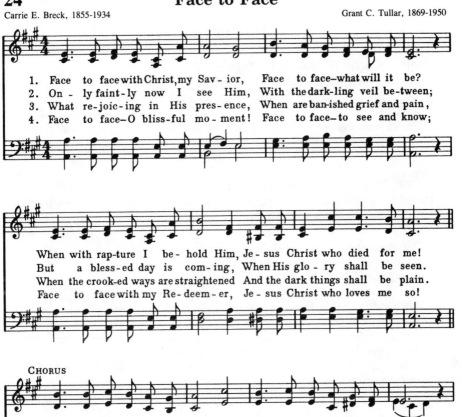

1. Face to face with Christ, my Sav - ior, Face to face—what will it be?
2. On - ly faint-ly now I see Him, With the dark-ling veil be-tween;
3. What re-joic-ing in His pres-ence, When are ban-ished grief and pain,
4. Face to face—O bliss-ful mo - ment! Face to face—to see and know;

When with rap-ture I be - hold Him, Je - sus Christ who died for me!
But a bless-ed day is com-ing, When His glo - ry shall be seen.
When the crook-ed ways are straightened And the dark things shall be plain.
Face to face with my Re-deem - er, Je - sus Christ who loves me so!

CHORUS

Face to face I shall be-hold Him, Far be-yond the star-ry sky;

Face to face, in all His glo - ry, I shall see Him by and by!

Face to Face

Author—Carrie E. Breck, 1855-1934
Composer—Grant C. Tullar, 1869-1950

> Beloved, now are we the sons of God, and it doth not yet appear what we shall be: but we know that, when He shall appear, we shall be like Him; for we shall see Him as He is. And every man that hath this hope in him purifieth himself, even as He is pure.
>
> 1 John 3:2, 3

In his book, *Written Because*, the composer, Grant C. Tullar, tells about the rather unusual circumstances that prompted the writing of this hymn. He calls the hymn his "jelly song" and explains in this way:

> An almost-empty jelly dish at the supper table in the M.E. parsonage at Rutherford, New Jersey, where I was assisting in a series of evangelistic meetings, was responsible for the writing of "Face to Face."
>
> My fondness for jelly was not long a secret, and my hostess did her best to see that a reasonable supply was always on the table. The three of us had spent the afternoon calling on the sick, so we were a bit hurried in the preparation for supper that evening, and the jelly dish was neglected. It had only a wee dab of jelly in it, and as I passed it to the others, I possibly showed fear lest they should not refuse it...But host and hostess refused it, and as I started to help myself I said, "So this is all for me, is it?"
>
> At that instant, "all for me" as a theme for a song thrust itself upon my mind with such force that I placed the dish again on the table without taking any jelly, and excusing myself, went to the piano and wrote the melody and a few verses, the first one beginning:

> All for me the Savior suffered,
> All for me He bled and died.

> The pastor asked if he might sing it at the service, that night, before I preached. He told the people the story of its writing, and declared he had found the secret of getting Mr. Tullar to write good songs—"Don't feed him too much jelly!"
>
> We discussed the new song before retiring, that night, and I promised to revise the words somewhat...but that was never done, because when the postman came the next morning, he brought me a letter from Mrs. Breck with several poems in it, and as I started to read the first one, I discovered that it exactly fitted my music written the night before!... No word of her poem nor my music needed to be changed. The architect had planned both of them so perfectly, that from that day on, "Face to Face" has been winning its way into hearts and lives all over the world.

86

The author, Carrie E. Breck, was born on January 22, 1855, at Walden, Vermont. She lived most of her life with her husband and five daughters in Portland, Oregon. Mrs. Breck was known as a deeply-committed Christian and a life-long Presbyterian. She wrote more than 2,000 poems, a number of which have become hymn texts, including "When Love Shines In" and "Help Somebody Today." Mrs. Breck has left the following account of her busy life as a wife, mother, and writer: "I penciled verses under all conditions; over a mending basket, with a baby on my arm, and sometimes even when sweeping or washing dishes—my mind moved in poetic meter." Interestingly, it was said of Carrie Breck that "she could not carry a tune and had no natural sense of pitch, but she had a keen sense of rhythm and loved music."

The composer, Grant Colfax Tullar, was born on August 5, 1869 at Bolton, Connecticut. His mother died when he was two years of age, and the early years of his life were lived in extreme hardship. He was converted at the age of nineteen, at a Methodist camp meeting, out of a drunken, dissipated life. Soon Tullar discovered a gift for singing, playing the organ, and composing gospel songs. He was ordained to the Methodist ministry and pastored a church for a short time before entering into the evangelistic field, assisting such evangelists as Sam Jones, Major George A. Hilton, and others. In 1893, Tullar formed a partnership with Isaac H. Meredith and founded the Tullar-Meredith Publishing Company, which successfully published an unusual quantity of sacred music, including many of Tullar's original texts and tunes. Several of his songs still in use today include "Nailed to the Cross" and "Shall I Crucify My Savior?" Mr. Tullar also assisted with the music for the hymn "I Would Be True" (No. 43).

"Face to Face" first appeared in the collection, *Sermons in Song*, No. 2 (1899), published by the Tullar-Meredith Company, New York.

A story is told in *Unfamiliar Stories of Familiar Hymns*, by William Hart, of a missionary couple, the Rev. and Mrs. R. W. Porteous, missionaries with the former China Inland Mission board, and their use of this hymn while expecting momentary death from a band of Chinese terrorists. The missionaries tell of being led to a lonely spot on a hill and being told "This is the place!" When the executioner took his long knife from his shoulder, the courageous couple, expecting immediate death, began to sing:

> Face to face with Christ my Savior,
> Face to face—what will it be
> When with rapture I behold Him,
> Jesus Christ who died for me?

To the missionary couple's surprise, no order was given. The executioner shouldered his axe-like knife and Mr. and Mrs. Porteous were released

and permitted to return to their headquarters in Shanghai. They often told
their story of their singing faith and their anticipation of seeing their Savior
"face to face" in the hour of expected death.

* * *

"We go to the grave of a friend saying,
'A man is dead'; but angels throng about him, saying,
'A man is born.'"

Henry Ward Beecher

"There is a land of pure delight
Where saints immortal reign;
Infinite day excludes the night,
And pleasures banish pain."

FACE TO FACE

"Oh, sometimes my faith sees Jesus coming o'er the stormy sea.
And the waves are stilled, the raging tempest past;
Then the clouds return again, clouds of care and grief and pain,
And the sweetness of His presence does not last.

"But some day I'll bide with Him, where no storm His face shall dim —
He who loves me and who saves me by His grace.
Here I walk by faith, not sight; but I'm walking toward the light,
And — what glory when I see Him face to face!

"Face to face — and that forever;
Face to face, where naught can sever;
I shall see Him in His beauty, face to face;
I have caught faint glimpses here,
Seen through many a falling tear,
But — what glory when I see Him face to face!"

Annie Johnson Flint

88

25

For All the Saints

SINE NOMINE

William W. How, 1823-1897

Ralph Vaughan Williams, 1872-1958

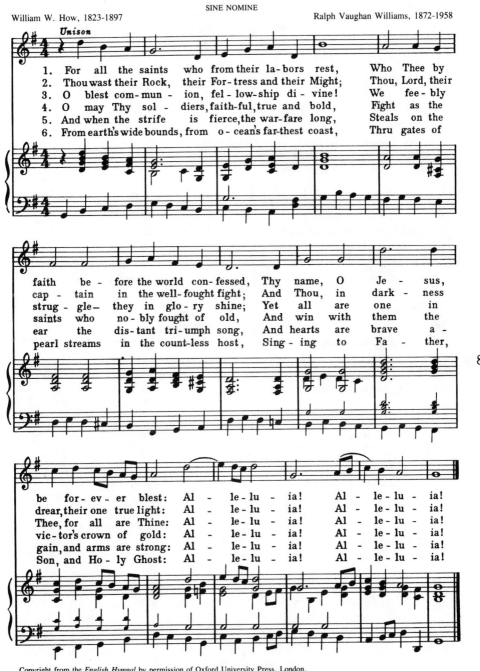

Unison

1. For all the saints who from their la-bors rest, Who Thee by faith be-fore the world con-fessed, Thy name, O Je - sus, be for-ev-er blest: Al - le-lu - ia! Al - le-lu - ia!
2. Thou wast their Rock, their For-tress and their Might; Thou, Lord, their cap - tain in the well-fought fight; And Thou, in dark - ness drear, their one true light: Al - le-lu - ia! Al - le-lu - ia!
3. O blest com-mun - ion, fel - low-ship di - vine! We fee - bly strug - gle— they in glo - ry shine; Yet all are one in Thee, for all are Thine: Al - le-lu - ia! Al - le-lu - ia!
4. O may Thy sol - diers, faith-ful, true and bold, Fight as the saints who no - bly fought of old, And win with them the vic - tor's crown of gold: Al - le-lu - ia! Al - le-lu - ia!
5. And when the strife is fierce, the war-fare long, Steals on the ear the dis-tant tri - umph song, And hearts are brave a - gain, and arms are strong: Al - le-lu - ia! Al - le-lu - ia!
6. From earth's wide bounds, from o - cean's far-thest coast, Thru gates of pearl streams in the count-less host, Sing - ing to Fa - ther, Son, and Ho - ly Ghost: Al - le-lu - ia! Al - le-lu - ia!

89

Copyright from the *English Hymnal* by permission of Oxford University Press, London.

For All the Saints

Author—William W. How, 1823-1897
Composer—Ralph Vaughan Williams, 1872-1958
Tune Name—"Sine Nomine"
Meter—10 10 10. with Alleluias

> Wherefore seeing we also are compassed about with so great a cloud of witnesses, let us lay aside every weight, and the sin which doth so easily beset us, and let us run with patience the race that is set before us. **Hebrews 12:1**

Bishop William W. How wrote the text of "For All the Saints", in 1864, for use in the Anglican Church liturgy commemorating All Saints Day, generally celebrated on the first Sunday in November. It was originally titled "Saints Day Hymn—Cloud of Witnesses—Hebrews 12:1." The text was intended to be a commentary on the clause of the Apostles' Creed, "I believe in the communion of saints." It is considered to be the finest hymn ever written for this purpose.

Bishop How was affectionately known by such titles as the "poor man's bishop" and the "people's bishop" through the city of London. His untiring energy and genuine interest in the spiritual welfare of the common people brought him the respect and love of all who knew him. The bishop once wrote a striking description of the characteristics, which he believed should be found in an ideal minister of the gospel:

90

> Such a minister should be a man pure, holy, and spotless in his life; a man of much prayer; in character meek, lowly, and infinitely compassionate; of tenderest love to all; full of sympathy for every pain and sorrow, and devoting his days and nights to lightening the burdens of humanity; utterly patient with insult and enmity; utterly fearless in speaking the truth and rebuking sin; ever ready to answer every call, to go wherever bidden, in order to do good; wholly without thought of self; making himself the servant of all; patient, gentle, and untiring in dealing with the soul he would save; bearing with ignorance, wilfulness, slowness, cowardice, in those of whom he expects most; sacrificing all, even life itself, if need be, to save some.

Those who knew Bishop How best said it was almost a perfect description of his own life and ministry. On his pastoral staff, he had engraved a Latin saying of the medieval monk, St. Bernard, which he often quoted: "Feed with the Word; feed with the life."

Surprisingly, however, Bishop How was one of the champions of liberal theology within the Anglican Church. In his attempt to reconcile science and the Bible, he once wrote: "Evolution is the wonderful way in which the Lord formed man out of the dust of the ground." Yet, despite his theological views regarding evolution and higher criticism, his hymns contain a strong evangelical message. Among the sixty hymns which he wrote are such enduring favorites as "O Word of God Incarnate" (*101 Hymn Stories*, No. 71), "O Jesus, Thou Art Standing," "We Give Thee But Thine Own," and "Jesus, Name of Wondrous Love." His hymns all embody the ideals he once stated for any worthy hymn: "A good hymn should be like a good prayer — simple, real, earnest, and reverent." It is generally agreed by hymnists that Bishop William How will long be regarded as one of the truly, important, English hymn writers of the Christian Church.

"For All the Saints" first appeared in *Hymns for Saints' Day, and Other Hymns* in 1864, compiled by Earl Nelson, a nephew of England's heroic Admiral Nelson. The text originally had eleven stanzas and began with the words "Thy saints," which were later changed to "the saints." Several of the omitted stanzas deserve attention:

> For the Apostles' glorious company
> Who, bearing for the cross o'er land and sea,
> Shook all the mighty world, we sing to Thee. Alleluia.

> For martyrs, who with raptured-kindled eye,
> Saw the bright crown descending from the sky,
> And died to grasp it, Thee we glorify. Alleluia.

The talented and beloved bishop died, while vacationing in Ireland, on April 10, 1897. He was greatly mourned by those whom he directly served as well as by the Christian church at large, for his writings, which included his sixty hymns as well as published sermons, poems, and essays.

The composer of this tune, "Sine Nomine" (literally means "without a name"), was Ralph Vaughan Williams, one of the most significant English composers of the 20th century. In addition to composing nine symphonies, several major works for chorus and orchestra, opera, ballet, film music, chamber music, and three organ preludes on Welsh hymn tunes, Vaughan Williams was a pioneer in collecting and publishing English folk music, from the time of the Tudor period to Henry Purcell, all of which greatly influenced his compositions and hymn tunes. It has been said that only two master composers throughout music history have concerned themselves seriously with composing tunes specifically for hymn texts — J. S. Bach and Ralph Vaughan Williams. He was editor of the *English Hymnal*, for which he composed the "Sine Nomine" tune, in 1906, especially for Bishop How's text. It is interesting to note that Eric Routley, noted English authority on hymnody, reports that at first this tune was rejected by many as being "jazz music." Today, however, it is judged by authorities to be one of the finest hymn tunes of this century.

Although evangelicals do not generally follow the church year as closely as do the Roman Catholics and the more liturgical Protestant groups, a day such as "All Saints Day" can be infused with a real evangelical, scriptural meaning. It can be emphasized that all believers are called to be saints. We can also honor the memory of our church members and loved ones who have died within the past year and reaffirm the glorious anticipation we have as believers of being eternally reunited with them as well as with the saints of all ages. Alleluia!

*　　*　　*

"How bright these glorious spirits shine!
Whence all their white array?
How came they to the blissful seats
Of everlasting day?
Lo! these are they, from sufferings great
Who came to realms of light,
And in the blood of Christ have washed
Those robes which shine so bright.

"Now with triumphal palms they stand
Before the throne on high,
And serve the God they love, amidst
The glories of the sky.
His presence fills each heart with joy,
Tunes every mouth to sing:
By day, by night, the sacred courts
With glad hosannas ring.

"Hunger and thirst are felt no more,
Nor suns with scorching ray;
God is their sun, whose cheering beams
Diffuse eternal day.
The Lamb who dwells amidst the throne
Shall o'er them still preside,
Feed them with nourishment divine,
And all their footsteps guide.

"'Mong pastures green He'll lead His flock
Where living streams appear;
And God the Lord from every eye
Shall wipe off every tear."

Scottish Paraphrases, 1781
From Revelation 7:13-17

92

26 Glorious Things of Thee Are Spoken

AUSTRIAN HYMN

John Newton, 1725-1807

Franz Joseph Haydn, 1732-1809

1. Glo - rious things of thee are spo - ken, Zi - on, cit - y of our God;
2. See, the streams of liv - ing wa - ters, Spring-ing from e - ter - nal love,
3. Round each hab - i - ta - tion hov-'ring, See the cloud and fire ap - pear

He whose word can - not be bro - ken Formed thee for His own a - bode:
Well sup - ply thy sons and daugh-ters And all fear of want re - move:
For a glo - ry and a cov -'ring, Show - ing that the Lord is near!

On the Rock of A - ges found-ed, What can shake thy sure re - pose?
Who can faint while such a riv - er Ev - er flows their thirst to as-suage?
Glo-rious things of Thee are spo - ken, Zi - on, cit - y of our God;

With sal - va-tion's walls sur-round-ed, Thou mayst smile at all thy foes.
Grace which, like the Lord, the Giv - er, Nev - er fails from age to age.
He whose word can - not be bro - ken Formed thee for His own a - bode.

Glorious Things of Thee Are Spoken

Author—John Newton, 1725-1807
Composer—Franz Joseph Haydn, 1732-1809
Tune Name—"Austrian Hymn"
Meter—87.87 Doubled
Scripture Reference—Psalm 87:3 and Isaiah 33:20-21

> Great is the Lord, and greatly to be praised in the city of our God, in the mountain of His holiness. Beautiful for situation, the joy of the whole earth is Mount Zion, on the sides of the north, the city of the great King. God is known in her palaces for a refuge.   Psalm 48:1, 2, 3

> John Newton, clerk, once an infidel and libertine, a servant of slavers in Africa, was by the rich mercy of our Lord and Saviour, Jesus Christ, preserved, restored, pardoned, and appointed to preach the faith he had long labored to destroy.

This fitting testimonial, written by Newton himself prior to his death, describes aptly the unusual and colorful life of this man, one of the great evangelical preachers of the eighteenth century. The granite tombstone bearing this inscription can still be seen in the small cemetery adjoining the parish churchyard in Olney, England, where John Newton ministered so effectively for fifteen years.

94

The story of John Newton's early life is generally quite well known. He was born on July 24, 1725, in London. His mother, a godly woman, died when he was not quite seven years of age. When he was eleven years old, he went to sea with his sea-captain father and followed this life for the next eighteen years. These years were filled with adventure but were one continuous round of rebellion and debauchery. He became known as one of the most vulgar and blasphemous of men. Following his dramatic conversion experience, in 1748, and his call later at the age of thirty-nine to the Christian ministry, Newton became pastor of the Anglican parish in the little village of Olney, near Cambridge, England, and began writing hymn texts that expressed his spiritual experiences and convictions. His most popular hymn, "Amazing Grace" (*101 Hymn Stories*, No. 6), is really a testimony of Newton's early life and conversion.

While pastoring the Olney Church, John Newton enlisted the aid of William Cowper, a friend and neighbor, who was a well-known writer of classic literature during this period, to aid him in his hymn writing. (See "O For a Closer Walk With God," No. 67) In 1779, their combined efforts produced the famous *Olney Hymns Hymnal*, one of the most important single contributions made to the field of evangelical hymnody. In this ambitious collection of 349 hymns, 67 were written by Cowper, with the remainder by Newton. The hymnal was divided into three parts: Part 1 contained texts based on Scripture texts, used especially to climax a sermon or to illustrate prayer meeting talks about Bible characters; Part 2 was devoted to "Occasional Subjects," texts relating to particular seasons or events; Part 3 was devoted to "The Progress and Changes of the Spiritual Life." This hymnal became the hymnbook of the Low or Evangelical churches within the Anglican Church and was reprinted both in England and America for a hundred years.

"Glorious Things of Thee Are Spoken" is from Part 1 of the *Olney Hymns* and is generally considered to be one of Newton's finest. It is said to be the only joyful hymn in the entire collection. The hymn gives a stirring description of God's protection of His chosen people. Expressions such as "He whose word cannot be broken formed thee for His own abode" show Newton's profound respect for the covenantal promises to the Jews as well as to the local church and its earthly ministry. The hymn originally had five verses. The final two stanzas, generally omitted, are worthy of attention:

Savior, if of Zion's city I through grace a member am,
Let the world deride or pity, I will glory in Thy name;
Fading is the worldling's pleasure, all his boasted pomp and show;
Solid joys and lasting treasure, none but Zion's children know.

Blest inhabitants of Zion, washed in the Redeemer's blood!
Jesus, whom their souls rely on, makes them kings and priests to God.
'Tis His love His people raises, over self to reign as kings,
And as priests, His solemn praises each for a thank-off'ring brings.

The tune, "Austrian Hymn," was composed by Franz Joseph Haydn for the Austrian national hymn text by Hauschka, "Gott Erhalte Franz den Kaiser," and was first performed on Emperor Franz II's birthday, February 12, 1797. Haydn later used the air as a theme for variations in the slow movement of his string quartet known as the "Emperor" of "Kaiser," Opus 76, No. 3. The music was first used as a hymn tune, in 1802, in Edward Miller's hymnal, *Sacred Music.* Its first appearance with John Newton's text was in *Hymns Ancient and Modern* (1889).

Franz Joseph Haydn was an eighteenth-century, Austrian musician who ranks as one of the master composers of all time. Though raised a Catholic, Haydn was a devout believer in Christ. He once wrote: "When I think of the divine Being, my heart is so full of joy that the notes fly off as from a spindle; and, as I have a cheerful heart, He will pardon me, if I serve Him cheerfully." Haydn always began each manuscript with the inscription "In Nomine Domini" and signed at the end "Soli Deo Gloria!"

95

Haydn was born in Rohau, Austria, on May 31, 1732. In 1761, he became musical director to the Hungarian family of Esterhazy and remained in this position for the next thirty years. During this time he composed more than one hundred symphonies, twenty-two operas, four oratorios, sixteen masses, and a great amount of chamber music. His most famous choral work was the oratorio, *The Creation*. All of his works are said to be characterized by the "joy of a heart devoted to God."

John Newton's majestic text wedded to this stirring music by Franz Haydn makes this a worthy and uplifting hymn of worship for any congregation.

*   *   *

"To the name of our salvation,
Laud and honor let us pay,
Which for many a generation
Hid in God's foreknowledge lay,
But with holy exultation
We may sing aloud today.

"Jesus is the name we treasure,
Name beyond what words can tell;
Name of gladness, name of pleasure,
Ear and heart delighting well;
Name of sweetness passing measure
Saving us from sin and hell.

"'Tis the name that whoso preacheth
Speaks like music to the ear;
Who in prayer this name beseecheth
Sweetest comfort findeth near;
Who its perfect wisdom reacheth,
Heavenly joy possesseth here."
Anonymous, 15th century
Translated by John M. Neale

96

"Lord, for that Word, the Word of life which fires us,
Speaks to our hearts and sets our souls ablaze;
Teaches and trains, rebukes us and inspires us,
Lord of the Word, receive your people's praise."
Unknown

27 God Be With You

Jeremiah E. Rankin, 1828-1904

William G. Tomer, 1833-1896

1. God be with you till we meet a-gain, By His coun-sels
2. God be with you till we meet a-gain, 'Neath His wings pro-
3. God be with you till we meet a-gain, When life's per-ils
4. God be with you till we meet a-gain, Keep love's ban-ner

guide, up-hold you, With His sheep se-cure-ly fold you—
tect-ing hide you, Dai-ly man-na still pro-vide you—
thick con-found you, Put His arms un-fail-ing round you—
float-ing o'er you; Smite death's threat'ning wave be-fore you—

CHORUS

God be with you till we meet a-gain. Till we meet,___ till we

meet, Till we meet at Je - sus' feet, Till we
till we meet,

meet,___ till we meet— God be with you till we meet a-gain.

God Be With You

Author—Jeremiah E. Rankin, 1828-1904
Composer—William G. Tomer, 1833-1896

The grace of our Lord Jesus Christ be with you. Amen.   Romans 16:20

This popular benediction hymn, along with "Blest Be the Tie That Binds" (*101 Hymn Stories*, No. 12), has closed more religious services during the past century than all other hymns combined. "God Be With You" was written and published, in 1882, by the Rev. Jeremiah Eames Rankin, who was, at that time, pastor of the First Congregational Church of Washington, D.C. The poem originally had eight stanzas, but today the first, second, fourth, and seventh stanzas are all that are commonly sung. The omitted final stanza, however, is worthy of attention:

> God be with you till we meet again
> Ended when for you earth's story,
> Israel's chariot sweeps to glory;
> God be with you till we meet again.

98   Jeremiah Rankin was born in Thornton, New Hampshire, on January 2, 1828. He was a graduate of Middlebury College in Vermont and received his theological training at the Andover Theological Seminary in Massachusetts. He held the pastorates of several prominent congregational churches in New England and Washington, D.C. until 1889, when he became president of Howard University, Washington, D.C., the noted school for Negro education. Dr. Rankin was always known as a powerful and effective preacher; and he attracted large crowds, not only with his speaking, but also with his emphasis on congregational singing, especially in his evangelistic, Sunday evening services. Rankin wrote much verse and compiled and edited a number of gospel songbooks, including: the *Gospel Temperance Hymnal* (1878), *Gospel Bells* (1883), and *German-English Lyrics, Sacred and Secular* (1897). He is also the author of the well-known gospel song, "Tell It to Jesus."

Mr. Rankin has left the following account regarding the writing of "God Be With You":

It was written in 1882 as a Christian goodby. It was called forth by no person or occasion, but was deliberately composed as a Christian hymn on etymology (origin) of "good-by" which is "God with you." The first stanza was sent to two different composers, one of musical note, the other wholly unknown and not thoroughly educated in music. I selected the composition of the latter, and with some slight changes it was published. It was first sung on Sunday evening at the First Congregational Church in Washington, of which I was then pastor. I attribute its popularity in no little part to the music at which it was my function to preside; but Mr. Tomer should have his full share of the honor.

William Gould Tomer was born on October 5, 1833. He served in the Union Army during the Civil War and then became a public school teacher in New Jersey. When he composed the music for this text upon Dr. Rankin's request, he was serving as music director at the Grace Methodist Episcopal Church in Washington, D.C. Later, he returned to New Jersey, where he spent his remaining years teaching school. This hymn was sung at his own funeral, in 1896.

"God Be With You" was widely used in the Moody and Sankey meetings throughout North America and England. It also became the "official" closing song for the Christian Endeavor Conventions around the world and as such was translated into many different languages. Dr. Rankin was always deeply interested in the work of Christian Endeavor. He once wrote the following concerning its use of his hymn:

It has had no sweeter recognition than that given it by its adoption by the Young People's Society of Christian Endeavor. Long, long may they sing it!

Still today, no finer farewell can be expressed by Christians to one another as they leave a place of worship than the sincere wish, "God be with you till we meet again."

*   *   *

AN ANCIENT PRAYER
"God be in my head, and in my understanding;
God be in mine eyes, and in my looking;
God be in my mouth, and in my speaking;
God be in my heart, and in my thinking;
God be at mine end, and at my departing. Amen."

Unknown

28 God of Our Fathers

NATIONAL HYMN

Daniel C. Roberts, 1841-1907

George W. Warren, 1828-1902

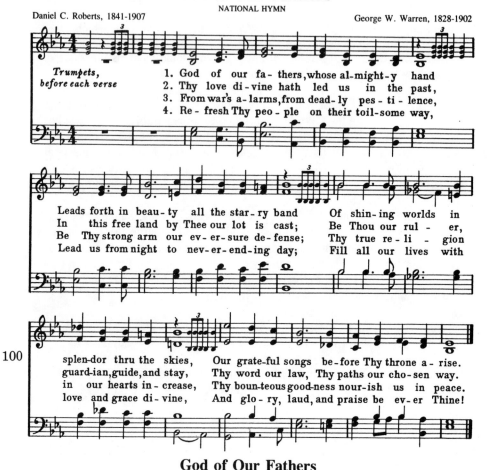

Trumpets,
before each verse

1. God of our fa-thers,whose al-might-y hand
2. Thy love di-vine hath led us in the past,
3. From war's a-larms,from dead-ly pes-ti-lence,
4. Re-fresh Thy peo-ple on their toil-some way,

Leads forth in beau-ty all the star-ry band
In this free land by Thee our lot is cast;
Be Thy strong arm our ev-er-sure de-fense;
Lead us from night to nev-er-end-ing day;

Of shin-ing worlds in
Be Thou our rul-er,
Thy true re-li-gion
Fill all our lives with

splen-dor thru the skies, Our grate-ful songs be-fore Thy throne a-rise.
guard-ian,guide,and stay, Thy word our law, Thy paths our cho-sen way.
in our hearts in-crease, Thy boun-teous good-ness nour-ish us in peace.
love and grace di-vine, And glo-ry, laud, and praise be ev-er Thine!

God of Our Fathers

Author—Daniel C. Roberts, 1841-1907
Composer—George W. Warren, 1828-1902
Tune Name—"National Hymn"
Meter—10 10. 10 10

If my people, which are called by my name, shall humble themselves, and pray, and seek my face, and turn from their wicked ways; then will I hear from heaven, and will forgive their sin, and will heal their land.   2 Chronicles 7:14

This stirring patriotic hymn has become increasingly popular since it was first written by an American Episcopalian minister, in 1876. Today it is included in nearly every published hymnal in this country. "God of Our Fathers" is the product of the Rev. Daniel C. Roberts, at that time pastor of a small rural church in Brandon, Vermont. It was written to commemorate the one hundredth anniversary of our country's Declaration of Independence and was sung for the first time at Brandon's Fourth of July celebration to the music of the old, Russian national anthem. This tune, which has since come to be known as the "Russian Hymn," is used exclusively today with the hymn "God the Omnipotent!" Later, Roberts submitted his text anonymously to the committee revising the Episcopal hymnal, and it was included in their 1892 edition, wedded with the "Russian Hymn" tune. At the time of our national Centennial observance commemorating the adoption of the Constitution, Robert's hymn text was chosen as the official hymn for that event. The committee commissioned the organist of the St. Thomas Episcopal Church in New York City, George William Warren, however, to compose an original tune for Robert's text. This new tune, with its dramatic trumpet calls before each stanza, contributed much to the growing popularity of the hymn. The hymn first appeared with its new tune, the "National Hymn," in 1894, in the official hymnal of the Episcopal Church, and Robert's text has been used exclusively with this music to the present time.

The hymn text represents Daniel Robert's one claim to literary fame. Evidently, he was a very modest man. In 1901, he wrote: "I remain a country parson, known only within my own small world." Concerning his hymn he once stated: "My little hymn has thus had a very flattering official recognition. But that which would really gladden my heart, popular recognition, it has not received."

Although popular recognition for Robert's hymn text was slow in coming, he did receive various honors before his death in Concord, New Hampshire, on October 31, 1907. He was given a Doctor of Divinity degree by Norwich University, was made president of the New Hampshire Historical Society, as well as president of the State Normal School in Vermont, and Chaplain of the National Guard of New Hampshire. Following service in the Union Army during the Civil War and later ordination to the Episcopal ministry in 1866, Roberts served parishes in Vermont and Massachusetts, and for many years he was the vicar of the St. Paul's Church in Concord, New Hampshire.

The composer of the "National Hymn" tune, George William Warren, was known as an accomplished organist, while serving Episcopal churches in Albany, Brooklyn, and New York City. He also composed various anthems and hymn tunes and, in 1888, edited *Warren's Hymns and Tunes as Sung at St. Thomas' Church*. Later, Warren received an honorary Doctor of Music Degree from Racine College, in Wisconsin, in recognition of his church music accomplishments.

This text, with its recognition of God's providential guidance of our nation in the past and our need for reliance on Him for the future, combined with its stirring, inspirational music, is a very usable hymn for any national celebration.

29 God Understands

Oswald J. Smith, 1890-

B. D. Ackley, 1872-1958

1. God un-der-stands your sor-row, He sees the fall - ing tear,
2. God un-der-stands your heart-ache, He knows the bit - ter pain;
3. God un-der-stands your weak-ness, He knows the tempt - er's pow'r;

And whis-pers, "I am with thee," Then fal - ter not, nor fear.
O, trust Him in the dark-ness, You can - not trust in vain.
And He will walk be - side you How-ev - er dark the hour.

REFRAIN

He un-der-stands your long-ing, Your deep-est grief He shares;

Then let Him bear your bur - den, He un - der-stands, and cares.

Copyright 1937, © Renewed 1965 The Rodeheaver Co. (A Div. of Word, Inc.) All rights reserved. International Copyright secured. Used by permission.

God Understands

Author—Oswald J. Smith, 1890-1986
Composer—B. D. Ackley, 1872-1958

> Blessed be God, even the Father of our Lord Jesus Christ, the Father of all mercies, and the God of all comfort; who comforteth us in all our tribulation, that we may be able to comfort them which are in trouble, by the comfort wherewith we ourselves are comforted of God.
> 2 Corinthians 1:3, 4

"How wonderful to know that God understands! He knows the deepest longing of the heart. Best of all, He shares our grief and pain and He sympathizes with us. Earth has no sorrow that He cannot heal. We can go to Him in every kind of trouble and find relief. He knows what is best and He does what is best, for He never makes a mistake."

These are the words of Oswald J. Smith, one of the great evangelical preachers and missionary statesmen of this century. In his book, *The Story of My Hymns*, Dr. Smith relates the following account regarding the writing of this particular song:

My youngest sister and her husband, Rev. and Mrs. Clifford Bicker, were preparing for their first furlough. Two little children had been born in Peru. Shortly before the boat sailed, Clifford was instantly killed in an automobile accident and my little sister, leaving her husband's body in South America, came home with her two fatherless boys—a widow at twenty-six.

To her, I dedicated "God Understands" and she got it before leaving the field. It was a comfort to Ruth. It has been a comfort to thousands of others.

Never will I forget the day, in the year 1935, that Ruth stepped off the train at the Union Station, Toronto, with her two boys, who later, thank God, became ministers of the Gospel. It was a sad home-coming.

Mr. B. D. Ackley wrote the touching melody to which it is now sung. It is a great favorite at funeral services. America's outstanding soloists have recorded it and sung it throughout the country.

For many years now, Dr. Oswald J. Smith has been associated with the People's Church of Toronto, Canada, as its founder and pastor. This church has become well-known for its great missionary outreach. In addition to pastoring, Dr. Smith's preaching and promoting of missionary activities has taken him into sixty-six foreign countries. He has also authored a number of books and has composed more than 1200 hymns and religious poems. He is the author of the beloved hymn "Deeper and Deeper," (*101 Hymn Stories*, No. 19). Several of Dr. Smith's other well-known gospel songs include "Joy in Serving Jesus," "The Glory of His Presence," "The Song of the Soul Set Free," "The Savior Can Solve Every Problem," and the one made especially popular by Homer Rodeheaver, "Then Jesus Came."

The names of the two Ackley brothers, Benton D. and Alfred Henry, have long been prominent in the gospel music field. Both were associated with the Rodeheaver Publishing Company in the promotion of gospel music, and each contributed numerous songs to these publications. (See "He Lives", No. 33).

B. D. Ackley was born on September 27, 1872, at Spring Hill, Pennsylvania, and died on September 3, 1958, at Winona Lake, Indiana. After serving as organist at several churches in New York City and Brooklyn, he joined the Billy Sunday-Homer Rodeheaver evangelistic team, in 1907, and traveled with them as their pianist and secretary for a number of years. Later, Ackley served as composer and editor for the Rodeheaver Publishing Company. In 1930, he met Dr. Oswald J. Smith for the first time, and together they collaborated on more than one hundred gospel songs. In all, B. D. Ackley has composed more than 3,000 hymn tunes. In recognition of his contribution to sacred music, Mr. Ackley was awarded the honorary, Doctor of Sacred Music Degree from Bob Jones University shortly before his home-going in 1958.

104

* * *

"Extraordinary afflictions are not always the punishment of extraordinary sins, but sometimes the trial of extraordinary graces. Sanctified afflictions are often spiritual promotions."

Matthew Henry

BE STILL MY SOUL
"Be still, my soul: thy God doth undertake
To guide the future as He has the past.
Thy hope, thy confidence let nothing shake;
All now mysterious shall be bright at last.
Be still my soul: the waves and winds still know
His voice who ruled them while He dwelt below."
Katharina Von Schlegel

30 God Will Take Care of You

Civilla D. Martin, 1869-1948

W. Stillman Martin, 1862-1935

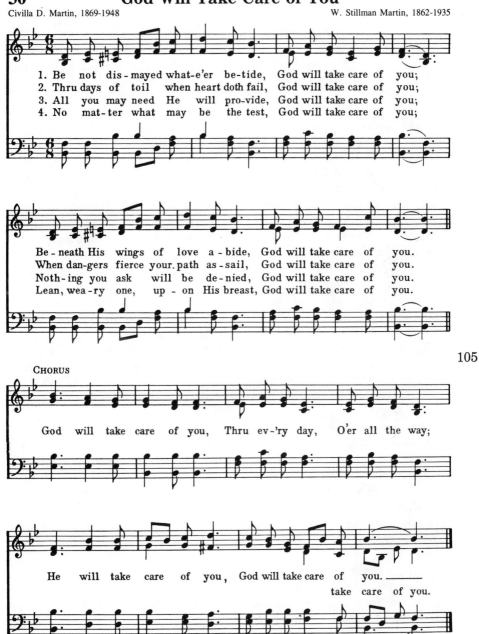

1. Be not dis-mayed what-e'er be-tide, God will take care of you;
2. Thru days of toil when heart doth fail, God will take care of you;
3. All you may need He will pro-vide, God will take care of you;
4. No mat-ter what may be the test, God will take care of you;

Be-neath His wings of love a-bide, God will take care of you.
When dan-gers fierce your path as-sail, God will take care of you.
Noth-ing you ask will be de-nied, God will take care of you.
Lean, wea-ry one, up-on His breast, God will take care of you.

CHORUS

God will take care of you, Thru ev-'ry day, O'er all the way;

He will take care of you, God will take care of you. ____
take care of you.

God Will Take Care Of You

Author—Civilla D. Martin, 1869-1948
Composer—W. Stillman Martin, 1862-1935

> There hath no temptation taken you but such as is common to man; but God is faithful, who will not suffer you to be tempted above that ye are able, but will with the temptation also make a way to escape, that you may be able to bear it. 1 Corinthians 10:13

This popular hymn of spiritual encouragement was written, in 1904, by Mr. and Mrs. Stillman Martin. It was composed while the Martins were spending several weeks as guests at the Practical Bible Training School at Lestershire, New York, where Mr. Martin was involved in helping the president of the school, John A. Davis, prepare a songbook. The Reverend W. Stillman Martin, a well-known Baptist evangelist, was invited to preach at a church some distance from the Bible school. That Sunday morning, Mrs. Martin became suddenly ill, making it impossible for her to accompany her husband to his preaching engagement. Mr. Martin seriously considered cancelling his speaking assignment, since it would be needful for him to be gone from her for a considerable time. Just then, however, their young son spoke up and said, "Father, don't you think that if God wants you to preach today, He will take care of Mother while you are away?" Agreeing, Mr. Martin kept his preaching appointment, and the service proved to be unusually blessed of God, with several people professing Christ as Savior as a result of the sermon.

Returning later that evening, Mr. Martin found his wife greatly improved in health, and while he was gone she had, in fact, been busily engaged in preparing a new hymn text, inspired by the chance remark of their young son earlier that day. That same evening, Stillman Martin composed the music for his wife's words just as they are still sung today. The next year, this hymn appeared in a new collection, *Songs of Redemption and Praise*, compiled for the school by W. S. Martin and President John Davis. "God Will Take Care of You" soon became a favorite hymn of Christian people everywhere.

Civilla Durfee Martin was born on August 21, 1869, in Nova Scotia. She taught school and studied music for a time before marrying Dr. Martin. Following their marriage, she traveled and aided him greatly in his ministry and evangelistic campaigns. Together they collaborated in writing a number of gospel songs. Mrs. Martin is also known for writing the popular, gospel song text "His Eye Is on the Sparrow," in which she collaborated with Charles Gabriel. Mrs. Martin died in Atlanta, Georgia, on March 9, 1948.

Walter Stillman Martin was born at Rowley, Essex County, Massachusetts, in 1862. After receiving his education at Harvard

University, he was ordained to the Baptist ministry. Dr. Martin became well known throughout the country for his Bible conference and evangelistic ministries. In 1916, Mr. and Mrs. Martin became members of the Disciples of Christ denomination, when he became a professor of Bible at the Atlantic Christian College in North Carolina. After 1919, Mr. and Mrs. Martin made their home in Atlanta, Georgia, while continuing their ministries until his home-going on December 16, 1935.

One of the lessons that any Christian leader soon realizes in ministering to God's people is that all believers need much encouragement and comfort from time to time. The hymn has been greatly used of God for this purpose.

*   *   *

STEP BY STEP

"Child of my love, fear not the unknown morrow,
Dread not the new demand life makes of thee;
Thy ignorance doth hold no cause for sorrow
Since what thou knowest not is known to Me.

"Thou canst not see today the hidden meaning
Of my command, but thou the light shalt gain;
Walk on in faith, upon my promise leaning,
And as thou goest all shall be made plain.

"One step thou seest — then go forward boldly,
One step is far enough for faith to see;
Take that, and thy next duty shall be told thee,
For step by step thy Lord is leading thee."
Author unknown

JEHOVAH JIREH ("The Lord Will Provide" — Genesis 22:14)
"My feeble hope in miracles had waned,
My faith that He would soon provide was strained,
Then, prompted by His Spirit, my heart cried,
Jehovah Jireh! My Savior will provide.

"My needs were great but greater than my need
Was He — Jehovah Jirah, so quick to heed
And help, to hold, to hide me from the storm
And shelter through the darkest night till morn."
Charles U. Wagner

107

31   Hark! The Herald Angels Sing

MENDELSSOHN

Charles Wesley, 1707-1788

Felix Mendelssohn, 1809-1847

1. Hark! the her-ald an-gels sing, "Glo-ry to the new-born King;
2. Christ, by high-est heav'n a-dored, Christ, the ev-er-last-ing Lord:
3. Hail the heav'n-born Prince of Peace! Hail the Sun of Right-eous-ness!
4. Come, De-sire of Na-tions, come! Fix in us Thy hum-ble home:

Peace on earth, and mer-cy mild— God and sin-ners rec-on-ciled!"
Late in time be-hold Him come, Off-spring of a vir-gin's womb.
Light and life to all He brings, Ris'n with heal-ing in His wings.
Rise, the wom-an's con-q'ring seed, Bruise in us the ser-pent's head.

Joy-ful, all ye na-tions, rise, Join the tri-umph of the skies;
Veiled in flesh the God-head see, Hail th'in-car-nate De-i-ty!
Mild He lays His glo-ry by, Born that man no more may die;
Ad-am's like-ness now ef-face, Stamp Thine im-age in its place:

With th'an-gel-ic hosts pro-claim, "Christ is born in Beth-le-hem."
Pleased as man with men to dwell, Je-sus, our Em-man-u-el.
Born to raise the sons of earth, Born to give them sec-ond birth,
Sec-ond Ad-am from a-bove, Re-in-state us in Thy love.

Hark! the her-ald an-gels sing, "Glo-ry to the new-born King!"

Hark! the Herald Angels Sing

Author—Charles Wesley, 1707-1788
Composer—Felix Mendelssohn, 1809-1847
Tune Name—"Mendelssohn"
Meter—77.77 Doubled with Refrain

> But thou, Bethlehem Ephratah, though thou be little among the thousands of Judah, yet out of thee shall He come forth unto Me that is to be ruler in Israel; whose goings forth have been from of old, from everlasting.   Micah 5:2

"Hark! the Herald Angels Sing" is another of the more than 6,500 hymns from the pen of Charles Wesley that have enriched Christian hymnody. It is thought to have been written approximately one year after his dramatic, Aldersgate conversion experience of 1738. This text, along with "Jesus, Lover of My Soul" (*101 Hymn Stories*, No. 45), is generally considered to be one of Wesley's finest. According to John Julian, noted hymnologist, this is one of the four most popular hymns in the English language. It certainly has become one of the classic, Christmas carol hymns to the present time, sung thousands of times every year all around the world. The text first appeared in *Hymns and Sacred Poems* (1739), with the first stanza beginning:

109

> Hark, how all the welkin (archaic for "heavens"-"sky") rings,
> Glory to the King of Kings!

The text was altered to its present form in George Whitefield's, *Collection of 1753*. In its original version, the text consisted of ten four-line stanzas. Although there have been various alterations made on this text through the years, the present version is still basically the product of Charles Wesley.

Like so many of Wesley's hymns, this text is really a condensed course in biblical doctrine in poetic form. Following the re-telling of the angelic visit to the shepherds in the initial stanza, the succeeding verses teach such spiritual truths as the virgin birth, Christ's deity, the immortality of the soul, the second or new birth, and a concern for Christ-like living. As the late Eric Routley, noted English hymnist, observes in his book, *Hymns and Human Life*: "These [Wesley] hymns were composed in order that men and women might sing their way, not only into experience, but also into knowledge; that the cultured might have their culture baptized and the ignorant might be led into truth by the gentle hand of melody and rhyme."

Charles Wesley is also the author of the hymns "A Charge to Keep I Have" (No. 1) and "Depth of Mercy" (No. 20). Other Charles Wesley hymns include "Christ the Lord is Risen Today" (*101 Hymn Stories*, No. 13) and "O for a Thousand Tongues" (*ibid.*, No. 65).

The tune, "Mendelssohn" was contributed by one of the master composers of the early nineteenth century, Felix Mendelssohn. He was born into a Jewish-Christian home on February 3, 1809, in Hamburg, Germany, and died at Leipzig, Germany, on November 4, 1847. Mendelssohn was a highly acclaimed boy prodigy, making his first public appearance as a pianist, at the age of nine. Felix Mendelssohn was not only a noted performer and conductor, but also a prolific composer throughout his brief life-time. His works included symphonies, chamber music, concertos, as well as much organ, piano, and vocal music. His most popular work still widely performed today is the oratorio, *The Elijah*, first performed in England on August 26, 1846. The "Mendelssohn" hymn tune was adapted from the composer's *Festgesang*, Opus 68, composed in 1840. This was a work that Mendelssohn wrote to commemorate the 400th anniversary of the invention of printing. The hymn setting of this music was made by William H. Cummings, a noted English musician and scholar, and was first published in Richard Chope's *Congregational Hymn and Tune Book* of 1857. Although other tunes have been tried with Wesley's text, the "Mendelssohn" has become the recognized music for this carol hymn.

110 Felix Mendelssohn is also the composer of the "Consolation" tune used for "Still, Still With Thee" (No. 79) and the "Munich" tune, used for the hymn "O Word of God Incarnate" (*101 Hymn Stories*, No. 71).

It is interesting to note briefly the history of our Christmas carol hymns. The word "carol" is derived from the word "carola," which means a ring dance. Carols, then, have long been thought of as an early form of sacred folk music, dating in time from the early middle ages. During this period they seem to have been an integral part of the early mystery and miracle plays which were widely used by the medieval church for teaching its religious dogmas. The carols were sung during these plays as an intermezzo between the various scenes, much like the role of a modern-day orchestra between the scenes of a drama production. Then, in 1627, the English Puritan parliament abolished the celebration of Christmas and all other "worldly festivals." During the remainder of the seventeenth century and well into the eighteenth century, there was a scarcity of these folk-like carol hymns in England. Charles Wesley's "Hark! the Herald Angels Sing" represents one of the relatively few, important carol hymns to have been written during this time.

* * *

"The hinge of history is on the door of a Bethlehem stable."

Ralph W. Sockman

32 Have Thine Own Way, Lord!

ADELAIDE

Adelaide A. Pollard, 1862-1934   George C. Stebbins, 1846-1945

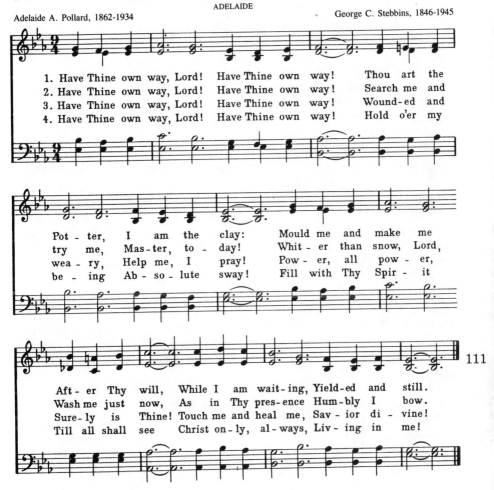

1. Have Thine own way, Lord! Have Thine own way! Thou art the
2. Have Thine own way, Lord! Have Thine own way! Search me and
3. Have Thine own way, Lord! Have Thine own way! Wound-ed and
4. Have Thine own way, Lord! Have Thine own way! Hold o'er my

Pot - ter, I am the clay: Mould me and make me
try me, Mas-ter, to - day!   Whit - er than snow, Lord,
wea - ry, Help me, I pray!   Pow - er, all pow - er,
be - ing Ab - so - lute sway! Fill with Thy Spir - it

Aft - er Thy will, While I am wait-ing, Yield-ed and still.
Wash me just now, As in Thy pres-ence Hum-bly I bow.
Sure-ly is Thine! Touch me and heal me, Sav - ior di - vine!
Till all shall see Christ on-ly, al-ways, Liv-ing in me!

111

Have Thine Own Way, Lord!

Author—Adelaide A. Pollard, 1862-1934
Composer—George C. Stebbins, 1846-1945
Tune Name—"Adelaide"
Meter—5.4.5.4. Doubled
Scripture Reference—Jeremiah 18:3, 4

But now, O Lord, Thou art our Father; we are the clay, and Thou our potter; and we all are the work of Thy hand.   Isaiah 64:8

It really doesn't matter what you do with us, Lord—just have your way with our lives...

This simple expression, prayed by an elderly woman at a prayer meeting one night, was the source of inspiration that prompted the writing of this popular consecration hymn, in 1902. From that time to the present, it has been an influential hymn in aiding individuals to examine and submit their lives to the Lordship of Christ.

The author of this hymn text, Adelaide A. Pollard, was herself experiencing a "distress of soul" during this time. It appears that it was a period in her life when she had been unsuccessful in raising funds to make a desired trip to Africa for missionary service. In this state of discouragement, she attended a little prayer meeting one night and was greatly impressed with the prayer of an elderly woman, who omitted the usual requests for blessings and things, and simply petitioned God for an understanding of His will in life. Upon returning home that evening, Miss Pollard meditated further on the story of the potter, found in Jeremiah 18:3, 4:

Then I went down to the potter's house, and, behold, he wrought a work on the wheels. And the vessel that he made of clay was marred in the hand of the potter: so he made it again another vessel, as seemed good to the potter to make it.

Before retiring that evening, Adelaide Pollard completed the writing of all four stanzas of this hymn as it is sung today.

Adelaide Addison Pollard was known as a remarkable, saintly woman but one who lived the life of a mystic. She was born on November 27, 1862, at Bloomfield, Iowa. She was named, Sarah, by her parents, but because of her later dislike for this name, she adopted the name, Adelaide. After an early training in elocution and physical culture, she moved to Chicago, Illinois, during the 1880's and taught in several girls' schools. During this time, she became rather well-known as an itinerant Bible teacher. Later, she became involved in the evangelistic ministry of Alexander Dowie, assisting him in his healing services. She, herself, claimed to have been healed of diabetes in this manner. Still later, she became involved in the ministry of another evangelist named Sanford, who was emphasizing the imminent return of Christ. Miss Pollard desired to travel and minister in Africa, but when these plans failed to materialize, she spent several years teaching at the Missionary Training School at Nyack-on-the-Hudson. She finally got to Africa for a short time, just prior to World War I and then spent most of the war years in Scotland. Following the war, she returned to America and continued to minister throughout New England, even though by now she was very frail and in poor health.

Miss Pollard wrote a number of other hymn texts throughout her life, although no one knows exactly how many, since she never wanted any recognition for her accomplishments. Most of her writings were signed simply AAP. "Have Thine Own Way, Lord!" is her only hymn still in use today.

The music for this text was supplied by George Coles Stebbins, one of the leading gospel musicians of this century. The hymn first appeared in 1907 in Stebbins' collection, *Northfield Hymnal with Alexander's Supplement*. That same year, it also appeared in two other popular hymnals, Ira Sankey's *Hallowed Hymns New and Old* and Sankey and Clement's *Best Endeavor Hymns*.

In 1876, George Stebbins was invited by D. L. Moody to join him in his evangelistic endeavors. For the next twenty-five years, Stebbins was associated with Moody and Sankey and such other leading evangelists as George F. Pentecost and Major D. W. Whittle as a noted song leader, choir director, composer, and compiler of many gospel song collections. He has supplied the music for such popular gospel hymns as: "Saved by Grace" (No. 76), "Ye Must Be Born Again" (No. 101), "There Is a Green Hill Far Away" (*101 Hymn Stories*, No. 96), "Jesus, I Come," "Take Time to be Holy," "Savior, Breathe an Evening Blessing," and many others. He has left an interesting autobiography of his life and times entitled *Memoirs and Reminiscences*, published in 1924. George C. Stebbins lived a fruitful life for God to the age of ninety-one, passing away on October 6, 1945, at Catskill, New York.

113

* * *

"I AM WILLING—
To receive what Thou givest,
To lack what Thou withholdest,
To relinquish what Thou takest,
To surrender what Thou claimest,
To suffer what Thou ordainest,
To do what Thou commandest,
To wait until Thou sayest 'Go.'"
Unknown

33

He Lives

Alfred H. Ackley, 1887-1960

Alfred H. Ackley, 1887-1960

1. I serve a ris-en Sav-ior, He's in the world to-day; I know that He is
2. In all the world a-round me I see His lov-ing care, And tho my heart grows
3. Re-joice, re-joice, O Chris-tian, lift up your voice and sing E - ter-nal hal-le-

liv-ing, what-ev-er men may say; I see His hand of mer-cy, I
wea-ry I nev-er will de-spair; I know that He is lead-ing thru
lu-jahs to Je-sus Christ the King! The hope of all who seek Him, the

hear His voice of cheer, And just the time I need Him He's al-ways near.
all the storm-y blast, The day of His ap-pear-ing will come at last.
help of all who find, None oth-er is so lov-ing, so good and kind.

114

Chorus

He lives, He lives, Christ Je-sus lives to-day! He walks with me and
He lives, He lives,

talks with me a - long life's nar-row way. He lives, He lives, sal-
He lives, He lives,

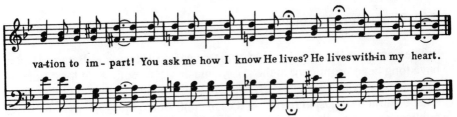

va-tion to im-part! You ask me how I know He lives? He lives with-in my heart.

Copyright 1944 by Homer A. Rodeheaver. © Renewed 1962, The Rodeheaver Co. (A Div. of Word, Inc.) All rights reserved. International Copyright secured. Used by permission.

He Lives

Author and Composer—Alfred H. Ackley, 1887-1960

> He is not here: for He is risen, as He said. Come, see the place where the Lord lay.
>
> Matthew 28:6

"Why should I worship a dead Jew?"

This challenging question was posed by a sincere young Jewish student who had been attending evangelistic meetings conducted by the author and composer of this hymn, Alfred H. Ackley.

In his book, *Forty Gospel Hymn Stories*, George W. Sanville records Mr. Ackley's answer to this searching question, which ultimately prompted the writing of this popular gospel hymn:

> He lives! I tell you, He is not dead, but lives here and now! Jesus Christ is more alive today than ever before. I can prove it by my own experience, as well as the testimony of countless thousands.

Mr. Sanville continues:

> Mr. Ackley's forthright, emphatic answer, together with his subsequent triumphant effort to win the man for Christ, flowered forth into song and crystallized into a convincing sermon on "He Lives!" His keenly alert mind was sensitive to suggestions for sermons, and sermons in song. In his re-reading of the resurrection stories of the Gospels, the words "He is risen" struck him with new meaning. From the thrill within his own soul came the convincing song—"He Lives!" The scriptural evidence, his own heart, and the testimony of history matched the glorious experience of an innumerable cloud of witnesses that "He Lives," so he sat down at the piano and voiced that conclusion in song. He says, "The thought of His ever-living presence brought the music promptly and easily."

The hymn first appeared in *Triumphant Service Songs*, a hymnal published by the Rodeheaver Company, in 1933. It has been a favorite with evangelical congregations to the present time.

The names of the two Ackley brothers, Alfred Henry and Benton D., have long been prominent in the gospel music field. Both were long-time associates with the Rodeheaver Publishing Company in the compilation and promotion of gospel music, and each contributed many songs to these publications. (See "God Understands" No. 29).

A. H. Ackley was born on January 21, 1887, at Spring Hill, Pennsylvania. He received a thorough education in music, including study in composition at the Royal Academy of Music in London, England. As a performer, he was recognized as an accomplished cellist. Following graduation from the Westminster Theological Seminary, he was ordained to the Presbyterian ministry, in 1914. While serving Presbyterian pastorates in Pennsylvania and California, Ackley always maintained a keen interest in the writing of hymns and hymn tunes. It is estimated that he wrote well over 1,000 gospel songs and hymns in addition to aiding in the compilation of various hymnals and songbooks for the Rodeheaver Company. In recognition of his contribution to sacred music, he was awarded the honorary Doctor of Sacred Music Degree from John Brown University. Mr. Ackley died at Whittier, California, on July 3, 1960.

Recently, I had the privilege of visiting the Holy Land and of standing in the garden tomb, where it is believed our Lord was buried and resurrected. What a spiritual blessing it was to realize anew, that we worship and serve One who broke the bonds of death and now ever liveth to make intercession for us.

116

* * *

THE LORD IS RISEN

"The Lord is risen indeed;
Now is His work performed;
Now is the mighty Captive freed,
And death's strong castle stormed.

"The Lord is risen indeed:
The grave has lost its prey;
With Him is risen the ransomed seed,
To reign in endless day.

"The Lord is risen indeed:
He lives, to die no more;
He lives, the sinner's cause to plead,
Whose curse and shame He bore.

"Then, angels, tune your lyres,
And strike each cheerful chord;
Join, all ye bright celestial choirs,
To sing our risen Lord!"

Thomas Kelly

34   He the Pearly Gates Will Open

Fredrick A. Blom, 1867-1927
Trans. by Nathaniel Carlson, 1879-1957

Elsie Ahlwen, 1905-

1. Love di-vine, so great and won-drous! Deep and might-y, pure, sub-lime!
2. Like a spar-row hunt-ed, fright-ened, Weak and help-less—so was I;
3. Love di-vine, so great and won-drous! All my sins He then for-gave!
4. In life's e-ven-tide, at twi-light, At His door I'll knock and wait;

Com-ing from the heart of Je-sus—Just the same thru tests of time.
Wound-ed, fall-en, yet He healed me—He will heed the sin-ner's cry.
I will sing His praise for-ev-er, For His blood, His pow'r to save.
By the pre-cious love of Je-sus I shall en-ter heav-en's gate.

CHORUS

He the pearl-y gates will o-pen, So that I may en-ter in;

For He pur-chased my re-demp-tion And for-gave me all my sin.

117

Arr. © Copyright 1968 by Singspiration, Inc. All rights reserved. Used by permission.

He the Pearly Gates Will Open

Author—Fredrick A. Blom, 1867-1927
English translation by Nathaniel Carlson, 1879-1957
Composer—Elsie R. Ahlwen, 1905-

But as it is written, eye hath not seen, nor ear heard, neither have entered into the heart of man, the things which God hath prepared for them that love Him.

1 Corinthians 2:9

This is another of the heart-warming Swedish songs that has become meaningful not only to Swedish descendants but to Christians world-wide, having been translated into more than a dozen languages. Other popular hymns of Scandinavian origin found in most evangelical hymnals include: "More Secure Is No One Ever" (No. 59), "Thanks to God" (No. 85), and "Day by Day" (*101 Hymn Stories*, No. 17).

The author of this text, Fredrick Arvid Blom, was born on May 21, 1867, near Enkoping, Sweden. He came to the United States in the 1890's and became an officer in the Salvation Army, in Chicago. Later Blom studied at North Park College and Seminary and then pastored Mission Covenant (now Evangelical Covenant) churches until 1915. Through various circumstances, Mr. Blom fell into deep sin and eventually spent time in prison. He explained, "I drifted from God...and became embittered with myself, the world, and not the least with ministers who looked on me with suspicion, because I was a member of the Socialist party." Sometime later, Blom was restored in his fellowship with God at a Salvation Army meeting and once again resumed a pastorate at a Swedish Congregational Church in Titusville, Pennsylvania, until returning to Sweden in 1921. There he pastored several churches until his death on May 24, 1927, at Uddevalla, Sweden.

118

It is generally believed that Fredrick Blom wrote the text for these verses either in prison or shortly after his spiritual restoration. The words no doubt reflect his back-slidden condition, especially verses two and three, as well as the joy of his renewed fellowship with the Lord.

Like a sparrow hunted, frightened, weak and helpless—so was I;
Wounded, fallen, yet He healed me—He will heed the sinner's cry.

Love divine, so great and wondrous! All my sins He then forgave!
I will sing His praise forever, for His blood, His pow'r to save.

Blom evidently wrote a number of other hymns throughout his ministry, but only this one is known and sung in our country.

The English translation of this Swedish text was made by Nathaniel Carlson, an Evangelical Free Church pastor. Carlson translated numerous songs from the Swedish language and also wrote original texts and composed a number of tunes. His works were published between 1929 and 1932 in three different editions, titled *Songs of Trust and Triumph*.

The composer, Elsie R. Ahlwen, was also born in Sweden and came to the United States as a young woman. After her studies at the Moody

Bible Institute, Chicago, Illinois, she became a full-time evangelist in reaching the Swedish immigrant population in the Chicago area. The Swedish words for the refrain, "Han skall oppna parleporten," ("He the pearly gates will open") had been known to Miss Ahlwen for some time, and she often sang them to her own melody in her evangelistic ministry. One day while conducting a service in Chicago, Miss Ahlwen was approached by an elderly man who presented her with the words for the four stanzas, which had previously been written by Fredrick Blom following his backslidden and spiritual renewal experience. Upon completion of the music for the entire text, the hymn came to be the popular theme song of Elsie Ahlwen's ministry.

Miss Ahlwen later married Daniel A. Sundeen, a businessman, who shared in her ministry as well as in the raising of a family. Upon the sudden death of her husband in 1962, Mrs. Sundeen penned these words: "It is difficult to see beyond the bend in the road where your loved one disappeared. But how good it is to know that, when My Lord calls me, the Pearly Gates will open—not because of my worthiness, but because He purchased my salvation."

Since her retirement, Elsie R. Ahlwen-Sundeen has resided in Manchester, New Hampshire.

*   *   *

"If the Father deigns to touch with divine power the cold and pulseless heart of the buried acorn and to make it burst forth from its prison walls, will He leave neglected on the earth the soul of man made in the image of his creator?"

William Jennings Bryan

THE BEST IS YET TO COME

"My heart is glad, I'm saved by grace, to Christ my life I give;
And He's prepared for me a place, where I with Him shall live.

"In heaven's land, heav'ns glory land, we'll live eternally;
Our home prepared by Christ's dear hand, and there His face we'll see.

"Heav'n has no night, Christ is its light, its sun shall ne'er go down;
There clothed we'll be in garments white, from Christ receive a crown.

"In heav'n with Christ, we'll sing with joy, no tears our eyes will dim;
And sin shall ne'er our hope destroy, when we're at home with Him.

"Blessed rest with Him to live in heav'ns land with God's own Son.
Even here His peace He'll give — But the best is yet to come."

N. Frykman
Swedish trans. by Ethel Larson Palm

35 Higher Ground

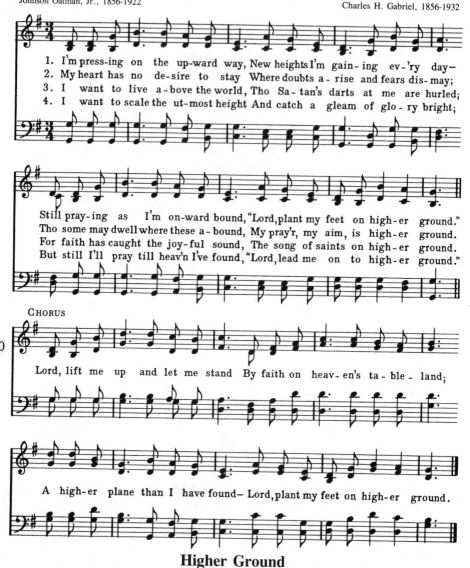

Higher Ground

Author—Johnson Oatman, Jr., 1856-1922
Composer—Charles H. Gabriel, 1856-1932

I press toward the mark for the prize of the high calling of God in Christ Jesus.
Philippians 3:14

...this hymn once took high rank among the holiness people, and secured a lasting place in American hymnology. Nothing can bring forth more shouts at a camp meeting of "Glory," "Hallelujah," than the singing of "Higher Ground." *Biographies of Gospel Song and Hymn Writers* by J. H. Hall

Johnson Oatman, Jr. was born near Medford, New Jersey, on April 21, 1856. He became a member of the Methodist Episcopal Church, when he was nineteen years of age. Soon he was licensed to preach and was ordained by his denomination, although he never actually pastored a church. In his early life, he was actively involved in the family's mercantile business, and, upon his father's death, entered the insurance business. In 1892, he started writing gospel songs, and, from then till his death, in 1926, he wrote approximately 3,000 gospel hymn texts. It is reported that Oatman generally averaged four to five new texts each week, throughout this period of his life, receiving no more than $1.00 for each of his songs. His texts were always in great demand by the leading gospel musicians of his day, such as Kirkpatrick, Excell, and Charles Gabriel.

Johnson Oatman is also the author of such popular hymn texts as "Count Your Blessings." (See *101 Hymn Stories*, No. 16) and "No, Not One!"

The composer of this music, Charles Hutchinson Gabriel, was born on August 18, 1856, in Wilton, Iowa. Gabriel is generally considered to be the most popular and influential, gospel song writer during the Billy Sunday-Homer Rodeheaver evangelistic crusade decade, 1910-20. In his association with the Rodeheaver Publishing Company as music editor, Gabriel continued his prolific musical output, until his death on September 15, 1932, in Los Angeles, California. It is estimated that Charles Gabriel was involved in the writing of more than 8,000 gospel songs as well as in the editing of numerous compilations and hymnals. In many of his songs he authored both the text and music. Often Gabriel attributed his texts to his pseudonym, "Charlotte G. Homer."

Charles Gabriel also supplied the music for the gospel hymn "O That Will Be Glory" (*101 Hymn Stories*, No. 70). Other well-known gospel favorites written or composed by Charles Gabriel include: "More Like the Master," "Send the Light," "My Savior's Love," "He Is So Precious to Me," "He Lifted Me," and "O It Is Wonderful."

"Higher Ground" was first published, in 1898, in the collection, *Songs of Love and Praise*, No. 5, compiled by John R. Sweney, Frank M. Davis, and J. Howard Entwisle. In his autobiography, *Sixty Years of Gospel Song*, Gabriel recalls that he composed this tune after his return to Chicago in September, 1892, and sold it for the grand sum of five dollars.

121

*   *   *

"There is not a heart but has its moments of longing, yearning for something better, nobler, holier than it knows now."

Henry Ward Beecher

His Way With Thee

Cyrus S. Nusbaum, 1861-1937

Cyrus S. Nusbaum, 1861-1937

1. Would you live for Je-sus and be   al-ways pure and good? Would you walk with
2. Would you have Him make you free, and fol-low at His call? Would you know the
3. Would you in His king-dom find a   place of con-stant rest? Would you prove Him

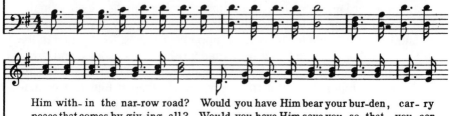

Him with- in the nar-row road? Would you have Him bear your bur-den, car- ry
peace that comes by giv-ing all? Would you have Him save you, so that you can
true in prov-i - den-tial test? Would you in His serv-ice la- bor   al-ways

CHORUS

all your load? Let Him have His way with thee.
nev-er fall? Let Him have His way with thee.   His pow'r can make you what you
at your best? Let Him have His way with thee.

ought to be, His blood can cleanse your heart and make you free, His love can

fill your soul, and you will see 'Twas best for Him to have His way with thee.

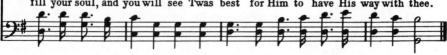

His Way With Thee

Author and Composer—Cyrus S. Nusbaum, 1861-1937

But the Lord is faithful, who shall establish you, and keep you from evil.

2 Thessalonians 3:3

Cyrus Silvester Nusbaum was ordained to the Methodist Church ministry in 1886. He went on to become one of the outstanding evangelists of his time, especially throughout the southwest area of our country. However, this hymn was born during a time of deep discouragement, following Mr. Nusbaum's first year of ministry. He gives the following account:

I had spent my first year in pastoral work. Having been appointed to serve as pastor in one of the poorest circuits in our district, I had struggled hard during the year to take care of the seven preaching places and congregations. It had been a most difficult task, strenuous and discouraging, and the income pitifully small. At the end of the conference year, my wife and I gathered our few necessary belongings, and, with the assistance of one of our members, we arrived at the railroad station in order to take the train to the place where the conference was to meet that year.

Naturally, we had prayed and hoped that, at the conference, I might be appointed to a better charge, but when the Bishop read the appointments the last night of the conference, I was named as pastor of the same old circuit. It was with heavy hearts that we repaired to our lodging place that night. Mrs. Nusbaum sensibly retired early, but I remained in the little parlor with no one to disturb me.

I was very unhappy and a spirit of rebellion seemed to possess me. About midnight, I finally knelt in prayer beside my chair. After some struggle, a deep peace came stealing into my heart. I told the Lord that I would be willing to let Him have His way with me regardless of the cost. With that feeling, of surrender to the will of God, came the inspiration for the song, now so well-known throughout Christendom.

123

"His Way With Thee" first appeared in *Gospel Praises*, compiled by Kirkpatrick, Hall and Gilmour, 1899. Although Mr. Nusbaum wrote words and music for a number of other hymns, this is the only one still in common usage.

* * *

"With eager heart and will on fire, I strove to win my great desire.
'Peace shall be mine,' I said; but life grew bitter in the barren strife.

"My soul was weary, and my pride was wounded deep;
    to Heaven I cried,
'God grant me peace or I must die;' the silent stars gave no reply.

"Broken at last, I bowed my head, forgetting all myself, and said—
'Whatever comes, His will be done;' and in that moment
    peace was won."

37 Holy Ghost, With Light Divine

MERCY

Andrew Reed, 1787-1862

Louis M. Gottschalk, 1829-1869
Arr. Edwin P. Parker, 1836-1925

1. Ho - ly Ghost, with light di - vine, Shine up - on this heart of mine;
2. Ho - ly Ghost, with pow'r di - vine, Cleanse this guilt-y heart of mine;
3. Ho - ly Ghost, with joy di - vine, Cheer this sad-dened heart of mine;
4. Ho - ly Spir - it, all di - vine, Dwell with-in this heart of mine;

Chase the shades of night a - way, Turn my dark - ness in - to day.
Long hath sin with-out con - trol Held do - min - ion o'er my soul.
Bid my man - y woes de - part, Heal my wound-ed, bleed-ing heart.
Cast down ev - 'ry i - dol-throne, Reign su - preme and reign a - lone.

Holy Ghost, With Light Divine

Author—Andrew Reed, 1787-1862
Composer—Louis M. Gottschalk, 1829-1869
Arranger—Edwin P. Parker, 1836-1925
Tune Name—"Mercy"
Meter—77.77

Behold, I send the promise of my Father upon you; but tarry ye in the city of Jerusalem, until ye be endued with power from on high.

Luke 24:49

"As the earth can produce nothing unless it is fertilized by the sun, so we can do nothing worthwhile for God without the energizing Holy Spirit's power operative in our lives."

Unknown

"I used to ask God to help me. Then I asked if I might help Him. I ended up by asking Him to do His work through me."

Hudson Taylor

Holy Ghost, With Light Divine

One of the marks of spiritual maturity in any believer's life is the growing awareness of the Holy Spirit's presence and power for daily living. How natural it often seems to attempt to live our lives and even minister for God in our own strength. The words of this hymn can serve as a worthy prayer for personal devotions, as we begin each new day.

"Holy Ghost, With Light Divine" has been, for many years, one of the church's important, teaching hymns regarding the Holy Spirit's ministry in a Christian's life. In a very simply-stated manner, the text tells us that we need a sensitivity to the Holy Spirit's presence, in order to have clear directions for our lives (verse one). Then, we are reminded that we need the Holy Spirit's ministry to enable us to live lives of purity and power (verse two). We also need the work of the Holy Spirit to balance the emotional sorrows of life with "joy divine" (verse three). Finally, we need the all-prevailing control by the Holy Spirit, if our lives are to be totally committed and conformed to God (verse four).

The text first appeared, in 1817, in a publication by its author, Andrew Reed, in his *Supplement to Watts's Psalms and Hymns*. It reappeared, in 1842, in Reed's next collection-*Hymn Book, Prepared From Dr. Watts's Psalms and Hymns, and Other Authors With Some Originals*. Andrew Reed titled his hymn text "Prayer to the Holy Spirit." In all, Reed contributed twenty hymns to these volumes. Another of Reed's hymn texts still in use today is also addressed to the Holy Spirit—"Spirit Divine, Attend Our Prayers." Several of the verses from this fine text are as follows:

125

Spirit divine, attend our prayers, and make this house Thy home;
Descend with all Thy gracious powers, O come, great Spirit, come!

Come as the light; to us reveal our emptiness and woe,
And lead us in those paths of life, whereon the righteous go.

Come as the fire, and purge our hearts like sacrificial flame;
Let our whole soul an offering be, to our Redeemer's name.

Following Reed's death on February 25, 1862 in London, his hymns, together with the hymns of his wife, Eliza Reed, were published in the *Wycliffe Supplement*, in 1872.

Andrew Reed was born on November 27, 1787, in London, England. He was ordained to the Congregational Church ministry, in 1811. In addition to serving as pastor of the New Road Chapel, St. George's-in-the-East, London, from 1811 to 1861, he was also known as an ardent philanthropist, largely responsible for founding such social agencies, in England, as the London Orphan Asylum and the Royal Hospital for Incurables. In 1834, while visiting Congregational churches in the United States, Andrew Reed was awarded the Doctor of Divinity Degree by Yale College in recognition of his many achievements.

The tune's name, "Mercy," is a result of the tune's early association with Charles Wesley's hymn "Depth of Mercy." (See No. 20). It first appeared, in 1854, as an adaptation from a secular, classical piano number by Louis M. Gottschalk, a composition titled "The Last Hope." Louis Moreau Gottschalk was born on May 8, 1829, in New Orleans, Louisiana and died on December 18, 1869, in Rio de Janeiro, Brazil. He was recognized as the first American-born piano virtuoso, and his concerts were in great demand both in the United States and South America. His performances were distinctive for the use of his own compositions, including "The Last Hope," which Gottschalk used to close each performance and from which the "Mercy" tune was later adapted.

The arranger of this tune, Edwin Pond Parker, was also an ordained Congregational church minister and served the Center Church, Hartford, Connecticut, for a period of fifty years. In addition to his pastoral duties, Parker always had a keen interest in hymnology. He wrote and arranged more than two hundred hymns as well as assisting in the compilation of several hymnals.

Because of the preference that many have today for the term "Holy Spirit" rather than "Holy Ghost," the hymn text has been changed in many of the present hymnals to this form, "Holy Spirit, Light Divine."

126   *   *   *

> "Holy Spirit, dwell with me;
> I myself would holy be;
> Separate from sin, I would
> Choose and cherish all things good;
> And whatever I can be,
> Give to Him who gave me Thee!"
>   Thomas T. Lynch

38   I Am Trusting Thee, Lord Jesus

BULLINGER

Frances Ridely Havergal, 1836-1879   Ethelbert W. Bullinger, 1837-1913

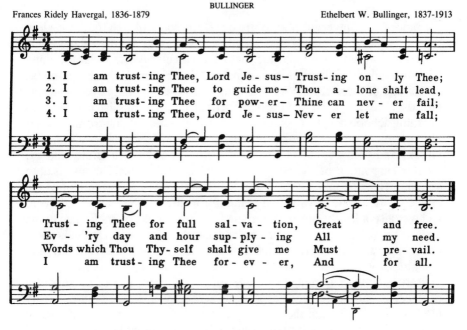

1. I am trust-ing Thee, Lord Je - sus— Trust-ing on - ly Thee;
2. I am trust-ing Thee to guide me— Thou a - lone shalt lead,
3. I am trust-ing Thee for pow-er— Thine can nev - er fail;
4. I am trust-ing Thee, Lord Je - sus— Nev - er let me fall;

Trust - ing Thee for full sal - va - tion, Great and free.
Ev - 'ry day and hour sup-ply - ing All my need.
Words which Thou Thy-self shalt give me Must pre - vail.
I am trust - ing Thee for - ev - er, And for all.

I Am Trusting Thee, Lord Jesus

Author—Frances Ridley Havergal, 1836-1879
Composer—Ethelbert W. Bullinger, 1837-1913
Tune Name—"Bullinger"
Meter—85.83

Blessed is the man that trusteth in the Lord, and whose hope the Lord is.Jeremiah 17:7

"I Am trusting Thee, Lord Jesus—Trusting only Thee."

This is another of the child-like, but beautiful expressions from the soul of the esteemed English poetess, Frances Ridley Havergal, often referred to as "the Sweetest Voice of Hymnody." Though highly educated and cultured, Miss Havergal always maintained a simple, child-like faith and confidence in her Lord. She is generally called "the consecration poet," since her hymns so reflect this quality. Her entire life was characterized by spiritual saintliness. It is said that she never wrote a line of verse without first fervently praying over it, and then she gave God all the credit for its composition:

I believe my King suggests a thought, and whispers me a musical line or two, and then I look up and thank Him delightedly and go on with it. That is how my hymns come.

Frances R. Havergal was born on December 14, 1836, in Astley, Worcestershire, England, into a cultured, religious family. Her father, William Havergal, was an influential Anglican clergyman, who for many years was also involved in improving and composing English hymnody. At the age of three, Frances could read, and at the age of seven, she was already writing verses. She received her education at English and German boarding schools and enjoyed exceptional advantages of culture and travel. She became a natural linguist, mastering French, German, Italian, Latin, Greek, and Hebrew. Miss Havergal was also a devoted Bible student, memorizing much of the New Testament as well as the Psalms, Isaiah, and the Minor Prophets. She was a brilliant pianist and interpreter of the music of the masters, especially Handel, Mendelssohn, and Beethoven, and was also a lovely singer. Her numerous little books of poems and hymn texts are now treasured all over England and America. Perhaps the keynote of them is her own expression: "Thy will be done is not a sigh, but only a song."

Frances Havergal, though seventeen years younger, was a contemporary of America's best-known, gospel song writer of this era, Fanny Crosby (1820-1915). Although these two gifted women never met, each was an ardent admirer of the other. The following is a letter sent by Miss Havergal to Fanny Crosby:

Dear blind sister over the sea—
An English heart goes forth to thee.
We are linked by a cable of faith and song,
Flashing bright sympathy swift along.
One in the East and one in the West,
Singing for Him whom our souls love best.
Singing for Jesus! Telling His love
All the way to our home above,
Where the severing sea, with its restless tide
Never shall hinder and never divide.
Sister, what shall our meeting soon be
When our hearts shall sing and our eyes shall see?

Frail in health all of her life, Miss Havergal one day caught a severe cold which caused inflamation of the lungs. When told that her life was in danger, she exclaimed, "If I am really going, it is too good to be true!" At another time she responded, "Splendid! To be so near the gates of heaven." At the very end, it is reported that she sang clearly, but faintly, another of her hymns, "Jesus, I Will Trust Thee, Trust Thee With My Soul." Then, according to reports by her sister,

She looked up steadfastly, as if she saw the Lord; and surely nothing less heavenly could have reflected such a glorious radiance upon her face. For ten minutes we watched that almost visible meeting with her King, and her countenance was so glad, as if she were already talking to Him! Then she tried to sing; but after one sweet, high note her voice failed, and as her brother commended her soul into the Redeemer's hand, she passed away.

Frances Havergal died at the early age of forty-two on June 3, 1879, in Swansea, Wales. On her tombstone at Astley, Worcestershire, is carved her favorite text, 1 John 1:7—"The blood of Jesus Christ His Son cleanseth us from all sin."

The composer of the music, Ethelbert W. Bullinger, was born at Canterbury, England, December 15, 1837, a direct descendent of Johann H. Bullinger, the great Swiss Reformer. He was an Anglican clergyman, known as an able Greek and Hebrew scholar, receiving an honorary D.D. degree from the Archbishop of Canterbury, in 1881, in recognition of his accomplishments. Throughout his life, he maintained a keen interest in church music and composed several other hymn tunes. This is the only one, however, still in common usage. It was composed in 1874 and first appeared in *Wesley's Hymns and New Supplement* (1877). He was also the author of many books including: *The Companion Bible, Commentary on Revelation, The Giver and His Gifts* now titled *Word Studies on the Holy Spirit, Great Cloud of Witnesses in Hebrews Eleven, Number in Scripture,* and *The Witness of the Stars.*

"I Am Trusting Thee, Lord Jesus" was said to be Miss Havergal's 129 favorite of all her hymns. It was written at Ormont, Dessous, Switzerland, in 1874. A copy of the text was found in her personal Bible after her death.

Frances R. Havergal is also the author of the hymns "I Gave My Life for Thee" (*101 Hymn Stories,* No. 34) and "Take My Life and Let It Be" (*ibid.,* No. 87).

* * *

"Dare to look up to God and say, Deal with me in the future as Thou wilt; I am of the same mind as Thou art; I am Thine; I refuse nothing that pleases Thee; lead me where Thou wilt; clothe me in any dress Thou choosest."

Discourses by Epictetus

39 I Must Tell Jesus

ORWIGSBURG

Elisha A. Hoffman, 1839-1929

Elisha A. Hoffman, 1839-1929

1. I must tell Je - sus all of my tri - als, I can-not bear these bur - dens a - lone; In my dis - tress He kind-ly will help me, He ev - er loves and cares for His own.

2. I must tell Je - sus all of my trou-bles, He is a kind, com-pas - sion-ate Friend; If I but ask Him, He will de - liv - er, Make of my trou - bles quick-ly an end.

3. Tempt-ed and tried, I need a great Sav - ior, One who can help my bur - dens to bear; I must tell Je - sus, I must tell Je - sus, He all my cares and sor - rows will share.

4. O how the world to e - vil al - lures me! O how my heart is tempt-ed to sin! I must tell Je - sus, and He will help me O - ver the world the vic - t'ry to win.

CHORUS

I must tell Je - sus! I must tell Je-sus! I can-not bear my bur-dens a - lone; I must tell Je - sus! I must tell Je - sus! Je-sus can help me, Je-sus a - lone.

I Must Tell Jesus

Author and Composer—Elisha A. Hoffman, 1839-1929
Tune Name— "Orwigsburg"
Meter—10 9. 10 9 with refrain

> For in that He Himself hath suffered being tempted, He is able to succour them that
> are tempted.   Hebrews 2:18

The author and composer of this hymn, Elisha A. Hoffman, gives the following account of its writing:

> During a pastorate in Lebanon, Pennsylvania, there was a woman to whom God permitted many visitations of sorrow and affliction. Coming to her home one day, I found her much discouraged. She unburdened her heart, concluding with the question, "Brother Hoffman, what shall I do? What shall I do?" I quoted from the word, then added, "You cannot do better than to take all of your sorrows to Jesus. You must tell Jesus."
>
> For a moment she seemed lost in meditation. Then her eyes lighted as she exclaimed, "Yes, I must tell Jesus."
>
> As I left her home I had a vision of that joy-illuminated face...and I heard all along my pathway the echo, "I must tell Jesus...I must tell Jesus."

131

Reaching his study, Rev. Mr. Hoffman penned the words quickly for what has become one of his best-loved songs. And before very long, he had composed the melody to fit the words as well. The hymn first appeared in the 1894 edition of *Pentecostal Hymns*, of which Mr. Hoffman was one of the music editors. The tune "Orwigsburg" is named for Orwigsburg, Pennsylvania, where Elisha Hoffman was born on May 7, 1839.

Elisha Albright Hoffman, though never formally trained in music, has contributed more than 2,000 gospel songs to Christian hymnody. For most of his hymns, Mr. Hoffman supplied both the words and the music. Several of his still popular gospel songs include: "Are You Washed in the Blood?", "Is Your All on the Altar?", "What a Wonderful Savior!", "Leaning on the Everlasting Arms" and "Glory to His Name."

In addition to his song writing and assisting in the compilation and editing of fifty different song books, Hoffman pastored several Evangelical and Presbyterian churches throughout the country. He also served with the Evangelical Association Publishing House in Cleveland, Ohio, for eleven years. It is through his gospel songs, however, that Elisha Hoffman ministered most effectively to the greatest number of people around the world.

40   I Need Thee Every Hour

Annie S. Hawks, 1835-1918
Chorus—Robert Lowry, 1826-1899

Robert Lowry, 1826-1899

1. I need Thee ev-'ry hour, Most gra - cious Lord; No ten - der voice like
2. I need Thee ev-'ry hour, Stay Thou near by; Temp-ta-tions lose their
3. I need Thee ev-'ry hour, In joy or pain; Come quick-ly and a -
4. I need Thee ev-'ry hour, Most Ho - ly One; O make me Thine in -

CHORUS

Thine Can peace af - ford.
pow'r When Thou art nigh.   I need Thee, O I need Thee, Ev-'ry hour I
bide, Or life is vain.
deed, Thou bless - ed Son!

132

need Thee! O bless me now, my Sav - ior— I come to Thee!

I Need Thee Every Hour

Authors—Annie S. Hawks, 1835-1918
         Chorus—Robert Lowry, 1826-1899
Composer—Robert Lowry, 1826-1899
Scripture Reference—John 15:5

In the day of my trouble I will call upon Thee; for Thou wilt answer me. Psalm 86:7

This deeply, personal hymn was written out of the daily experiences of a busy housewife and mother, Annie Hawks, in the year 1872.

Annie Sherwood Hawks was born in Hoosick, New York, on May 28, 1835. At a very early age, she displayed a gift for writing verse and by the age of fourteen, was contributing poetry regularly to various newspapers. In all, she wrote more than 400 poems, though this hymn text is the only one still in common usage. In 1859, Annie Sherwood married Charles Hawks, and three children were born into this home. For much of her life she lived in Brooklyn, New York, and was a member of the Hanson Place Baptist Church, where for eight years Dr. Robert Lowry, himself a prominent, gospel poet and musician, was her pastor. Mr. Lowry recognized Mrs. Hawks' poetic gifts and encouraged her to use these abilities for writing hymn texts. Annie Hawks has left the following account regarding the writing of her one immortal hymn:

> One day as a young wife and mother of 37 years of age, I was busy with my regular household tasks during a bright June morning, in 1872. Suddenly, I became filled with the sense of nearness to the Master, and I began to wonder how anyone could ever live without Him, either in joy or pain. Then, the words were ushered into my mind and these thoughts took full possession of me—"I need Thee every hour...."

Later, Mrs. Hawks showed these four stanzas to Dr. Lowry, who was very much impressed with them. Lowry quickly composed the music for the verses and also added a refrain. Dr. Lowry had the conviction that a refrain or chorus was necessary for any hymn to give it completeness as well as to provide an opportunity for everyone, especially the children, to be part of the congregational singing. The hymn first appeared in a small collection of hymns prepared especially for the National Baptist Sunday School Association Convention held in Cincinnati, Ohio, in that same year of 1872. It was sung by the delegates with great appreciation. The following year, it was included in a new songbook, *The Royal Diadem*, compiled by Lowry and William Doane, with the heading "Without Me Ye Can Do Nothing"—John 15:5 Later the song was widely used and popularized by Ira Sankey in the large Moody-Sankey campaigns, both in this country and throughout Great Britain, where it became a favorite with many of God's people.

133

Sixteen years after writing her hymn text, Mrs. Hawks experienced the death of her husband, which, she has written, "cast a shadow of great loss over my life." Mrs. Hawks has left this account regarding the spiritual help she received from her own hymn during this very difficult period of her life:

> I did not understand at first why this hymn had touched the great throbbing heart of humanity. It was not until long years after, when the shadow fell over my way, the shadow of a great loss, that I understood something of the comforting power in the words, which I had been permitted to give out to others in my hour of sweet serenity and peace.

The composer of the music for this text, Dr. Robert Lowry, was recognized and honored as an outstanding Baptist minister in his various pastorates through the eastern areas of our country. He was born in Philadellphia on March 12, 1826. Lowry served Baptist churches in Pennsylvania, New York City, Brooklyn, and New Jersey and was a professor of rhetoric at Bucknell University for a six-year period. He was known as a man of rare administrative ability, an excellent preacher, and a thorough Bible student. Music and hymnology were his favorite studies, though he always thought of them as avocations. Later, however, with the death of William Bradbury, in 1868, the Biglow Publishing Company selected Robert Lowry to be its music editor. In typical fashion, Lowry applied himself vigorously to the study of music and became highly knowledgable in the field. It is said that the quality of his publications did much to stimulate and improve the cause of sacred music in this country.

Although Robert Lowry had no formal training in musical composition, he has contributed many fine hymns to our evangelical hymnals and has compiled and published a great number of songbook collections, especially geared for Sunday school use. From the soul and pen of this dedicated pastor-musician have come such other gospel hymn favorites as: "Christ Arose" (No. 15), "Nothing But the Blood," and "Shall We Gather at the River" (See *Singing With Understanding*, page 36. He has composed just the music for such well-known hymns as: "All the Way My Savior Leads Me" (*101 Hymn Stories*, No. 5), "Savior, Thy Dying Love," and the stirring text by Isaac Watts, "We're Marching to Zion."

134

* * *

A VOICE
"The Father, too, does He not see and hear?
And seems He far who dwells so very near?
Fear not, my child, there is no need to fear.

"The days may darken and the tempest lower;
Their power is nothing to the Father's power;
Lift up thy heart and watch with me this hour."
Samuel Valentine Cole

41   I Surrender All

Judson W. Van De Venter, 1855-1939   Winfield S. Weeden, 1847-1908

1. All to Je-sus I sur-ren-der, All to Him I free-ly give;
2. All to Je-sus I sur-ren-der, Hum-bly at His feet I bow;
3. All to Je-sus I sur-ren-der, Make me, Sav-ior, whol-ly Thine;
4. All to Je-sus I sur-ren-der, Lord, I give my-self to Thee;

I will ev-er love and trust Him, In His pres-ence dai-ly live.
World-y pleas-ures all for-sak-en, Take me, Je-sus, take me now.
Let me feel the Ho-ly Spir-it— Tru-ly know that Thou art mine.
Fill me with Thy love and pow-er, Let Thy bless-ings fall on me.

CHORUS

I sur-ren-der all, I sur-ren-der all,
I sur-ren-der, I sur-ren-der all, I sur-ren-der, I sur-ren-der all,

All to Thee, my bless-ed Sav-ior, I sur-ren-der all.

135

I Surrender All

Author—Judson W. Van de Venter, 1855-1939
Composer—Winfield S. Weeden, 1847-1908

> He that findeth his life shall lose it; and he that loseth his life for my sake shall find it.   Matthew 10:39

This hymn text was written by the author as he recalled the day that he had surrendered his life to Christ and dedicated himself completely to Christian service. It was first published, in 1896, in the collection, *Gospel*

Songs of Grace and Glory compiled by Weeden, Van de Venter and Leonard. Mr. Van de Venter has left this account of the writing of his hymn text:

> The song was written while I was conducting a meeting at East Palestine, Ohio, and in the home of George Sebring (founder of the Sebring Campmeeting-Bible Conference in Sebring, Ohio, and later developer of the town of Sebring, Florida). For some time, I had struggled between developing my talents in the field of art and going into full-time evangelistic work. At last the pivotal hour of my life came, and I surrendered all. A new day was ushered into my life. I became an evangelist and discovered down deep in my soul a talent hitherto unknown to me. God had hidden a song in my heart, and touching a tender chord, He caused me to sing.

Judson Van de Venter was born on a farm near Dundee, Michigan, on December 5, 1855. Following graduation from Hillsdale College, he became an art teacher and later a supervisor of art in the public schools of Sharon, Pennsylvania. He was also an active layman in his Methodist Episcopal Church. It was during this time that Van de Venter became especially involved in evangelistic meetings being held in his church. Recognizing his unusual talent for Christian service, his friends began urging him to give up teaching and become an evangelist. For the next five years, Mr. Van de Venter wavered between the challenge of the ministry and that of becoming a recognized artist. Following his decision to surrender his life to Christ, he traveled extensively throughout the United States, England, and Scotland in evangelistic work. He was assisted for many years by his associate and singer, Winfield S. Weeden.

Dr. Billy Graham, foremost evangelist of our century, wrote this tribute to Mr. Van de Venter in the book, *Crusade Hymn Stories*, edited by Cliff Barrows:

> One of the evangelists who influenced my early preaching was also a hymnist who wrote "I Surrender All"—the Rev. J. W. Van de Venter. He was a regular visitor at the Florida Bible Institute (now Trinity Bible College) in the late 1930's. We students loved this kind, deeply spiritual gentleman and often gathered in his winter home at Tampa, Florida, for an evening of fellowship and singing.

The composer of the music for this hymn text, Winfield S. Weeden, was a long-time associate with Mr. Van de Venter in evangelistic work. Weeden was born on March 29, 1847, at Middleport, Ohio. Before his evangelistic ministry, he had been active for a number of years in teaching singing schools throughout his area. He was said to have been an effective song leader and a gifted vocalist. He compiled several collections, including *The Peacemaker* (1894), *Songs of the Peacemaker* (1895), and *Songs of Sovereign Grace* (1897). On his tombstone is inscribed the title of this hymn, "I Surrender All."

Judson W. Van de Venter and Winfield Weeden also collaborated in writing the popular gospel hymn "Sunlight."

42   I'd Rather Have Jesus

Mrs. Rhea F. Miller, 1894-1966   George Beverly Shea, 1909-

1. I'd rath-er have Je-sus than sil-ver or gold, I'd rath-er be
2. I'd rath-er have Je-sus than men's ap-plause, I'd rath-er be
3. He's fair-er than lil-ies of rar-est bloom, He's sweet-er than

His than have rich-es un-told; I'd rath-er have Je-sus than hous-es
faith-ful to His dear cause; I'd rath-er have Je-sus than world-
hon-ey from out the comb; He's all that my hun-ger-ing spir-

REFRAIN

or land, I'd rath-er be led by His nail-pierced hand: Than to be the
wide fame, I'd rath-er be true to His ho-ly name:
it needs—I'd rath-er have Je-sus and let Him lead:

137

king of a vast do-main Or be held in sin's dread sway! I'd

rath-er have Je-sus than an-y-thing This world af-fords to-day.

Copyright 1922, 1950. © Renewed 1939, 1966 by Chancel Music, Inc. Assigned to The Rodeheaver Co. (A Div. of Word, Inc.) All rights reserved. International Copyright secured. Used by permission.

I'd Rather Have Jesus

Author—Mrs. Rhea F. Miller, 1894-1966
Composer—George Beverly Shea, 1909-
Scripture Reference—Psalm 71:23; Matthew 16:24-26

For to me to live is Christ, and to die is gain.   Philippians 1:21

The name of George Beverly Shea is certainly well known to evangelical Christians. Since 1947, he has been the featured soloist with the Billy Graham Evangelistic Association and has been seen and heard around the world, through his many recordings, television rallies, and the "Hour of Decision" radio program. His singing of gospel music is always characterized with a warmth and simplicity of style accompanied by a rich, bass-baritone vocal quality. Without question, "I'd Rather Have Jesus" is the best-loved song that Mr. Shea sings and one for which he composed the music himself. It is the first song he ever wrote and one which has become his "trademark" to the present time.

George Beverly Shea was born into the home of fine Christian parents in Winchester, Ontario, Canada, on February 1, 1909. His father was a faithful minister of the gospel for the Wesleyan Methodist Church, and his mother was a strong spiritual and musical influence in his life. As young George was growing up in parsonages in New York and New Jersey, his friends and family became very much aware of his fine musical talent and full, resonant voice. He began to sing regularly in his father's church as well as for services in other local churches. Following high school, George attended Houghton College in New York during 1928-29, but family financial problems caused him to leave after one year and take employment as a clerk in an insurance office in New York City. During this time, he lived with his parents while his father was pastoring in Jersey City. In his book, *Songs That Touch the Heart*, Bev Shea tells this story:

138

Once again Mother—my musical guardian—had a part. A lover of beauty, be it a flower, a bird, a poem, an ennobling quotation—whatever—Mother was a collector. . . she loved to share poetry and she always had some verse in hand copied from a book or clipped from a magazine. It was her practice of leaving such writings on the piano music rack which led to my writing "I'd Rather Have Jesus" when I was twenty years old. The same Sunday morning I read those wonderful words for the first time, I wrote music for them and used the song that same day in my father's church service. Of course, Mrs. Rhea F. Miller is the catalyst. Without her inspiring lyrics, there would have been no song. . . . Over the years, I've not sung any song more than "I'd Rather Have Jesus," but I never tire of Mrs. Miller's heartfelt words.

During the nearly nine years that Shea worked for the Mutual of New York Life Insurance Company, he continued his vocal training and singing in churches and for local Christian broadcasts. One day a director of a network radio station heard him sing and arranged for him to audition for a national program with the Lynn Murray Singers. Bev was thrilled with the prospect of singing on a network radio program, of being heard by large numbers of people, and having a chance to make "big money" for a change. After passing the audition test, Bev Shea just didn't feel right about accepting this "once in a life-time" offer to be in secular work. "No" was a strange word to such an offer, as positions such as these were rare during those depression days, and thousands of young singers would have leaped at such an opportunity.

On June 16, 1934, Bev married his teen-age sweetheart, Eram Scharfe, and together they raised two children. The family moved to Chicago, where Bev took a position on the staff of radio station WMBI. In June of 1944, Bev Shea realized his ambition to sing the gospel on a national radio program, "Club Time." A well-known aluminum firm, headed by a devoted Christian businessman, Herbert J. Taylor, sponsored Shea's program for the next several years, a program heard by thousands of listeners each week. Then during the 1940's and 50's, Shea was active, singing in large Youth for Christ rallies throughout America and Canada. And now for more than three decades, Bev Shea has ministered with the Billy Graham Evangelistic Team, around the world as well as on radio and television. In 1956, George Beverly Shea was given an honorary doctorate degree from Houghton College in recognition of his many years of effective Christian ministry.

139

Whenever Bev Shea speaks to young people, his words of advice, based on the scriptural truths taught in Matthew 16:24-26, are usually these: "God will always guide your life when you give the direction over to Him."

...If any man will come after me, let him deny himself, and take up his cross, and follow Me. For whosoever will save his life shall lose it; and whosoever will lose his life for my sake shall find it.

Bev's favorite scripture verse, one that he generally attaches to his signature, is found in Psalm 71:23:

My lips shall greatly rejoice when I sing unto Thee; and my soul, which Thou hast redeemed.

The power that this song has had in influencing and changing lives for God will be fully evaluated only in eternity. There are countless testimonies by individuals whose lives have been changed by the singing of this one hymn:

A thousand grim marines sat on a South Pacific Island, during the days of World War II, listening to a gospel message punctuated with gunfire in the distance. When the chaplain sat down, a marine stood to his feet to sing the closing hymn. As the shell-scarred palms swayed nearby, more than half of that company came forward to profess faith in Christ as their Savior. The marine soloist, a former opera singer, had just concluded singing "I'd Rather Have Jesus..."

George Beverly Shea has also written several other songs which have gained popular acceptance—"The Wonder of It All," and "I Will Praise Him in the Morning."

* * *

WHAT JESUS IS

"To the artist, He is the one altogether lovely—Song of Solomon 5:15
To the architect, He is the chief cornerstone—1 Peter 2:6
To the astronomer, He is the sun of righteousness—Malachi 4:2
To the baker, He is the bread of life—John 6:35
To the banker, He is the hidden treasure—Matthew 13:44
To the builder, He is the sure foundation—Isaiah 28:16
To the carpenter, He is the door—John 10:7
To the doctor, He is the great physician—Jeremiah 8:22
To the educator, He is the great teacher—John 3:2
To the engineer, He is the new and living way—Hebrews 10:20
To the farmer, He is the sower and Lord of harvest—Luke 10:2
To the florist, He is the rose of Sharon—Song of Solomon 2:1
To the geologist, He is the rock of ages—1 Corinthians 10:4
To the horticulturist, He is the true vine—John 15:1
To the judge, He is the only righteous judge of man—2 Timothy 4:8
To the juror, He is the faithful and true witness—Revelation 3:14
To the jeweler, He is the pearl of great price—Matthew 13:46
To the lawyer, He is counselor, lawgiver, and true advocate—Isaiah 9:6
To the newspaper man, He is tidings of great joy—Luke 2:10
To the oculist, He is the light of the eyes—Proverbs 29:13
To the philanthropist, He is the unspeakable gift—2 Corinthians 9:15
To the philosopher, He is the wisdom of God—1 Corinthians 1:24
To the preacher, He is the Word of God—Revelation 19:13
To the sculptor, He is the living stone—1 Peter 2:4
To the servant, He is the good master—Matthew 23:8-10
To the statesman, He is the desire of all nations—Haggai 2:7
To the student, He is the incarnate truth—1 John 5:6
To the theologian, He is the author and finisher of our faith—
Hebrews 12:2
To the toiler, He is the giver of rest—Matthew 11:28
To the sinner, He is the Lamb of God who takes the sin away—John 1:29

To the Christian, He is the Son of the Living God, the Savior, the Redeemer, and the Loving Lord."

Unknown

43 I Would Be True

PEEK

Howard A. Walter, 1883-1918   Joseph Yates Peek, 1843-1911

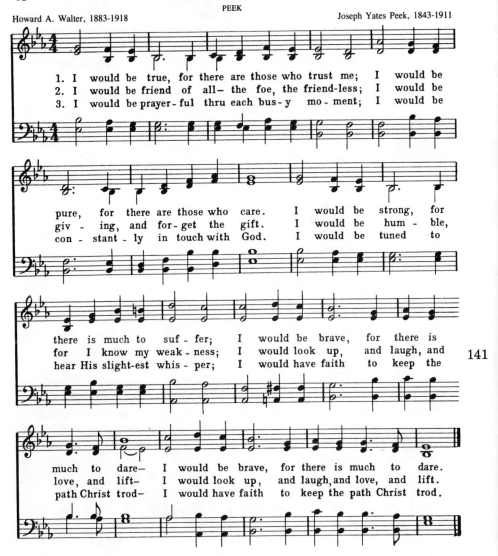

1. I would be true, for there are those who trust me; I would be
2. I would be friend of all— the foe, the friend-less; I would be
3. I would be prayer-ful thru each bus-y mo-ment; I would be

pure, for there are those who care. I would be strong, for
giv - ing, and for-get the gift. I would be hum - ble,
con - stant - ly in touch with God. I would be tuned to

there is much to suf - fer; I would be brave, for there is
for I know my weak - ness; I would look up, and laugh, and
hear His slight-est whis - per; I would have faith to keep the

much to dare— I would be brave, for there is much to dare.
love, and lift— I would look up, and laugh, and love, and lift.
path Christ trod— I would have faith to keep the path Christ trod.

I Would Be True

Author—Howard A. Walter, 1883-1918
Composer—Joseph Yates Peek, 1843-1911
Tune Name—"Peek"
Meter—11 10. 11 10

I have chosen the way of truth: Thy judgments have I laid before me. Psalm 119:30

"I Would Be True," written by a young man in his early twenties, has proven to be one of the most appealing hymns for young people ever written to the present time. The author, Howard A. Walter, went to Japan, in 1906, to spend a year teaching English at the Waseda University. It was his desire to write a statement of his philosophy of life to share with his mother back home. Howard titled the first three stanzas of his poem "My Creed." Mrs. Henry Walter, greatly impressed and pleased with her son's convictions, sent a copy of the poem to *Harper's Magazine*, where it was published in the May, 1907 issue. During the summer of 1909, Howard Walter showed his "My Creed" text to an itinerant, Methodist lay-preacher, Joseph Yates Peek. Although Peek possessed no technical expertise in music, he immediately began whistling a tune for the words. Peek in turn contacted a friend, Grant Colfax Tullar, an accomplished organist and well-known songwriter, who notated and harmonized the music in its present form. The fourth stanza of this hymn was not added by Howard Walter until several years later.

142

Howard Arnold Walter was born on August 19, 1883, at New Britain, Connecticut. He was graduated with high honors from Princeton University in 1905. This was followed by his teaching experience at the Waseda University of Tokyo, Japan. Returning to the United States, Walter prepared for the ministry at Hartford Seminary and was ordained by the Congregational Church denomination, serving as an assistant minister at the Asylum Hill Congregational Church in Hartford, Connecticut for three years. In 1913, he joined the executive staff of the YMCA and left for Lahore, India, to teach and reach the Mohammedan students there. In 1918, during a severe influenza epidemic, the dynamic life of this young man came to an abrupt end. Howard Walter's life has often been cited as an outstanding example of his own earlier creedal statement. Hartford Seminary has placed Howard A. Walter's name on its honor roll, where it may still be seen today. In his home church, the First Congregational Church of Christ in New Britain, Connecticut, a memorial tablet was placed on February 14, 1926, on which the first two stanzas of this hymn text are inscribed.

The author of the music, Joseph Yates Peek, was born on February 27, 1843, at Schenectady, New York. After achieving considerable success as a florist, he became an itinerant Methodist preacher, in 1904, and did considerable traveling throughout this country. Although he had no formal musical training, he maintained a keen interest in music throughout his life, playing the violin, banjo, and piano. Less than two months before his death on March 17, 1911, Joseph Peek realized his life-long ambition, that of becoming a fully-ordained, Methodist preacher.

Grant Colfax Tullar, who assisted Joseph Peek in notating and harmonizing this music, is also the composer for the well-known gospel song "Face to Face" (No. 24).

James Procter (dates unknown)

Robert Harkness, 1880-1961

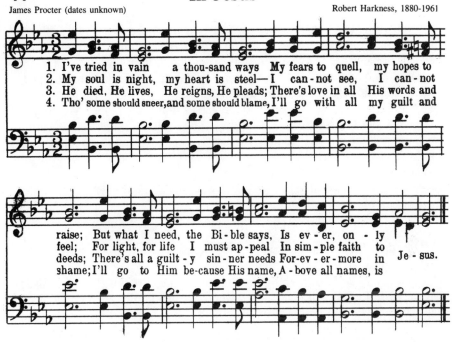

1. I've tried in vain a thou-sand ways My fears to quell, my hopes to raise; But what I need, the Bi-ble says, Is ev-er, on-ly
2. My soul is night, my heart is steel—I can-not see, I can-not feel; For light, for life I must ap-peal In sim-ple faith to
3. He died, He lives, He reigns, He pleads; There's love in all His words and deeds; There's all a guilt-y sin-ner needs For-ev-er-more in Je-sus.
4. Tho' some should sneer, and some should blame, I'll go with all my guilt and shame; I'll go to Him be-cause His name, A-bove all names, is

In Jesus

Author—James Procter, dates unknown
Composer—Robert Harkness, 1880-1961

The fool hath said in his heart, There is no God.   Psalm 14:1

> Though some should sneer, and some should blame,
> I'll go with all my guilt and shame;
> I'll go to Him because His name
> Above all names is Jesus.

These are the words of a man who had been an avowed atheist for most of his life but who later became a believer in Jesus Christ and a follower of the Christian faith. The composer of the music, Robert Harkness, shares this account:

"In November, 1903, while I was privileged to be associated with the late R. A. Torrey in his world-wide campaigns, we had meetings in the city of Manchester, England. At the close of an afternoon session, toward the end of November, a lady approached me, as I was leaving the platform, and timidly handed me an envelope.

'Mr. Harkness, would you read the verses in this envelope? Maybe you can set them to music.'

'I opened the envelope and immediately began to read these interesting words:

> I've tried in vain a thousand ways my fears to quell,
> My hopes to raise.
> But what I need, the Bible says, is ever, only Jesus.

'My dear lady, that's a very unusual text. Where did you get it?' The lady began to relate the following story:

'The verses were written by my brother, James Procter. He was raised in an old-fashioned Christian home, where we had family prayers. He lived as a boy in a good spiritual environment, attending Sunday school and church regularly. But in his early teens, he began to read the writings of the Free Thinkers and other infidels. He read the error of these writers to such an extent that his own faith in God became shaken. Finally, he renounced all interest in the Christian faith and the Bible. He later joined the Free Thinkers' Society in Manchester, soon becoming its president.

'During these early years of infidelity and searching for life's meaning, James Procter penned the first two stanzas of this hymn. In the second verse, he especially described his own attitudes as an unbeliever with these words:

> My soul is night, my heart is steel—
> I cannot see, I cannot feel;
> For light, for life I must appeal
> In simple faith to Jesus.

'Later, while serving as president of the Free Thinkers' Society in Manchester, England, James Procter experienced a serious illness. Fearing that the end of his life was at hand, he one day requested his sister to send for a minister of the gospel. A faithful man of God came to his bedside and led Procter to a saving faith in Christ. The illness took a turn for the better and his sister described this experience during his convalescence:

'One day as I sat at my brother's bedside, he said, "Sister, go over to that old bureau and look through some papers in the top right drawer. You will find a sheet on which are two verses of a poem. I want to finish that text right now."

'I went over to the bureau and soon located the paper and began to read, "I've tried in vain. . . ."'

'Yes, yes, that's it. Now let me dictate the last two verses to you.'

'With great excitement, my brother repeated these words slowly, while I wrote them down with much care:

> He died, He lives, He reigns, He pleads;
> There's love in all His words and deeds—
> There's all a guilty sinner needs
> Forever more in Jesus.
>
> 'Tho some should sneer and some should blame,
> I'll go with all my guilt and shame
> I'll go to Him because His name
> Above all names is Jesus.

'That closing verse was especially meaningful to my brother as it represented his personal testimony to his many long-time friends, the other members of the Free Thinkers' Society. You can well imagine my delight on that November day of 1903, when the noted gospel musician, Robert Harkness, expressed a real interest in my brother's text.'

"I thanked this dear lady for her kindness in giving me these words, written by her brother, and for sharing with me this unusual experience. I promised her that I would do my best to set them to some appropriate music. Our campaign meetings ended in Manchester at the end of November. Just before Christmas of 1903, I traveled by train from Edinburgh to London to spend the Christmas season with relatives. It was a dull, foggy day. Visibility seemed to be nil, as I casually looked through some papers in my pocket as the train rambled its way to London. To my surprise, there was the paper with the four verses of 'In Jesus.' As I read the words anew, the musical suggestion came quickly and the music was written, just as it has been used to the present time."

Robert Harkness was born in Bendigo, Australia, on March 2, 1880. He traveled extensively with the Torrey-Alexander gospel team and also with J. Wilbur Chapman in evangelistic meetings. Harkness was recognized as one of the finest gospel pianists of his day. He also wrote instructional books on the techniques of evangelistic hymn-playing that have been very influential, including a one-volume correspondence course published by the Lillenas Publishing Company. Robert Harkness personally composed or arranged more than 2,000 gospel songs. Several of these are still familiar favorites with many Christians: "Our Great Savior" (No. 73), "Why Should He Love Me So?", "Hiding in the Shadow of the Rock," "No Longer Lonely," "Sometime, All Sorrow Will Be O'er," "Thine, Lord,"

145

"Only Believe and Live," and "When I See My Savior Hanging on Calvary."

Mr. Harkness continued to be active in Christian service until his death at the age of eighty-one on May 8, 1961, in London, England. He gave extensive personal performances throughout this country in a program called "The Music of the Cross." His inspiring piano solos will long be remembered by many.

Through the years, men in their vain deceits have tried to discredit both our Savior, the Living Word, as well as the Scriptures, the written Word of God. But human reasoning alone will never truly satisfy the yearning of any life, since man is a special creation — endowed with a spirit that is meant to relate to the corresponding faculty of God. One can never be a truly complete person, until this spiritual union is accomplished. Like the author of this hymn text, when one is faced with the crises of life and the prospect of an endless eternity, that spirit within the human breast cries out for far more comfort and assurance than mere human reasoning alone can afford. For now and for eternity, "What I need, the Bible says, is ever, only Jesus."

*　　*　　*

146　　"Atheism is the death of hope, the suicide of the soul."

Anonymous

"Atheism is rather in the lip than in the heart of man."

Sir Francis Bacon: *Essays: Of Atheism*

THE ANVIL— GOD'S WORD

"Last eve I passed beside a blacksmith's door,
And heard the anvil ring the vesper chime;
Then looking in, I saw upon the floor
Old hammers, worn with beating years of time.

"'How many anvils have you had,' said I,
'To wear and batter all these hammers so?'
'Just one,' said he, and then, with twinkling eye,
'The anvil wears the hammers out, you know.'

"And so, thought I, the anvil of God's Word,
For ages skeptic blows have beat upon;
Yet, though the noise of falling blows was heard,
The anvil is unharmed — the hammers gone."

Unknown

45   In My Heart There Rings a Melody

Elton M. Roth, 1891-1951

Elton M. Roth, 1891-1951

1. I have a song that Je-sus gave me, It was sent from heav'n a-bove; There nev-er was a sweet-er mel-o-dy, 'Tis a mel-o-dy of love.
2. I love the Christ who died on Cal-v'ry, For He washed my sins a-way; He put with-in my heart a mel-o-dy, And I know it's there to stay.
3. 'Twill be my end-less theme in glo-ry, With the an-gels I will sing; 'Twill be a song with glo-rious har-mo-ny, When the courts of heav-en ring.

CHORUS

In my heart there rings a mel-o-dy, There rings a mel-o-dy with heav-en's har-mo-ny; In my heart there rings a mel-o-dy; There rings a mel-o-dy of love.

147

Copyright 1924. Renewal 1951 by Hope Publishing Co., Carol Stream, IL 60188. All rights reserved. Used by permission.

In My Heart There Rings a Melody

Author and Composer—Elton M. Roth, 1891-1951

O sing unto the Lord a new song; for He hath done marvelous things: His right hand, and His holy arm, hath gotten Him the victory.   Psalm 98:1

The author and composer of this favorite gospel song, Elton Menno Roth, was born on November 27, 1891, at Berne, Indiana. At the age of fourteen, he directed his first church choir. Later, he attended the Moody Bible Institute as well as the Fort Wayne Bible School of Indiana. Roth also did further, serious, music study with several, prominent, European music teachers. For a time, he traveled extensively with several evangelists as their song leader and choir director. Mr. Roth then taught for a period of time at several different Bible schools and colleges, including a six-year period at the Missionary Training Institute in Nyack, New York.

Elton Roth later moved to Los Angeles, where he became increasingly known as a distinguished church musician, singer, composer, and conductor. In the 1930's, he organized a professional group known as the Ecclesia Choir, which performed many concerts throughout this country. Mr. Roth also published many anthems and more than 100 sacred songs, for which he composed the music and generally the text as well. It is interesting to note, however, that of all of Elton Roth's compositions, only this simple gospel hymn, written in his early ministry, is still in general use.

148

Mr. Roth has given the following details about "In My Heart There Rings a Melody," written in 1923, while he was engaged in evangelistic meetings in Texas:

One hot summer afternoon, I took a little walk to the cotton mill just outside of town. On my way back through the burning streets of this typical plantation village, I became weary with the oppressive heat, and paused at a church on the corner.

The door being open, I went in. There were no people in the pews, no minister in the pulpit. Everything was quiet, with a lingering sacred presence. I walked up and down the aisle and began singing, "In My Heart There Rings a Melody," then hurried into the pastor's study to find some paper. I drew a staff and sketched the melody, remaining there for an hour or more to finish the song, both words and music.

That evening I introduced it by having over two hundred boys and girls sing it at the open air meeting, after which the audience joined in the singing. I was thrilled as it seemed my whole being was transformed into a song.

The hymn first appeared in printed form in Roth's *Campaign Melodies*, published in 1924. The following year it appeared in the Hope Publishing Company's *Hymns of Praise, No. 2*. It has been a favorite with evangelical people to the present time.

46   # In Times Like These

Ruth Caye Jones, 1902-1972   Ruth Caye Jones, 1902-1972

1. In times like these you need a Sav-ior, In times like these you need an an-chor; Be ver-y sure, be ver-y sure Your an-chor holds and grips the Sol-id Rock!
2. In times like these you need the Bi-ble, In times like these O be not i-dle; Be ver-y sure, be ver-y sure Your an-chor holds and grips the Sol-id Rock!
3. In times like these I have a Sav-ior, In times like these I have an an-chor; I'm ver-y sure, I'm ver-y sure My an-chor holds and grips the Sol-id Rock!

REFRAIN

This Rock is Je-sus, Yes, He's the One; This Rock is Je-sus, The on-ly One!

1,2. Be ver-y sure, be ver-y sure Your an-chor holds and grips the Sol-id Rock!
3. I'm ver-y sure, I'm ver-y sure My an-chor holds and grips the Sol-id Rock!

149

© Copyright 1944. Renewal 1971 by R. C. Jones. Assigned to Singspiration, Inc. All rights reserved. Used by permission.

In Times Like These

Author and Composer—Ruth Caye Jones, 1902-1972

> Then Simon Peter answered Him, Lord, to whom shall we go? Thou hast the words of eternal life.   John 6:68

This meaningful and popular gospel song has been a favorite with God's people, since it was first written during the height of World War II. It was written in the midst of a busy housewife's day and came, said its author, as a direct inspiration from the Holy Spirit. Mrs. Jones related that all she did was write down what was given to her from God Himself. Though it was written as a response to the stresses and strains of wartime living, yet it has been used and appropriated by many of God's children for their particular difficult situations. It has been used in almost every kind of unusual pressure in the Christian life: for funerals, missionary departures, and as a source of challenge to those who are far from God and need His personal salvation. Mrs. Jones was told numerous times of the blessing that "In Times Like These" brought to a needy individual at a special time of need. She also stated that she too learned first hand of the comfort and encouragement that the words of this song can provide, in difficult days, as she experienced times of convalescence, following a serious surgery.

150

Mrs. Jones was actively involved in a music ministry with the other members of her family. The musical, Jones family was well-known throughout the Eastern areas of our country, having produced for many years the popular radio program, "A Visit With the Joneses." Mrs. Jones' son, the Rev. Bert Jones, has also been a popular recording artist and has been recognized for his unusual talent as a gospel organist, of both electric and pipe organs.

The popularity of "In Times Like These" is evidenced by the number of ways in which the song has been arranged and published in many Singspiration Company collections since its first appearance in 1944. It is a good example of a simple, straight-forward gospel song that God has ordained to minister to many who need periodic reminders of its vital truth.

*   *   *

"Jesus, I love Thee, Thou art to me
Dearer than ever mortal can be;
Jesus, I love Thee, Savior Divine,
Earth has no friendship constant as Thine;
Thou wilt forgive me when I am wrong,
Thou art my comfort, Thou art my song!
Jesus, I love Thee, yes, Thou are mine,
Living or dying, still I am Thine!"

47 It Came Upon the Midnight Clear

CAROL

Edmund H. Sears, 1810-1876

Richard S. Willis, 1819-1900

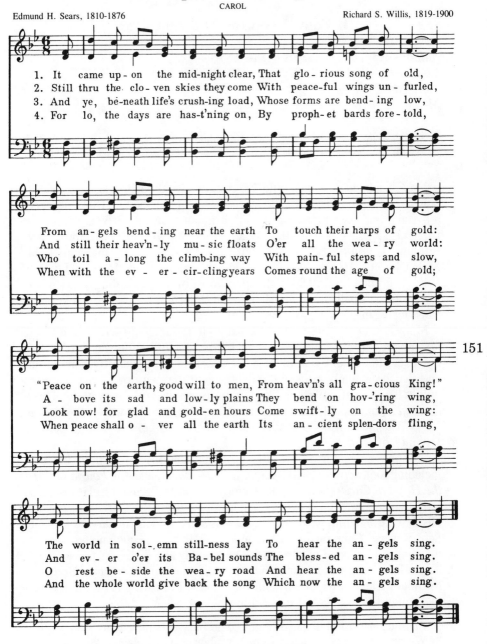

1. It came up-on the mid-night clear, That glo-rious song of old, From an-gels bend-ing near the earth To touch their harps of gold: "Peace on the earth, good will to men, From heav'n's all gra-cious King!" The world in sol-emn still-ness lay To hear the an-gels sing.

2. Still thru the clo-ven skies they come With peace-ful wings un-furled, And still their heav'n-ly mu-sic floats O'er all the wea-ry world: A-bove its sad and low-ly plains They bend on hov-'ring wing, And ev-er o'er its Ba-bel sounds The bless-ed an-gels sing.

3. And ye, be-neath life's crush-ing load, Whose forms are bend-ing low, Who toil a-long the climb-ing way With pain-ful steps and slow, Look now! for glad and gold-en hours Come swift-ly on the wing: O rest be-side the wea-ry road And hear the an-gels sing.

4. For lo, the days are has-t'ning on, By proph-et bards fore-told, When with the ev-er-cir-cling years Comes round the age of gold; When peace shall o-ver all the earth Its an-cient splen-dors fling, And the whole world give back the song Which now the an-gels sing.

It Came Upon the Midnight Clear

Author—Edmund H. Sears, 1810-1876
Composer—Richard S. Willis, 1819-1900
Tune Name—"Carol"
Meter—CM (86.86 Doubled)

> And suddenly there was, with the angel, a multitude of the heavenly host praising God, and saying, "Glory to God in the highest, and on earth peace, good will toward men."
>
> Luke 2:13, 14

No Christmas season would be complete without the singing of this beloved carol hymn. Since the text was first published in 1849, scarcely a hymnal has been printed in which it is not included. It was one of the first carol hymns ever written by an American writer. The author, Rev. Edmund Hamilton Sears, was born on April 6, 1810, in Sandisfield, Massachusetts. He received his theological training at the Harvard Divinity School, graduating in 1837. He spent most of the remaining years of his life pastoring small Unitarian Churches at Wayland, Lancaster, and Weston, Massachusetts.

Many, no doubt, are surprised that a Unitarian could write such a fine text about the events surrounding Christ's nativity. It was often said, however, that Sears was more a Unitarian in name than by conviction, and that he actually believed and preached the deity of Christ from his pulpit. This is particularly evident in his *Sermons and Songs of the Christian Life*, a book published one year before his death. He wrote, "Although I was educated in the Unitarian denomination, I believe and preach the Divinity of Christ."

Edmund Sears wrote a number of publications throughout his life, including *Regeneration, Foregleams of Immortality*, and *The Fourth Gospel, the Heart of Christ*, both of which enjoyed a wide circulation. He authored only two hymn texts, however, each intended for the Christmas season. His first carol hymn, written while he was still a student in Harvard Divinity School, was "Calm on the Listening Ear of Night." Though not as popular, this hymn is included in various hymnals today and is still frequently used. There is a close resemblance between this text and "It Came Upon the Midnight Clear," written fifteen years later. Following is the first stanza of Edmund Sears' initial carol hymn:

> Calm on the list'ning ear of night comes heaven's melodious strains,
> Where wild Judea stretches forth her silver-mantled plains;
> Celestial choirs, from courts above, shed sacred glories there;
> And angels, with their sparkling lyres, make music in the air.

It Came Upon the Midnight Clear

"It Came Upon the Midnight Clear" was first published in the *Christian Register*, on December 29, 1849. It is generally considered to be one of the first hymn carols to emphasize the social implications of the angels' message—that of achieving peace and good will toward our fellowmen in the midst of social difficulty. The writing of this text occurred at a time in American history when there was much unrest. There was the foreboding of the tensions between the North and South, which finally erupted a decade later in the Civil War. In New England, there was much social upheaval as a result of the industrial revolution there. It was also the time of the frantic "forty-niner" gold rush to California. This hymn text, then, addresses these concerns—it is for those who are "beneath the crushing load," and urges us to listen once again to the singing of the angels. The final stanza is the great verse of hopeful optimism—the golden age... "when peace shall over all the earth its ancient splendors fling, and the whole world gives back the song, which now the angels sing."

The tune for this carol hymn, "Carol," was contributed by a rather well-known American musician of the nineteenth century, Richard Storrs Willis. Willis was born on February 10, 1819, in Boston, Massachusetts, and died on May 7, 1900, in Detroit, Michigan. Part of his musical training included six years of composition study in Germany, where he became an intimate friend of Felix Mendelssohn, who was greatly interested in his compositions. After Willis' return to the United States, in 1848, he served as a music critic for the *New York Tribune* and several other newspapers. His own publications included *Church Chorals and Choir Studies* (1850), *Our Church Music* (1856), *Waif of Song* (1876), and *Pen and Lute* (1883). Willis' tune, "Carol," was originally used with another hymn text, "See Israel's Gentle Shepherd Stand," which was an adaptation of Study No. 23 in his collection, *Church Chorals and Choir Studies*, published in 1850. This is the same collection that also contained the first translated appearance of the old German hymn, "Fairest Lord Jesus!" (*101 Hymn Stories*, No. 21). Richard Willis' tune "Carol" has proven to be a worthy melodic vehicle for Edmund Sears' text as generations around the world continue to sing and enjoy this carol each Christmas season.

*   *   *

A CHRISTMAS HYMN

"What babe newborn is this that in a manger cries?
Near on her lowly bed his happy mother lies.
Oh, see the air is shaken with white and heavenly wings—
This is the Lord of all the earth, this is the KING OF KINGS!"

R. W. Gilder

Jesus Calls Us

GALILEE

Mrs. Cecil F. Alexander, 1818-1895   William H. Jude, 1851-1922

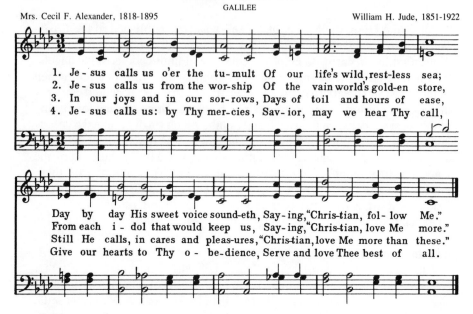

1. Je - sus calls us o'er the tu - mult Of our life's wild, rest-less sea;
2. Je - sus calls us from the wor-ship Of the vain world's gold-en store,
3. In our joys and in our sor-rows, Days of toil and hours of ease,
4. Je - sus calls us: by Thy mer-cies, Sav- ior, may we hear Thy call,

Day by day His sweet voice sound-eth, Say- ing,"Chris-tian, fol- low Me."
From each i - dol that would keep us, Say- ing,"Chris-tian, love Me more."
Still He calls, in cares and pleas-ures,"Chris-tian, love Me more than these."
Give our hearts to Thy o - be-dience, Serve and love Thee best of all.

Jesus Calls Us

Author—Mrs. Cecil F. Alexander, 1818-1895
Composer—William H. Jude, 1851-1922
Tune Name—"Galilee"
Meter—87.87
Scripture Reference—Matthew 4:18; Mark 1:16-18

If any man serve Me, let him follow Me; and where I am, there shall my servant be; if any man serve Me, him will my Father honor.   John 12:26

This is another of the quality hymn texts written by Cecil Frances (Humphreys) Alexander, recognized as one of Great Britain's, finest, women hymn writers. It is one of the few of Mrs. Alexander's hymn texts not specifically written for children; nearly all of her more than 400 poems and hymn texts were intended for reaching and teaching children with the gospel. One of her popular publications, *Hymns for Little Children*, published in 1848, was widely circulated with more than a quarter of a million copies sold. It was always Mrs. Alexander's contention that spiritual truths could best be taught to children through the use of suitable songs. Another of her well-beloved hymns, "There Is a Green Hill Far Away" (*101 Hymn Stories*, No. 96), was written for the purpose of teaching children the meaning of the phrase from the Apostles' Creed, "suffered under Pontius Pilate, was crucified, dead, and buried." Her many other hymns covered a wide range of doctrinal subjects such as Baptism, the Ten Commandments, and the Lord's Prayer.

Following her marriage, in 1850, to the distinguished churchman, Dr. William Alexander, who later became archbishop for all of Ireland, Mrs. Alexander devoted her literary talents to helping her husband with his ministry, including writing appropriate poems that he could use with his sermons. On one occasion, after he had preached a sermon on "The Burial of Moses," Mrs. Alexander prepared for her husband these lines which are still considered classic today:

> By Nebo's lonely mountain, On this side of Jordan's wave,
> In a vale in the land of Moab, There lies a lonely grave.
> But no man built that sepulchre, and no man saw it e'er;
> For the angels of God upturned the sod, and laid the dead man there.

One fall day, two years after their marriage, Dr. Alexander asked his wife if she could write a poem for a sermon he was planning to preach the following Sunday, November 30. This is the Sunday in the liturgical church year known as St. Andrew's Day, commemorating the calling of Andrew by Jesus as recorded in Matthew 4:18-20 and Mark 1:16-18.

> Now as He walked by the Sea of Galilee, He saw Simon and Andrew, his brother, casting a net into the sea; for they were fishers. And Jesus said unto them, Come after Me, and I will make you become fishers of men. And straightway they forsook their nets, and followed Him (Mark 1:16, 17, 18).

155

St. Andrew's Day has traditionally been an important day in the liturgical worship of the Anglican Church. Andrew is the patron saint of Scotland, and the oblique cross on which tradition has had him crucified is part of the Union Jack of the British flag.

The following Sunday Dr. Alexander closed his sermon with the new five-verse, four-line poem written by his wife. The second stanza, omitted in most non-liturgical hymnals, reads as follows:

> As, of old, Saint Andrew heard it,
> By the Galilean lake,
> Turned from home and toil and kindred,
> Leaving all for His dear sake.

The other four stanzas have been widely used in all churches to challenge God's people to hear Christ's call and then to follow, serve, and love Him best of all.

The tune, "Galilee," was composed for this text by William Herbert Jude, born in Westleton, Suffolk, England, in 1851. He was a distinguished organist and was the editor of several music publications, including a number of choir anthems and an operetta, *Innocents Abroad*. Jude was also known throughout Great Britain and Australia as a music lecturer and recitalist. The tune "Galilee" was named for the beautiful lake in the area of Tiberius where Jesus met Simon Peter and Andrew. The tune first appeared with Mrs. Alexander's text in *The Congregational Church Hymnal*, London, in 1887.

* * *

"God never shuts one door but He opens another."

Irish Proverb

FOLLOW ME

" 'Take up thy Cross,' the Savior said,
'If thou wouldst my disciple be;
Deny thyself, the world forsake,
And humbly follow after Me.'

"Take up thy cross, and follow Christ;
Nor think till death to lay it down;
For only he who bears the Cross
May hope to wear the glorious crown."

Charles W. Everest

"Take my will, and make it Thine;
It shall be no longer mine.
Take my heart—it is Thine own;
It shall be Thy royal throne.

"All to Jesus now I give,
From this hour for Him to live;
While before His cross I bow,
He doth hear my humble vow."

Unknown

49   Jesus, I My Cross Have Taken

ELLESDIE

Henry F. Lyte, 1793-1847

From Leavitt's *Christian Lyre,* 1831
Attr. to Wolfgang A. Mozart, 1756-1791
Arr. by Hubert P. Main, 1839-1925

1. Je - sus, I my cross have tak - en, All to leave and fol - low Thee;
2. Let the world de - spise and leave me, They have left my Sav - ior too;
3. Man may trou - ble and dis - tress me, 'Twill but drive me to Thy breast;
4. Haste thee on from grace to glo - ry, Armed by faith and winged by prayer;

Des - ti - tute, de - spised, for - sak - en— Thou from hence my all shalt be.
Hu - man hearts and looks de - ceive me— Thou art not, like man, un - true.
Life with tri - als hard may press me— Heav'n will bring me sweet - er rest.
Heav'n's e - ter - nal day's be - fore thee— God's own hand shall guide thee there.

157

Per - ish ev - 'ry fond am - bi - tion— All I've sought and hoped and known!
And while Thou shalt smile up - on me, God of wis - dom, love, and might,
O 'tis not in grief to harm me While Thy love is left to me;
Soon shall close thy earth - ly mis - sion, Swift shall pass thy pil - grim days;

Yet how rich is my con - di - tion— God and heav'n are still my own!
Foes may hate, and friends may shun me— Show Thy face, and all is bright!
O 'twere not in joy to charm me Were that joy un - mixed with Thee!
Hope shall change to glad fru - i - tion, Faith to sight, and prayer to praise!

Jesus, I My Cross Have Taken

*Author—*Henry F. Lyte, 1793-1847
*Music—*From Leavitt's "Christian Lyre," 1831
    Attributed to Wolfgang A. Mozart, 1756-1791
Arranged by Hubert P. Main, 1839-1925
Tune Name—"Ellesdie"
*Meter—*87.87 Doubled

> Then said Jesus unto His disciples, if any man will come after Me, let him deny himself, and take up his cross, and follow Me.   Matthew 16:24

Shortly after his ordination to the Anglican Church ministry, in 1815, Henry Lyte was asked to visit a fellow clergyman who was terminally ill. The visit revealed the fact that neither of these ministers really had a personal faith in Christ or had ever had a genuine conversion experience. They began to search the Scriptures together, and soon both made a sincere commitment to God. That experience made a great change in Lyte's life and in his future preaching. He became a skilled student of the Bible and a tireless preacher of the gospel. Though Lyte suffered throughout his lifetime with a frail body that was always prone to tuberculosis, he was known as a man strong in spirit and faith. It is thought that this hymn text was written by Henry Lyte, in 1824, to commemorate his earlier conversion experience and commitment to the Christian gospel.

158

Henry Francis Lyte was born on June 1, 1793, near the city of Kelso, Scotland. As a youngster, he and his family were plagued with severe poverty with young Henry eventually becoming an orphan. Yet despite these hardships, the young man managed to graduate from Trinity College in Dublin, Ireland. While in school he won several honors for "writing the best English verse." After serving several smaller parishes, he was transferred to a community of fisherman at Lower Brixham, in Devonshire, England. Here he ministered faithfully to these humble people for the next twenty-three years of his life. During this time he also wrote some eighty hymn texts, including such favorites as "Abide With Me" (*101 Hymn Stories*, No. 2) and "Praise My Soul, the King of Heaven." Another of Lyte's notable accomplishments in this village was the development of a Sunday school of more than 800 children, all of which influenced a great change in the moral and religious tone of that hardened community.

"Jesus, I My Cross Have Taken" reflects Lyte's own personal attitude toward the "cross" of his suffering and the fact that he had found refuge in Christ alone in learning to accept and use suffering in a spiritual manner. It is thought that in addition to Lyte's bodily afflictions, a difficulty with some individuals within his church also weighed heavily upon his spirit.

This is possibly alluded to in such expressions from the second and third stanzas as: "human hearts and looks deceive me...," "man may trouble and distress me...," "foes may hate, and friends may shun me...;" Yet the glad anticipation of God's hereafter made these "pilgrim days" inconsequential for Lyte, since "hope shall change to glad fruition, faith to sight, and prayer to praise."

In addition to his reputation as an effective parish pastor, Henry F. Lyte was also recognized as a poet and musician. Among his published works are *Sacred Poetry* (1824), *Tales on the Lord's Prayer* (1826), *Poems, Chiefly Religious* (1833), and *The Spirit of the Psalms* (1836). "Jesus, I My Cross Have Taken," originally a six-stanza poem, first appeared in Lyte's *Sacred Poetry*, simply signed "G." In his *Poems, Chiefly Religious*, Henry Lyte acknowledged authorship of it for the first time.

In 1831, Joshua Leavitt, a Congregationalist, compiled and published an important American hymnal, the *Christian Lyre*. It was prepared especially for use in Charles G. Finney's revival campaigns. It was so successful that there were eventually twenty-six editions printed. Leavitt's hymnal was innovative for that day, in that he printed the text and music on opposite sides of the page rather than placing the music in the back of the book, or not including music at all, as was the practice with other hymnals of that time. Also, Leavitt's new hymnal included arrangements of well-known secular melodies which could be used with the hymn texts. This practice met with violent opposition from the more formal churches.

159

Wolfgang A. Mozart was born in Salzburg, Austria, on January 27, 1756. At the age of six he was already widely recognized as a composer and a child prodigy on the piano. In all, Mozart wrote over 600 musical compositions during his brief lifetime. His works included every area of musical performance, including fifty symphonies, operas, chamber music, and sacred compositions. A number of hymn tunes have been adapted from these various works. Mozart died broken in health, at the age of thirty-five and was buried in a pauper's grave. Today, Wolfgang Amadeus Mozart is recognized as one of the master composers of all music history. It has often been said that, since the eighteenth century, he has been the yardstick by which to measure musical genius.

In many hymn collections, Wolfgang A. Mozart is credited as the source of this tune, although this fact has never been fully substantiated. The tune first appeared without any credit to Mozart in Joshua Leavitt's *Christian Lyre* of 1831. It reappeared, in 1873, in a hymnal, *Winnowed Hymns*, with the entry "Air, Mozart, Arr. H.P.M." It has been assumed that Hubert P. Main, a noted compiler of hymnals and gospel song books, simply harmonized the melody he found in that book attributed to Mozart. "Ellesdie" is said to be derived from the initial letters "L.S.D.," no doubt dedicated to an individual who is unknown today.

50 Jesus Paid It All

Elvina M. Hall, 1820-1889

John T. Grape, 1835-1915

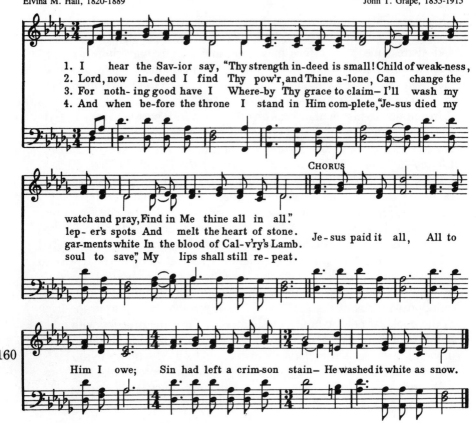

Jesus Paid It All

Author—Elvina M. Hall, 1820-1889
Composer—John T. Grape, 1835-1915

> Come now, and let us reason together, saith the Lord: Though your sins be as scarlet, they shall be as white as snow; though they be red like crimson, they shall be as wool.
> Isaiah 1:18

This hymn, often used for our communion services, speaks pointedly about the truth of the certainty of our personal relationship with God. The text was written by a lay woman named Elvina Hall. She wrote these words one Sunday morning, in 1865, while seated in the choir loft of the Monument Street Methodist Church of Baltimore, Maryland, supposedly listening to the sermon by her pastor, the Rev. George Schrick. During the course of the message, she began scribbling the words of the poem on the flyleaf of her church hymnal. Following the service, there might have been a conversation like this:

Mrs. Hall: Pastor Schrick...I enjoyed the message this morning, well...I mean—Oh, pastor, I really must confess that I wasn't listening too closely because, you see, once you started preaching about how we can really know God's forgiveness and love, I began thinking about all that Christ has already done to provide our redemption. These words came to me, and I just had to get them down on paper. And the only paper I had at the time was the flyleaf of this hymnal. Would you have time to look at these verses just now?

Pastor: Why of course, Elvina, and I certainly don't want you feeling guilty by any means for what you did during my sermon. In fact, I believe that what you did is proof of something I firmly believe—that when the Word of God finds root in our lives, it stimulates our creative abilities and makes it possible for the Holy Spirit to take these talents and use them to bring great spiritual blessing to His people for the days ahead. It's very possible, Elvina, that God has touched your life this morning, in this manner, even while I was preaching.

Mrs. Hall: Then you are not angry with me for writing this poem, when I really should have been listening to your sermon?

Pastor: Of course not. In fact, that reminds me of something else. Just several days ago, our good organist, John Grape, gave me a copy of a new tune he had recently composed. If I remember correctly, he titled it, "All to Christ I Owe," and do you know, Elvina, I think that tune might fit your poem. Yes, here's a copy of the music right in my Bible. Now you read that first stanza again, while I see how John's tune matches your words.

Mrs. Hall:

I hear the Savior say, "Thy strength indeed is small,
Child of weakness, watch and pray, find in Me thine all in all."

Pastor: Oh, that's wonderful, Elvina; the words and the tune match perfectly. Now all we need is a good refrain that will summarize everything into one strong, final statement.

Mrs. Hall:

Jesus paid it all, all to Him I owe;
Sin had left a crimson stain; He washed it white as snow.

Mrs. Elvina Mable Hall, author of the text, was born on June 4, 1820, in Alexandria, Virginia. She and her first husband were faithful members of the Monument Street Methodist Church for more than forty years. John T. Grape, composer of the tune, was a successful coal merchant in Baltimore, who, as he once said, "dabbled in music for my own amusement.'' For many years he was an active lay-worker in the Monument Street Church, working in the Sunday school as well as serving as the organist-choir director. This hymn in its present form first appeared in Philip Bliss's *Gospel Song Book Collection* (1874), and from that time to the present, it has enjoyed wide use in evangelical churches everywhere.

Again we marvel at the workings of God on our behalf. An obscure woman scribbles a poem on the flyleaf of her hymnal, an amateur church musician unknowingly creates a matching tune, an unknown pastor provides encouragement and another hymn is born, that has since found an important place in our church hymnals and in turn has ministered spiritual challenge and blessing to countless numbers of people for more than a century.

*　*　*

"The sufficiency of my merit is to know that my merit is not sufficient."
St. Augustine

"None but God can satisfy the longings of an immortal soul; that as the heart was made for Him, so He only can fill it."

Richard Chenevix Trench: *Notes on the Parables. Prodigal Son*

BUT WITH HIM—Oh, With Jesus!
"Are any words so blest?
With Jesus, everlasting joy
And everlasting rest!
With Jesus—all the empty heart
Filled with perfect love;
With Jesus—perfect peace below
And perfect bliss above.

"Why will you do without Him?
He calls and calls again, 'Come unto Me! Come unto Me!'
Oh, shall He wait in vain?
He wants to have you with Him;
Do you not want Him, too?
You cannot do without Him,
And He wants—even you."
Frances Ridley Havergal

51 Jesus, Savior Pilot Me

PILOT

Edward Hopper, 1818-1888

John E. Gould, 1822-1875

1. Je - sus, Sav - ior, pi - lot me O - ver life's tem-pes-tuous sea:
2. As a moth- er stills her child, Thou canst hush the o - cean wild;
3. When at last I near the shore, And the fear - ful break-ers roar

D.C. – Chart and com-pass come from Thee– Je - sus, Sav - ior, pi - lot me!
D.C. – Won-drous Sov-'reign of the sea, Je - sus, Sav - ior, pi - lot me!
D.C. – May I hear Thee say to me, "Fear not– I will pi - lot thee!"

Un-known waves be-fore me roll, Hid- ing rocks and treach-'rous shoal;
Bois-t'rous waves o - bey Thy will When Thou say'st to them, "Be still!"
'Twixt me and the peace-ful rest – Then, while lean-ing on Thy breast,

163

Jesus, Savior, Pilot Me

Author—Edward Hopper, 1818-1888
Composer—John E. Gould, 1822-1875
Tune Name—"Pilot"
Meter—77.77.77
Scripture Reference—Matthew 8:23-27

> Thou wilt show me the path of life. In Thy presence is fulness of joy; at Thy right
> hand there are pleasures for evermore.   Psalm 16:11

Just as our Lord often taught profound spiritual truths with earthly associations, so many of our fine hymns have been written with symbolic imagery that makes them more readily understood. There are hymns that speak of soldiers, pilgrims, shepherds, sheep, precious jewels, and many other relationships in life that are meaningful to us. "Jesus, Savior, Pilot Me" was written especially for sailors in language they knew well — charts, compasses, and the absolute need for a competent pilot to guide their crafts over the tempestuous seas.

This hymn text was written by an American Presbyterian minister named Edward Hopper and was first published in the year 1871. Hopper was born in New York City on February 17, 1818. His father was a merchant and his mother a descendant of the Huguenots, the persecuted French Protestant Reformers. Following his graduation from Union Theological Seminary in 1842, Hopper served, with distinction, two Presbyterian churches in the New York area. He was later awarded an honorary Doctor of Divinity degree from Lafayette College, in recognition of his pastoral accomplishments. In 1870, however, he began the most fruitful phase of his ministry, when he became pastor of a small church in the New York harbor area, known as the Church of Sea and Land. Here he ministered effectively, for the remaining years of his life, to the many sailors who made their way to and from their ships.

It was while ministering at his sailor's mission in New York City that Edward Hopper wrote this hymn text, especially for the spiritual needs of these sea-faring men. The theme of this hymn text was suggested by the gospel account recorded in Matthew 8:23-27, where Jesus calmed the raging sea of Galilee and, in so doing, quieted the fears of His disciples.

> And when He was entered into a ship, His disciples followed Him. And, behold, there arose a great tempest in the sea, insomuch that the ship was covered with the waves; but He was asleep. And His disciples came to Him, and awoke Him, saying, "Lord, save us; we perish." And He saith unto them, "Why are ye fearful, O ye of little faith?" Then He arose, and rebuked the winds and the sea; and there was a great calm. But the men marvelled, saying, "What manner of man is this, that even the winds and the sea obey Him?"

164

Hopper wrote the hymn anonymously as he did all of his works, and, for some time, no one ever knew that the pastor of the sailors was also the author of the sailors' favorite hymn. This was typical of Hopper's humble, gentle spirit in all that he did for God. The poem first appeared in *The Sailor's Magazine*, in 1871.

In 1880, a special anniversary celebration for the Seamen's Friend Society was held in New York City, and Edward Hopper was asked to write a new hymn for that occasion. Instead he brought and read "Jesus, Savior, Pilot Me," which had already become quite widely known in its inclusion in various hymnal publications. For the first time, the secret of Hopper's authorship of this hymn text became known.

Though this is the only hymn text that Edward Hopper has written that is still in common usage, it can be said of him as it can of many other hymn writers:

> Happy is the man who can produce one song which the world will keep on singing after its author shall have passed away.

"Jesus, Savior, Pilot Me" has been included in nearly every evangelical hymnal published until the present time. It is a hymn that has been especially meaningful to young people, sincerely concerned about knowing God's will for their future lives.

Originally Hopper's text included six stanzas, but hymnals today make use of only the first, fifth and sixth verses from the poem. Two of these omitted stanzas are, however, rather interesting expressions:

When the Apostles' fragile bark struggled with the billows dark,
On the stormy Galilee, Thou didst walk upon the sea;
And when they beheld Thy form, safe they glided through the storm.

Though the sea be smooth and bright, sparkling with the stars of night,
And my ship's path be ablaze with the light of halcyon days,
Still I know my need of Thee; Jesus, Savior, pilot me.

In 1888, at the age of seventy, Edward Hopper's prayer expressed in the third stanza of his own hymn had its fulfillment. He was found sitting in his study chair, pencil in hand, writing a new poem on the subject of heaven. This tribute was paid to him at his funeral:

Suddenly the gentle, affectionate spirit of Edward Hopper entered the heavenly "port," as he had requested, safely piloted by that never-failing friend, Jesus, whose Divine voice — in the words of the author's own text — was still tenderly whispering to him, "Fear not, I will pilot thee.

The composer of the music for this text was John E. Gould, a music store proprietor in New York City and later in Philadelphia. Mr. Gould also compiled and published eight books of church, Sunday school and secular songs. However, this is his only hymn tune still in use today.

Mr. Gould composed the music for "Jesus, Savior, Pilot Me" shortly after its writing by Edward Hopper, in 1871, and its anonymous appearance in *The Sailors' Magazine*. Later that same year, the text with this tune appeared in *The Baptist Praise Book*. This hymn could well have been the personal expression of Mr. Gould's own life, since he was suffering ill health at this time and wrote the music shortly before he sailed for Africa, seeking to improve his health. He died in Algiers, Africa, four years later. Though various tunes have been tried with this text through the years, John Gould's tune "Pilot" is the one still most widely used today.

* * *

"The billows swell, the winds are high,
Clouds overcast my wintry sky;
Out of the depths to Thee I call,
My fears are great, my strength is small.

"O Lord, the pilot's part perform,
And guide and guard me thro' the storm;
Defend me from each threat'ning ill,
Control the waves, say, 'Peace, be still.'
                                    William Cowper

52 Joy to the World!

ANTIOCH

Isaac Watts, 1674-1748

Possibly adapted from G. H. Handel, 1685-1759
Arr. by Lowell Mason, 1792-1872

1. Joy to the world! the Lord is come! Let earth receive her King; Let ev-'ry heart prepare Him room, And heav'n and nature sing, And heav'n and nature sing, And heav'n, and heav'n and nature sing.

2. Joy to the earth! the Savior reigns! Let men their songs employ; While fields and floods, rocks, hills and plains Repeat the sounding joy, Repeat the sounding joy, Repeat, repeat the sounding joy.

3. No more let sins and sorrows grow, Nor thorns infest the ground; He comes to make His blessings flow Far as the curse is found, Far as the curse is found, Far as, far as the curse is found.

4. He rules the world with truth and grace, And makes the nations prove The glories of His righteousness, And wonders of His love, And wonders of His love, And wonders, wonders of His love.

Joy to the World!

Author—Isaac Watts, 1674-1748
Composer—Possibly adapted from G. F. Handel, 1685-1759
Arranged by Lowell Mason, 1792-1872
Tune Name—"Antioch"
Meter—CM (86.86)
Scripture Reference—Psalm 98

> ...Fear not; for, behold, I bring you good tidings of great joy, which shall be unto all people.   Luke 2:10

Joy is the keynote of the entire Advent season, especially for the Christian, who realizes its spiritual significance — very God Himself invading this world and providing a means whereby sinful man might live eternally. This text is generally considered to be one of the most joyous Christmas hymns in existence, not in the sense of merry-making, but in the deep and solemn realization of what Christ's birth has meant to mankind.

This advent hymn is another of Watts' hymns from his well-known hymnal of 1719, *Psalms of David Imitated in the Language of the New Testament*. It was Isaac Watts' intent in writing this collection to give the Psalms a New Testament meaning and style. This he did, in the 1719 collection, by paraphrasing in Christian verse all of the 150 Psalms with the exception of twelve, which he felt were unfit for this purpose. "Joy to the World!" is a paraphrase of these verses taken from the last half of Psalm 98:

167

> Make a joyful noise unto the Lord, all the earth; make a loud noise, and rejoice, and sing praise. Let the floods clap their hands; let the hills be joyful together before the Lord; for He cometh to judge the earth; with righteousness shall He judge the world, and the people with equity.

Psalm 98 is a song of rejoicing at the marvelous ways in which God has protected and restored His chosen people. The Psalm anticipates the time when Jehovah will be the God of the whole earth and Israel's law will be accepted by all of the nations. Watts, however, has given this verse a fresh interpretation — a New Testament expression of praise for the salvation that began when God became incarnate as the Babe of Bethlehem and was destined to remove the curse of Adam's fall. Isaac Watts first titled his text "The Messiah's Coming and Kingdom."

Even as a boy, Isaac Watts displayed literary genius and an aptitude for study. At the age of five, he was learning Latin; at nine, Greek; at eleven, French; and at thirteen, Hebrew. In addition to his hymn writing, Watts became known as an ardent student of theology and philosophy, and, during his lifetime, he wrote many notable volumes which had a powerful influence upon English thinking, during the late seventeenth and early eighteenth centuries. As a seven year old, he wrote an acrostic, spelling out the letters of his name. This acrostic reflects not only the brilliance of young Watts but also the strong Calvinistic theology which characterized his entire life:

"I" — I am a vile, polluted lump of earth
"S" — So I've continued ever since my birth
"A" — Although Jehovah, grace doth daily give me
"A" — As sure this monster, Satan, will deceive me
"C" — Come therefore, Lord, from Satan's claws relieve me

"W" — Wash me in Thy blood, O Christ
"A" — And grace divine impart
"T" — Then search and try the corners of my heart
"T" — That I in all things may be fit to do
"S" — Service to Thee, and Thy praise too.

While Watts was still in his teens, he became very dissatisfied with the deplorable, Psalm singing characteristic of this time in the churches. The following was some of the typical doggeral being sung:

Ye monsters of the bubbling deep,
Your Master's praises spout;
Up from the sands ye docclings peep,
And wag your tails about.

One Sunday after returning from a service of this type of Psalm singing and being deeply concerned and critical of congregational singing, young Isaac was challenged by his father with the words, "Well then, young man, why don't you give us something better to sing?"

Watts, then eighteen years of age, accepted his father's challenge. The next Sunday he produced his first hymn, to which the congregational response was enthusiastic. For the next two years, young Watts wrote a new hymn text for his people every Sunday. He published a collection of 210 of these hymns, in 1707, in a book entitled *Hymns and Spiritual Songs*. This 1707 collection and the later 1719 hymnal represent important monuments in the development of English hymnody. They were the first real hymnals in the English language. Watts' preface in the *Hymns and Spiritual Songs* collection reflects his concern for congregational singing:

While we sing the praises of God in His Church, we are employed in that part of worship which of all others is the nearest akin to heaven, and 'tis pity that this of all others should be performed the worst upon earth.... That very action which should elevate us to the most delightful and divine sensations doth not only flat our devotion, but too often awakens our regret and touches all the springs of uneasiness within us.

In all, Isaac Watts wrote approximately 600 hymns throughout his lifetime. He has rightly been called the "Father of English Hymnody." Because of his bold departure from the traditional metrical Psalms and the use of "human composure hymns"—expressions based entirely on one's own thoughts and words—Watts was generally considered to be a radical churchman in his day. But today, more than two and one-half centuries later, our hymnals still contain such Watts' favorites as: "O God, Our Help in Ages Past"—a paraphrase of Psalm 90 (*101 Hymn Stories*, No. 66), "Jesus Shall Reign"—a setting of Psalm 72 (*ibid.*, No. 48), as well as "human composure" hymns such as "When I Survey the Wondrous Cross" (*ibid.*, No. 100), "I Sing the Mighty Power of God" (*ibid.*, No. 38), and "Am I a Soldier of the Cross?" (No. 6).

It is interesting to make a brief comparison between Isaac Watts and George Frederick Handel, who is generally credited with being the source of this hymn's music. Watts was a frail, five-foot tall, rather homely but gentle-mannered figure, while Handel was known as the robust, hot-tempered, cosmopolitan German master of the keyboard, opera and oratorio. Both men lived in London during this time and evidently knew each other.

The story of Handel's greatest contribution to sacred music, the oratorio *The Messiah* is generally familiar to most people. In 1741, Handel began writing the music for this biblical text, and, in the course of just twenty-four days completed all fifty-three numbers. *The Messiah* was given its first official public performance on April 13, 1742. It is undoubtedly the most frequently performed oratorio ever written, as well as the most highly esteemed. In 1836, Lowell Mason, an American choir director, composer, and public school educator, is thought to have rearranged a portion of Handel's *Messiah*, likely from some of the phrases in the numbers "Comfort Ye" and "Lift Up Your Heads," to fit the words of Watts' "Joy to the World." This adapted tune became known as the "Antioch" tune, and first appeared in Lowell Mason's *Modern Psalmist* in 1839. Though various other tunes have been used on occasion with Isaac Watts' text, "Antioch" has proven to be the most popular and lasting.

169

Lowell Mason is also the composer of the music for the hymns "A Charge to Keep I Have" (No. 1), "My Faith Looks Up to Thee," (No. 60), and the arranger of "O Day of Rest and Gladness" (No. 66). Other popular hymns for which Mason contributed the music include: "From Greenland's Icy Mountains" (*101 Hymn Stories*, No. 25), "Nearer, My God, to Thee" (*ibid.*, No. 61), and "When I Survey the Wondrous Cross" (*ibid.*, No. 100).

Through the combined talents of a frail English literary genius of the eighteenth century, a German-born, musical giant from the same period, and a nineteenth-century, American, choir director and educator, another great hymn was born that has since found a permanent place in the pages of our American church hymnals for use during every Advent season.

53 Leave It There

Charles A. Tindley, 1851-1933

Charles A. Tindley, 1851-1933

1. If the world from you with-hold of its sil _ ver and its gold, And you
2. If your bod - y suf-fers pain and your health you can't re - gain, And your
3. When your en - e - mies as - sail and your heart be-gins to fail, Don't for-
4. When your youth-ful days are gone and old age is steal-ing on, And your

have to get a - long with mea - ger fare, Just re - mem-ber, in His Word,
soul is al-most sink-ing in de - spair, Je - sus knows the pain you feel,
get that God in heav - en an - swers prayer; He will make a way for you
bod - y bends be-neath the weight of care, He will nev - er leave you then,

how He feeds the lit - tle bird— Take your bur-den to the Lord and leave it there.
He can save and He can heal— Take your bur-den to the Lord and leave it there.
and will lead you safe-ly thru— Take your bur-den to the Lord and leave it there.
He'll go with you to the end— Take your bur-den to the Lord and leave it there.

CHORUS

Leave it there,   leave it there,   Take your bur-den to the
Leave it there,   leave it there,

Lord and leave it there;   If you trust and nev - er doubt, He will
leave it there;

sure-ly bring you out— Take your bur-den to the Lord and leave it there.

Copyright 1916. Renewal 1944 by Hope Publishing Co., Carol Stream, IL 60188. All rights reserved. Used by permission.

Leave It There

Author and Composer—Charles A. Tindley, 1851-1933

> Why art thou cast down, O my soul? and why art thou disquieted in me? Hope thou in God; for I shall yet praise him for the help of his countenance.   Psalm 42:5

One day a worried parishioner approached Charles Tindley for a word of comfort. The kindly pastor replied: "Put all your troubles in a sack, take 'em to the Lord, and leave 'em there." This homespun response was the spark that later prompted the pastor, Charles Tindley, to pen the words and music of this familiar gospel hymn in 1916.

Charles Albert Tindley is known as the distinguished, negro Methodist pastor from Philadelphia. He was born into slavery on July 7, 1851, at Berline, Maryland. At the age of five, he was left an orphan. By his own determination, he taught himself to read and write. Later as a young man, he moved to Philadelphia, where he attended night school and took a correspondence course from the Boston School of Theology. Despite his lack of formal training, Tindley became known as a learned man; his many accomplishments included a mastery of both Hebrew and Greek. During these early years, he served as janitor of the Calvary Methodist Episcopal Church, which later called him to be its pastor, in 1902.

After his ordination to the Methodist ministry in 1885, Tindley served a number of smaller country churches throughout several of the eastern states, until his call to the Calvary Methodist Episcopal Church at the age of fifty-one. The church greatly prospered under his leadership, until it reached a membership of 12,500, including both negroes and whites, along with many other minority ethnic groups. In 1924, a larger building had to be built at Broad and Fitzwater Streets, and the church was renamed the Tindley Temple Methodist Church.

Charles Tindley was not only a very successful pastor, but he also wrote the words and music for many gospel songs, including such current favorites as "Nothing Between," "By and By," and "Stand by Me." It was Tindley's song, "I'll Overcome Some Day," written in 1901, that later served as the inspiration for the Civil Rights Movement theme song, "We Shall Overcome," during the 1950's and 1960's.

Charles A. Tindley completed his fruitful ministry for God on July 26, 1933, in Philadelphia, at the age of eighty-two.

*   *   *

"Blessed is the man who is too busy to worry in the daytime and too sleepy to worry at night."

Anonymous

54 Let Jesus Come Into Your Heart

Lelia N. Morris, 1862-1929

Lelia N. Morris, 1862-1929

1. If you are tired of the load of your sin, Let Je - sus come
2. If 'tis for pu - ri - ty now that you sigh, Let Je - sus come
3. If there's a tem - pest your voice can - not still, Let Je - sus come
4. If you would join the glad songs of the blest, Let Je - sus come

in - to your heart; If you de - sire a new life to be - gin,
in - to your heart; Foun - tains for cleans - ing are flow - ing near - by,
in - to your heart; If there's a void this world nev - er can fill,
in - to your heart; If you would en - ter the man - sions of rest,

Let Je - sus come in - to your heart.

CHORUS

Just now your doubt - ings give o'er, Just now re - ject Him no more; Just now throw o - pen the door— Let Je - sus come in - to your heart.

Let Jesus Come Into Your Heart

Words and Music by Lelia N. Morris, 1862-1929

Let the wicked forsake his way, and the unrighteous man his thoughts, and let him return unto the Lord, and He will have mercy upon him, and to our God, for He will abundantly pardon.   Isaiah 55:7

George Sanville, in his book, *Forty Gospel Hymn Stories*, relates the following account of this well-known invitation hymn written and composed by Lelia N. Morris in 1898:

At the Sunday morning service, Mountain Lake Park, Maryland, camp meeting, the minister preached with apostolic fervor. His zeal for saving souls charged his message with spiritual power. His handling of the theme, "Repentance," brought many to the altar. One was a woman of culture and refinement. As she knelt and prayed, she gave evidence of the inner struggle taking place. She wanted to do something—to give, not receive. Mrs. Morris quietly joined her at the altar, put her arms around her, and prayed with her. Mrs. Morris said, "Just now your doubtings give o'er." Dr. H. L. Gilmour, song leader of the camp meeting, added another phrase, "Just now reject Him no more." L. H. Baker, the preacher of the sermon, earnestly importuned, "Just now throw open the door." Mrs. Morris made the last appeal, "Let Jesus Come Into Your Heart."

173

Shortly thereafter Mrs. Morris completed the thought and added the music before the campmeetings closed. It was first published, in 1898, in the hymnal, *Pentecostal Praises*, compiled by William J. Kirkpatrick and Gilmour.

Lelia Naylor Morris was born on April 15, 1862, at Pennsville, Ohio. In 1881, she married Charles H. Morris and along with her husband became a very active worker in the Methodist Episcopal Church. Approximately ten years after her marriage, she became interested in writing gospel songs, especially as she visited and assisted in the various, holiness campmeetings throughout the East. Her husband reports that Lelia was a very quiet and reserved housewife and was deeply spiritual. He tells how she would write hymns as she went about her daily housework, keeping a handy writing pad tacked up in her kitchen for moments of inspiration.

In 1913, Leila's eyesight began to fail, and within a year her sight was completely gone. Yet despite this hardship, she continued to write gospel songs with the help of devoted friends. For a time she used a blackboard twenty-eight feet long with music staff lines on it, which had been constructed by her son. In all, Mrs. Morris wrote more than 1,000 hymn texts as well as many of the tunes. Several of her hymns still popular today include: "What If It Were Today?" "Nearer, Still Nearer," "The Fight Is On," "Sweeter As the Years Go By," and the beloved classic, "Stranger of Galilee."

55 Let the Lower Lights Be Burning

Philip P. Bliss, 1838-1876

Philip P. Bliss, 1838-1876

1. Bright-ly beams our Fa - ther's mer-cy From His light-house ev- er - more,
2. Dark the night of sin has set-tled, Loud the an - gry bil-lows roar;
3. Trim your fee - ble lamp, my broth-er! Some poor sail- or tem-pest- tossed,

But to us He gives the keep-ing Of the lights a - long the shore.
Ea - ger eyes are watch-ing, long-ing, For the lights a - long the shore.
Try- ing now to make the har - bor, In the dark-ness may be lost.

CHORUS

Let the low- er lights be burn-ing! Send a gleam a- cross the wave!

Some poor faint- ing, strug-gling sea-man You may res-cue, you may save.

Let the Lower Lights Be Burning

Author and Composer—Philip P. Bliss, 1838-1876

Let your light so shine before men, that they may see your good works, and glorify
your Father which is in heaven.   Matthew 5:16

Philip P. Bliss, a leading, gospel song writer of the late 19th century,
often received the inspiration for a hymn, while listening to a message
during a church service. Once an idea struck his alert mind, he worked
rapidly usually completing both the text and the music in one sitting.

One day, while traveling with Dwight L. Moody as the musician for an evangelistic campaign, Bliss was impressed by an illustration used by Mr. Moody for a message. Moody often told this terse, but moving story of a violent storm on Lake Erie:

> On a dark, stormy night, when the waves rolled like mountains and not a star was to be seen, a boat, rocking and plunging, neared the Cleveland harbor. "Are you sure this is Cleveland?" asked the Captain, seeing only light from the lighthouse.
> "Quite sure, sir," replied the pilot.
> "Where are the lower lights?"
> "Gone out, sir!"
> "Can you make the harbor?"
> "We must, or perish, sir."
> With a strong hand and a brave heart, the old pilot turned the wheel, But alas, in the darkness he missed the channel, and, with a crash upon the rocks, the boat was slivered and many a life lost in a watery grave.
> "Brethren," concluded Mr. Moody, "the Master will take care of the great lighthouse. Let us keep the lower lights burning."

"Let the Lower Lights Be Burning" first appeared in Bliss' earliest songbook, *The Charm*, in 1871, and later in the well-known collection, *Gospel Hymns*, published by Sankey and Bliss in that same year.

175

Philip P. Bliss was born in Clearfield County, Pennsylvania, on July 9, 1838. His youthful days were spent on a farm or in a lumber camp, where he experienced severe poverty. At an early age, young Bliss displayed unusual talent and interest in sacred music. Although he never received a formal training in music, his self-study made him a knowledgeable and proficient musician. At the age of twenty-five, Bliss sent a letter and a copy of his first music manuscript to Dr. George Root, wondering if he could sell his song to the Root and Cady Music Company, a leading music publishing house, in exchange for a flute. Root recognized the talent of this young man and immediately encouraged him with a new flute.

The next year, Bliss moved with his family from Pennsylvania to Chicago and became actively involved with the Root and Cady Company, as their representative in conducting music conventions and training institutes throughout the Midwest. During this time, Bliss' abilities as a gospel singer, song leader, and writer became increasingly recognized.

Bliss first met Dwight L. Moody in Chicago, during the summer of 1869, and soon began singing, frequently, in Moody's evangelistic meetings. The effectiveness of Bliss' singing in these services intensified Moody's conviction of the importance of music in an evangelistic ministry. Although Moody himself was not a singer, he has left the following account regarding his attitude about music:

I feel sure that the great majority of people do like singing. It helps to build up an audience—even if you preach a dry sermon. If you have singing that reaches the heart, it will fill the church every time. There is more said in the Bible about praise than prayer, and music and song have not only accompanied all scriptural revivals, but are essential in deepening spiritual life. Singing does at least as much as preaching to impress the Word of God upon people's minds. Ever since God first called me, the importance of praise expressed in song has grown upon me.

Philip Bliss continued to be a prolific composer of gospel hymns, until the time of the tragic train accident causing his untimely death, at the age of thirty-eight. (See "My Redeemer" *101 Hymn Stories*, No. 59) Several of Bliss's well-known compositions include: "Once for All" (No. 72), "Hold the Fort" (*101 Hymn Stories*, No. 30), "Jesus Loves Even Me" (*ibid.*, No. 46), as well as "Hallelujah, What a Savior," "Whosoever Will," "Wonderful Words of Life," "Almost Persuaded" and many more.

In 1874, Bliss compiled a small collection entitled *Gospel Songs*, and this has been the name by which all subsequent songs of this style became known. Soon Bliss joined forces with Ira D. Sankey in publishing many other gospel song collections, and these two men are generally credited with being the founders of the gospel song movement in this country. It has been well said that what Stephen Foster did in secular music—getting our nation to sing its distinctive folk music—Ira Sankey and P. P. Bliss did as validly and effectively in sacred music.

176

*   *   *

"We ought so to live Christ as to compel others to think about Christ."

Unknown

"Salvation may come quietly, but we cannot remain quiet about it."

Unknown

"I do not ask for mighty words to leave the crowd impressed,
But grant my life may ring so true my neighbor shall be blessed.
I do not ask for influence to sway the multitude;
Give me a 'word in season' for the soul in solitude.

"I do not ask to win the great—God grant they may be saved!
Give me the broken sinner, Lord, by Satan long-enslaved.
Though words of wisdom and of power rise easily to some
Give me a simple message Lord, that bids the sinner come."

Unknown

56 Living for Jesus

Thomas O. Chisholm, 1866-1960

C. Harold Lowden, 1883-1963

1. Liv-ing for Je-sus a life that is true, Striv-ing to please Him in all that I do, Yield-ing al-le-giance, glad-heart-ed and free— This is the path-way of bless-ing for me.

2. Liv-ing for Je-sus who died in my place, Bear-ing on Cal-v'ry my sin and dis-grace— Such love con-strains me to an-swer His call, Fol-low His lead-ing and give Him my all.

3. Liv-ing for Je-sus thru earth's lit-tle while, My dear-est treas-ure the light of His smile, Seek-ing the lost ones He died to re-deem, Bring-ing the wea-ry to find rest in Him.

CHORUS

O Je-sus, Lord and Sav-ior, I give my-self to Thee, For Thou in Thine a-tone-ment didst give Thy-self for me. I own no oth-er Mas-ter— my heart shall be Thy throne: My life I give, hence-forth to live, O Christ, for Thee a-lone.

177

Copyright 1917 Heidelberg Press. © Renewed 1945 C. Harold Lowden. Assigned to The Rodeheaver Co. (A Div. of Word, Inc.) All rights reserved. International Copyright secured. Used by permission.

Living for Jesus

Author—Thomas O. Chisholm—1866-1960
Composer—C. Harold Lowden—1883-1963
Tune Name—"Living"
Meter—10 10. 10 10. with Refrain

> I beseech you therefore, brethren, by the mercies of God that ye present your bodies a living sacrifice, holy, acceptable unto God, which is your reasonable service. And be not conformed to this world: but be ye transformed by the renewing of your mind, that ye may prove what is that good, and acceptable, and perfect, will of God.
>
> Romans 12:1, 2

The composer of this gospel hymn, C. Harold Lowden, has left the following account regarding the origin of this popular consecration hymn:

> In 1915, I wrote a "light and summery" type of gospel song entitled "The Sunshine Song" for children's services. It became quite popular, and many pastors wrote to me that the music should be saved, and a more general setting of words wedded to it. In 1917, I came across a copy of it in my files, and played it over. The rhythm and tempo suggested the words "Living for Jesus." The idea came to me that a deep consecration setting of words would be most appropriate.

178

> After much thought and prayer I decided to ask T. O. Chisholm to write the words. I mailed him a copy of the music and suggested the title and the type of refrain which I felt it deserved. In a day or so, Mr. Chisholm returned it to me, saying he didn't have the slightest idea as to the method used in writing words to music. Immediately, I sent the material back to him, telling him I believed God had led me to select him, and suggesting that he permit God to write the poem. Within a couple of weeks he had completed the writing of the words, just as they appear in the song today. More than a million copies have been sold, in song sheet form. It appeared in scores of hymnbooks of all denominations, and has been translated into more than fifteen languages and dialects.

The author, Thomas Obediah Chisholm, was born in a humble log cabin in Franklin, Kentucky, on July 29, 1866. After an early career as schoolteacher and editor of the weekly newspaper, *The Franklin Favorite*, he was converted to Christ at the age of twenty-seven under the ministry of Dr. Henry Clay Morrison, founder of Asbury College and Theological Seminary. In 1903, Chisholm was ordained to the Methodist ministry and pastored a Methodist Church at Scottsville, Kentucky, for a period of time. When his health began to fail, Thomas Chisholm moved his family to Winona Lake, Indiana, and became an insurance salesman and continued this work when he later moved to Vineland, New Jersey, in 1916. Writing, however, was always Mr. Chisholm's first love, and he wrote more than 1,200 poems, of which 800 were published in such periodicals as the *Sunday School Times*,

Moody Monthly, Alliance Weekly, and others. A number of Mr. Chisholm's poems have become well-known hymn texts: "Great Is Thy Faithfulness" (See *101 Hymn Stories,* No. 27), "He Was Wounded for Our Transgressions," "Christ Is Risen From the Dead," "O to Be Like Thee!" and "Trust in the Lord With All Your Heart."

Thomas O. Chisholm describes his purpose for writing as follows:

> I have sought to be true to the Word, and to avoid flippant and catchy titles and treatment. I have greatly desired that each hymn or poem might have some definite message to the hearts for whom it was written.

Mr. Chisholm concluded a long and fruitful ministry on February 29, 1960, at the Methodist Home for the Aged in Ocean Grove, New Jersey.

Carl Harold Lowden, the composer, was born on October 12, 1883, at Burlington, New Jersey. At the age of twelve, he sold his first song to the Hall-Mack Publishing Company, where later he was employed. Mr. Lowden taught music for several years at the Bible Institute of Pennsylvania (now the Philadelphia College of Bible). He also served as the minister of music for the Linden Baptist Church in Camden, New Jersey, for twenty-eight years. During another twelve-year period, Lowden was music editor for the Evangelical and Reformed Church Board (now the United Church of Christ). Mr. Lowden composed a number of hymn tunes and edited many songbook collections during his lifetime. His death occurred on February 27, 1963, at Collingswood, New Jersey.

179

"Living for Jesus" first appeared in a hymnal, in 1917, in a collection titled, *Uplifting Songs,* compiled by Lowden and Rufus W. Miller and published by the Heidelberg Press. The tune name "Living" was chosen by Mr. Lowden when the hymn was selected for inclusion in the 1956 edition of the *Baptist Hymnal.*

* * *

"Be like a watch! Have an open face, busy hands, full of good works, pure gold, and well regulated."

Unknown

"The service we render to others is really the rent we pay for our room on this earth."

Sir Wilfred Grenfell

"We can judge a man faithful or unfaithful only by his works."

Baruch Spinoza

More About Jesus

Eliza E. Hewitt, 1851-1920

John R. Sweney, 1837-1899

1. More a-bout Je-sus would I know, More of His grace to oth-ers show,
2. More a-bout Je-sus let me learn, More of His ho-ly will dis-cern;
3. More a-bout Je-sus— in His Word Hold-ing com-mun-ion with my Lord,
4. More a-bout Je-sus on His throne, Rich-es in glo-ry all His own,

More of His sav-ing full-ness see, More of His love who died for me.
Spir-it of God, my teach-er be, Showing the things of Christ to me.
Hear-ing His voice in ev-'ry line, Mak-ing each faithful say-ing mine.
More of His king-dom's sure in-crease, More of His com-ing—Prince of Peace.

REFRAIN

More, more a-bout Je-sus, More, more a-bout Je-sus;

More of His sav-ing full-ness see, More of His love who died for me.

More About Jesus

Author—Eliza E. Hewitt, 1851-1920
Composer—John R. Sweney, 1837-1899

That I may know Him, and the power of His resurrection, and the fellowship of His sufferings, being made conformable unto His death.   Philippians 3:10

The Christian gospel is thrilling to contemplate. On one hand, it is so simple that even a small child can understand and respond to its basic message—the necessity of placing one's faith in Christ. Yet, it is so pro-found that a lifetime is far too brief to fully comprehend it, since its message is really a person—a growing knowledge of and relationship to the eternal Son of God. Again and again throughout the ages, sincere men and women have cried out:

"That I may know Him..." "More, more about Jesus..."

And we must finally conclude even as St. Augustine did centuries ago: "Thou has created us for Thyself, O God, and our hearts can never be quieted till they find repose in Thee."

The author of this hymn text, Eliza Edmunds Hewitt, was an invalid for an extended period of her life. Out of this experience developed an intimate relationship with God and the Scriptures and a desire to share her feelings with others through writing. She became a prolific writer of Sunday school literature and children's poems. Eventually, her poems came to the attention of gospel musicians such as John R. Sweney, who began setting them to music. They collaborated on such favorites as "There Is Sunshine in My Soul Today" and "Will There Be Any Stars in My Crown?" Eliza Hewitt has also contributed other gospel hymn texts that are still widely sung today, such as: "Stepping in the Light," "Give Me Thy Heart," and "When We All Get to Heaven."

Eliza E. Hewitt was born on June 28, 1851, in Philadelphia, Pennsylvania. She graduated as valedictorian of her class at the Girls' Normal School in Philadelphia and spent her remaining years in that city. Eliza taught public school for a time but was soon confined to her bed for a considerable period with a spinal condition. It is thought that this problem was aggravated by or was the result of being struck across the back with a heavy slate by a boy who was being disciplined. Eliza's song, "There Is Sunshine in My Soul Today," is said to have been written as her expression of gratitude shortly after being relieved of a heavy cast for six months. Eventually, Eliza's physical condition improved, and she was able to continue an active life with her Christian ministries. Miss Hewitt was a close, personal friend of Fanny Crosby, and these two godly women met often for fellowship and discussion of their hymns. Eliza was also a first cousin of the gospel hymn writer, Edgar Page Stites. (See "Trusting Jesus," No. 93). In addition to working with John R. Sweney, Eliza Hewitt also collaborated with such other well-known gospel musicians as William J. Kirkpatrick, B. D. Ackley, Charles Gabriel, E. S. Lorenz and Homer Rodeheaver. She died on April 24, 1920, in Philadelphia, having made a notable contribution to the cause of Christ, through her hymnody.

The composer, John R. Sweney, was another of the influential musicians and leaders of the early, gospel song movement. He personally composed more than a thousand hymn tunes as well as editing or being associated with the publication of more than sixty gospel collections. In addition to working with Eliza Hewitt, he collaborated with such gospel

181

writers as Fanny Crosby in "My Savior First of All" (See *101 Hymn Stories*, No. 60). Other gospel favorites for which Mr. Sweney supplied music include: "Tell Me the Story of Jesus," "Fill Me Now," "Take the World, but Give Me Jesus," "Victory Through Grace," and "Beulah Land."

John R. Sweney was born in West Chester, Pennsylvania, on December 31, 1837. He became a respected music teacher and conductor in various schools and colleges around the country. For twenty-five years, Sweney served as a professor of music at the Pennsylvania Military Academy. Prior to 1871, most of his musical compositions had been of a secular nature. A spiritual crisis occurred in his life that year, however, and for the next twenty-eight years, Sweney devoted his talents to Christian ministries. He became recognized as one of the most successful song leaders of his time, always in great demand at the large Bible conferences throughout the country. John R. Sweney died on April 10, 1899, in Chester, Pennsylvania. At his funeral Ira D. Sankey sang "Beulah Land," a gospel song Mr. Sweney had composed nearly twenty-five years earlier.

John R. Sweney wrote the music especially for Eliza E. Hewitt's text, "More About Jesus," and the complete hymn first appeared in a collection, *Glad Hallelujahs*, published in 1887, edited by Wm. J. Kirkpatrick and John R. Sweney.

182

*   *   *

"Holiness is the architectural plan upon which God buildeth up His living temple."
Charles Haddon Spurgeon: *Holiness*

"He that sees the beauty of holiness, or true moral good, sees the greatest and most important thing in the world. . . . Unless this is seen, nothing is seen that is worth seeing; for there is no other true excellence or beauty."
Jonathan Edwards: *Treatise of Religious Affections*

"Things that once were wild alarms cannot now disturb my rest;
Closed with everlasting arms, pillowed on the loving breast.
O to lie forever here, doubt and care and self resign,
While He whispers in my ear—I am His and He is mine.

"His forever, only His—who the Lord and me shall part?
Ah, with what a rest of bliss, Christ can fill the loving heart.
Heav'n and earth may fade and flee, first-born light in gloom decline,
But while God and I shall be, I am His and He is mine."
George Robinson

58   **More Love to Thee**

Elizabeth P. Prentiss, 1818-1878   William H. Doane, 1832-1915

1. More love to Thee, O Christ, More love to Thee! Hear Thou the
2. Once earth-ly joy I craved, Sought peace and rest; Now Thee a-
3. Let sor-row do its work, Send grief and pain; Sweet are Thy
4. Then shall my lat-est breath Whis-per Thy praise; This be the

prayer I make On bend-ed knee; This is my ear-nest plea:
lone I seek— Give what is best; This all my prayer shall be:
mes-sen-gers, Sweet their re-frain, When they can sing with me,
part-ing cry My heart shall raise; This still its prayer shall be:

More love, O Christ, to Thee, More love to Thee, More love to Thee!

183

More Love to Thee

Author—Elizabeth P. Prentiss, 1818-1878
Composer—William H. Doane, 1832-1915
Tune Name—"More Love to Thee"
Meter—64.64.66.44

> And this I pray, that your love may abound yet more and more in knowledge and in all judgment; that ye may approve things that are excellent; that ye may be sincere and without offence till the day of Christ.   Philippians 1:9, 10

Mrs. Elizabeth Payson Prentiss, born in Portland, Maine, on October 26, 1818, was known throughout her life as a saintly woman, who continually practiced the presence of Christ. Those who knew her best described her as "a very, bright-eyed, little woman, with a keen sense of humor, who cared more to shine in her own happy household than in a wide circle of society." Though Elizabeth was strong in spirit, she was frail in body. Throughout her life she was a near invalid, scarcely knowing a moment free of pain. She once wrote these words:

I see now that to live for God, whether one is allowed ability to be actively useful or not, is a great thing, and that it is a wonderful mercy to be allowed even to suffer, if thereby one can glorify Him.

On another occasion she wrote:

To love Christ more is the deepest need, the constant cry of my soul. . .out in the woods, and on my bed, and out driving, when I am happy and busy, and when I am sad and idle, the whisper keeps going up for more love, more love, more love!

Early in life, Elizabeth demonstrated a gift for writing both prose and poetry. At the age of sixteen, she became a contributor to the *Youth's Companion*, a magazine of high spiritual and literary standards. After a period of teaching school in Massachusetts and Virginia, in 1845, she married Dr. George L. Prentiss, a Presbyterian minister, who later became a professor of Homiletics and Polity at Union Theological Seminary. Mrs. Prentiss continued to write and publish her literary works, and one of her books, *Stepping Heavenward*, sold over 200,000 copies in the United States alone.

184   "More Love to Thee" was written by Mrs. Prentiss during a time of great personal sorrow. While ministering to a church in New York City during the 1850's, the Prentiss' lost a child, and then a short time later their youngest child also died. For weeks, Elizabeth was inconsolable, and in her diary she wrote, "Empty hands, a worn-out, exhausted body, and unutterable longings to flee from a world that has so many sharp experiences." From her broken heart came this touching poem:

I thought that prattling boys and girls
Would fill this empty room;
That my rich heart would gather flowers
From childhood's opening bloom:
One child and two green graves are mine,
This is God's gift to me;
A bleeding, fainting, broken heart,
This is my gift to Thee.

During this period of grief, Mrs. Prentiss began meditating upon the story of Jacob in the Old Testament, and how God met him in a very special way during his moments of sorrow and deepest need. She prayed earnestly that she too might have a similar experience. She also thought about Sarah Adams' hymn text, "Nearer, My God, to Thee" (See *101 Hymn Stories*, No. 61). While she thus meditated and prayed, she began writing her own lines in almost the same metrical pattern that Sarah Adams had used in writing her poetic version of Jacob at Bethel. Mrs. Prentiss completed all four stanzas that same evening; but evidently she did not think very highly of her work, for she never showed the poem to anyone, not even her husband, for the next thirteen years. The poem was first printed in leaflet form, in 1869, and later appeared in the hymnal, *Songs of Devotion*. This hymn has since been translated into many languages, including Arabic and Chinese, indicating that it is a universal response from sincere believers around the world. Mrs. Elizabeth Prentiss died on August 13, 1878, at her summer home in Dorset, Vermont.

The composer of the music, William Howard Doane, was a successful businessman who wrote more than 2,000 gospel song tunes, but always as an avocation. He was Fanny Crosby's principal collaborator in writing gospel music, contributing music for such well-known hymn texts as: "Rescue the Perishing," (*101 Hymn Stories*, No. 76), "Pass Me Not," "I Am Thine, O Lord," "Near the Cross," "To God Be the Glory," and also the music for Lydia Baxter's hymn text, "Take the Name of Jesus With You" (No. 84). Mr. Doane left a fortune in trust, which has been used in many philanthropic causes, including the construction of Doane Memorial Music Building at the Moody Bible Institute in Chicago.

William H. Doane composed this music especially for Mrs. Prentiss' text and included it in his hymnal, *Songs of Devotion*, published in 1870.

185

* * *

"We are not to make the ideas of contentment and aspiration quarrel, for God made them fast friends...A man may aspire, and yet be quite content until it is time to rise; and both flying and resting are but parts of one contentment. The very fruit of the gospel is aspiration. It is to the heart what spring is to the earth, making every root, and bud, and bough desire to be more."

Henry Ward Beecher

"Gracious Spirit, Holy Ghost,
Taught by Thee, we covet most,
Of Thy gifts at Pentecost,
Holy, heavenly love.

"Love is kind, and suffers long,
Love is meek, and thinks no wrong,
Love than death itself more strong;
Therefore give us love.

"Faith and hope and love we see,
Joining hand in hand, agree;
But the greatest of the three,
And the best, is love."

Christopher Wordsworth

59

More Secure Is No One Ever

TRYGGARE KAN INGEN VARA

Lina Sandell Berg, 1832-1903

Swedish Melody

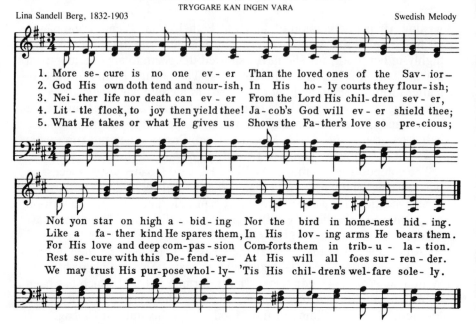

1. More se- cure is no one ev- er Than the loved ones of the Sav- ior—
2. God His own doth tend and nour-ish, In His ho- ly courts they flour-ish;
3. Nei- ther life nor death can ev - er From the Lord His chil-dren sev- er,
4. Lit - tle flock, to joy then yield thee! Ja - cob's God will ev - er shield thee;
5. What He takes or what He gives us Shows the Fa-ther's love so pre-cious;

Not yon star on high a - bid-ing Nor the bird in home-nest hid - ing.
Like a fa- ther kind He spares them, In His lov- ing arms He bears them.
For His love and deep com-pas - sion Com-forts them in trib- u - la - tion.
Rest se- cure with this De- fend- er— At His will all foes sur - ren - der.
We may trust His pur-pose whol- ly— 'Tis His chil-dren's wel-fare sole- ly.

More Secure Is No One Ever

Author—Lina Sandell Berg, 1832-1903
English Translation—a composite translation
Music—Swedish Melody
Tune Name—"Tryggare Kan Ingen Vara"
Meter—L.M. (88.88)

> The eternal God is thy refuge, and underneath are the everlasting arms.
>
> Deuteronomy 33:27

The nineteenth century witnessed the phenomenon of many gifted women taking a place of primary importance among the hymn writers of the Christian church. While Fanny Crosby was writing more than 8,000 hymn texts in this country, and Frances Ridley Havergal and Charlotte Elliott were writing hymns in England; Sweden, too, had its own outstanding representative, Lina Sandell Berg.

During the mid-nineteenth century, a powerful revival surge swept throughout the Scandinavian countries. Carl Olof Rosenius, Sweden's greatest lay-preacher, was a strong influence in the pietistic, free-church movement that arose out of the state Lutheran Church. An important factor in the spread of this movement was the emergence of many heart-warming, gospel songs that flowed from writers like Lina Sandell, whose lives had been touched by these revival fires. Throughout the second half of the century, Lina Sandell Berg was recognized as the foremost hymnist of Sweden, and this simple hymn was considered to be her finest.

Lina Sandell was born on October 3, 1832, in Froderyd, Smaland, Sweden. Her father, Jonas Sandell, was the parish pastor at Froderyd. Though a Lutheran, he was sympathetic to the pietistic emphasis of a personal salvation experience as against the church's stress upon ordinances, rites, and ritual; and he became an early leader in the renewal movement in southern Sweden.

When Lina was just twelve years of age, she had an experience that greatly shaped her entire life. As a younger child, she had been stricken with a paralysis that confined her to bed. Though the physicians considered her chance for a complete recovery hopeless, her parents always believed that God would one day restore her to health. One Sunday morning while her parents were in church, Lina began reading the Bible and praying earnestly, and when her parents returned, they found her dressed and walking. From this healing experience, Lina began to write verses expressing her gratitude and love for God, and at the age of sixteen, she published her first book of meditations and poems. One of her earliest hymn texts during this time was "Tryggare Kan Ingen Vara."

At the age of twenty-six, Lina had another experience which greatly influenced her life. She was accompanying her father aboard ship to Gothenberg across Lake Vattern. The ship gave a sudden lurch, and Lina's father fell overboard and drowned before the eyes of his devoted daughter. Although she had written a number of hymn texts prior to this tragic experience, now more songs than ever began to flow out of her broken heart, reflecting a simple, child-like trust in her Savior and a deep sense of His abiding presence in her life.

187

When Lina was thirty-five years of age, she married C. O. Berg, a wealthy Stockholm businessman. They enjoyed a happy married life, though they experienced sadness from the death of their first son, who died at birth. Later they founded an effective ministry with a Sailor's Mission in Sweden. Lina continued writing and merely signed her hymns "L. S.," by which she became affectionately known throughout Sweden. Lina Sandell Berg wrote approximately 650 hymns, before her death in 1903.

In spite of a frail body, Lina lived to be seventy-one years of age. At her funeral, the church choir sang "Tryggare Kan Ingen Vara," and the congregation joined in spontaneously. In 1953, ten thousand people gathered in the parsonage yard at Froderyd for the dedication of a bronze statue in her memory. The little cottage in which she lived for a time is now a public museum. Each year on Transfiguration Sunday, the people of the parish have a festive service in memory of Lina and her father.

Local tradition claims that it was while watching a flock of birds contentedly chirping in the refuge of the leafy boughs of a huge, ash tree outside of her home that Young Lina thought seriously about the security of God's children. From this inspiration, it is thought that she penned these tender words which have since become so appreciated by young and old alike. The tune is a typical Swedish folk melody with its characteristic lilting, singable style, making it ideally suited to this text. The text with this tune first appeared in the Swedish-American hymnal, *Sionsharpan*, in 1890. Its first translation into English was about 1925.

Lina Sandell Berg is also the author of the well-known Swedish hymn, "Day by Day" (*101 Hymn Stories*, No. 17). Other popular hymns of Swedish origin found in most evangelical hymnals include "He the Pearly Gates Will Open" (No. 34) and "Thanks to God!" (No. 85).

*   *   *

"Too wise to err, too good to be unkind—
Are all the movements of the Eternal mind."
John East-*Songs of My Pilgrimage*

188   TRUST
"How shall I know Him? In His dread control
Unnumbered planets wheel and seasons roll;
Light He commands and darkness, anthems low
Of sighing breezes, cloud and rain and snow;
His work the wonders that the lens reveals,
The blackbird's song and crashing thunder-peals;
By Him their treasures in the rocks are set;
He builds the tree and clothes the violet,
Spreads the unmeasured spaces of the sky,
Sends forth the dawn and paints the butterfly—
How shall I cabin Him in church or creed,
Or strive to bind Him in a book men read?
Yet, though in awe and wonderment I stand,
How shall I be afraid, in His great hand?"
Reginald C. Eva

60

My Faith Looks Up to Thee

OLIVET

Ray Palmer, 1808-1887   Lowell Mason, 1792-1872

1. My faith looks up to Thee, Thou Lamb of Cal - va - ry,
2. May Thy rich grace im - part Strength to my faint - ing heart,
3. While life's dark maze I tread And griefs a - round me spread,
4. When ends life's tran - sient dream, When death's cold sul - len stream

Sav - ior di - vine; Now hear me when I pray, Take all my
My zeal in - spire; As Thou hast died for me, O may my
Be Thou my guide; Bid dark - ness turn to day, Wipe sor-row's
Shall o'er me roll, Blest Sav - ior, then, in love, Fear and dis -

sin a - way, O let me from this day Be whol - ly Thine!
love to Thee Pure, warm and change-less be-- A liv - ing fire!
tears a - way, Nor let me ev - er stray From Thee a - side.
trust re-move— O bear me safe a - bove, A ran - somed soul.

189

My Faith Looks Up to Thee

Author—Ray Palmer, 1808-1887
Composer—Lowell Mason, 1792-1872
Tune Name—"Olivet"
Meter—664.6664

In whom we have boldness and confidence of access through our faith in Him.
Ephesians 3:12 (RSV)

Though there are in our hymnals many fine hymns related to the theme of faith and the necessity of placing our implicit trust and confidence in the finished work of Christ, this hymn is generally considered to be one of the finest on that subject. In fact, many students of hymnody have even termed this the finest American hymn ever written. It is interesting to note that the text was written by a twenty-two-year-old schoolteacher, who later became recognized as an outstanding, evangelical minister in this country.

The author, Ray Palmer, was born on November 12, 1808, in Little Compton, Rhode Island. His father was a judge in the community. Because of unexpected financial difficulties, young Ray was forced to discontinue his schooling at the age of thirteen and take a job as a store clerk in Boston. He began attending the historic, Park Street Congregational Church and there accepted Christ as Savior. Soon he felt the call of God to become a minister of the gospel. He resumed his education at Andover Academy and later graduated from Yale University, in 1830. While studying theology at the university, he took a part-time teaching position in a private girls' school in New York City.

Several months following his graduation from the university and while still living with the family of the lady who directed the girls' school where he taught, Palmer wrote the text for this hymn. He had experienced a very discouraging year in which he battled illness and loneliness. One night as he read a German poem picturing a needy sinner kneeling before the cross, Palmer was so moved, that he translated the lines into English and shortly added the four stanzas that eventually formed the text for "My Faith Looks Up to Thee." He recorded these thoughts:

190

> The words for these stanzas were born out of my own soul with very little effort. I recall that I wrote the verses with tender emotion. There was not the slightest thought of writing for another eye, least of all writing a hymn for Christian worship. It is well-remembered that when writing the last line, "Oh, bear me safe above, A ransomed soul!" the thought that the whole work of redemption and salvation was involved in those words, and suggested the theme of eternal praises, and this brought me to a degree of emotion that brought abundant tears.

Mr. Palmer copied the verses into his small notebook that he always carried with him and thought no more about the lines, except to read them occasionally for his own devotions. Two years later, he was visiting in Boston when he chanced to meet, on a busy street, his friend, Dr. Lowell Mason. In the course of the conversation, Dr. Mason asked young Palmer if he knew of any good texts that could be used for a new hymnal that Mason was in the process of compiling. Hesitatingly, Palmer showed the noted musician his little notebook. This is Palmer's account of that meeting:

> The little book containing the poem was shown him, and he asked for a copy. We stepped into a store together, and a copy was made and given to him, which, without much notice, he put into his pocket.

Two or three days afterward, we met again in the street, when scarcely waiting to salute me, he earnestly exclaimed: "Mr. Palmer, you may live many years and do many good things, but I think you will be best-known to posterity as the author of 'My Faith Looks Up to Thee.'"

Lowell Mason had in the meantime composed a melody for this text, a tune which he called "Olivet," in reference to the hymn's message. The hymn in its present form first appeared in print that same year, 1832, in a hymnal called *Spiritual Songs for Social Worship*, edited by Mason and his colleague, Thomas Hastings. And from that time to the present, nearly every evangelical hymnal has included this fine hymn.

Lowell Mason's prediction about this hymn certainly came true. Dr. Palmer did accomplish much throughout his lifetime, until his death at the age of seventy-nine. He pastored two Congregational churches in the East for thirty years and was the corresponding secretary of the American Congregational Missions Program, during the latter period of his life. He was the author of several popular volumes of religious verse and devotional essays. Palmer also wrote thirty-seven other fine hymns, for which he would never accept payment. Yet Ray Palmer is best remembered today for his first hymn, written when he was only twenty-two years of age.

Dr. Palmer's entire life was characterized by a warm and passionate devotion to Christ. He was described as a healthy, cheerful, and buoyant   191
man, greatly loved and admired by all who knew him. As Palmer grew older, he became deeply interested in the translation of the medieval Latin hymns, and to him belongs the distinction of being the first American writer to introduce this type of hymnody to the Christian church. His best known translation of a Latin text, one based on a poem by a twelfth-century monk named Saint Bernard of Clairvaux, (See "O Sacred Head Now Wounded, No. 70) is the hymn known as "Jesus, Thou Joy of Loving Hearts." It includes these meaningful lines:

> Jesus, Thou joy of loving hearts,
>   Thou fount of life, Thou light of men,
> From the blest bliss that earth imparts,
>   We turn unfilled to Thee again.
>
> Our restless spirits yearn for Thee,
>   Where'er our changeful lot is cast:
> Glad when Thy gracious smile we see,
>   Blest when our faith can hold Thee fast.

The name of Lowell Mason, composer of the music, also became well-known in musical circles, throughout our country, during the nineteenth century. His accomplishments were noteworthy. He has contributed the music for approximately 700 hymn texts, was involved in the compilation of more than eighty song and hymnbook collections, was instrumental in introducing music into the public school curriculum in Boston, in 1838, and later pioneered in the establishment of Normal Schools for training public school teachers. It has been said that for more than a generation, Lowell Mason provided our country with most of the trained, public school music teachers, as well as a large proportion of its trained religious and other professional musicians.

Lowell Mason is also the composer of the hymn "A Charge to Keep I Have" (No. 1) and arranger of "Joy to the World" (No. 52) and "O Day of Rest and Gladness" (No. 66). Other well-known hymn tunes composed by him include: "From Greenland's Icy Mountains" (*101 Hymn Stories*, No. 25), "Nearer, My God to Thee" (*ibid.*, No. 61), and "When I Survey the Wondrous Cross" (*ibid.*, No. 100).

In the providence of God, the literary talents of Ray Palmer and the musical abilities of Lowell Mason were blended together to give birth to a hymn that has ministered mightily to God's people for many decades.

* * *

"Orthodoxy can be learned from others; living faith must be a matter of personal experience."

J. W. Buchsel

"Faith is simply saying 'Amen' to God."

Merv Rosell

"Faith is to believe on the Word of God, what we do not see, and its reward is to see and enjoy what we believe."

St. Augustine

"Good when He gives, supremely good,
Nor less when He denies.
E'en crosses from His sovereign hand
Are blessings in disguise."

Unknown

61 My Jesus, I Love Thee

GORDON

William R. Featherston, 1846-1873

Adoniram J. Gordon, 1836-1895

1. My Jesus, I love Thee, I know Thou art mine— For Thee all the fol - lies of sin I re - sign; My gra - cious Re - deem - er, my Sav - ior art Thou: If ev - er I loved Thee, my Je - sus, 'tis now.

2. I love Thee be - cause Thou hast first lov - ed me And pur - chased my par - don on Cal - va - ry's tree; I love Thee for wear - ing the thorns on Thy brow: If ev - er I loved Thee, my Je - sus, 'tis now.

3. I'll love Thee in life, I will love Thee in death, And praise Thee as long as Thou lend - est me breath; And say when the death-dew lies cold on my brow, "If ev - er I loved Thee, my Je - sus, 'tis now."

4. In man-sions of glo - ry and end - less de - light, I'll ev - er a - dore Thee in heav - en so bright; I'll sing with the glit - ter - ing crown on my brow, "If ev - er I loved Thee, my Je - sus, 'tis now."

My Jesus, I Love Thee

Author—William R. Featherston, 1846-1873
Composer—Adoniram J. Gordon, 1836-1895
Tune Name—"Gordon"
Meter—11 11. 11 11

We love Him, because He first loved us.   1 John 4:19

It is difficult to realize that this beloved devotional hymn, which expresses so profoundly a believer's love and gratitude to Christ for what He has accomplished in redemption, was written by a teen-ager.

The author, William Ralph Featherston, (sometimes spelled *Featherstone*), was born on July 23, 1846, in Montreal, Canada, son of John and Mary Featherston. The family were members of the Wesleyan

Methodist Church of Montreal. It is thought that young Featherston penned these words at the time of his conversion experience, when only sixteen years of age. Though information about William Featherston is scarce, it is believed that he then sent the text to his aunt, Mrs. E. Featherston Wilson, living in Los Angeles, who in turn encouraged its publication. It is reported that the original copy of the poem, in the author's boyish handwriting, is still a cherished treasure in the family. Rather strangely, however, the hymn text appeared anonymously with a different tune in an English hymnal, *The London Hymn Book*, published in 1864.

The composer, Dr. A. J. Gordon, a well-known evangelical pastor of the Clarendon Street Baptist Church of Boston, Massachusetts, discovered this anonymous hymn in *The London Hymn Book* in 1870, and was attracted to its text. For several years Dr. Gordon had been working on assembling a new hymnal geared especially for Baptist congregations. As he meditated on the anonymous English hymn one day, he became dissatisfied with its existing melody, and as he later said, "In a moment of inspiration, a beautiful new air sang itself to me." The hymn in its present form first appeared in the hymnal, *The Service of Song for Baptist Churches*, compiled by S. L. Caldwell and A. J. Gordon and published in 1876. The hymn has been included in nearly every evangelical hymnal published to the present time. Dr. Gordon is also the composer for the rather well-known gospel song, "In Tenderness He Sought Me."

194

Adoniram Judson Gordon was born in New Hampton, New Hampshire, on April 19, 1836, and was named for the famed pioneer Baptist missionary to India-Burma. He died on February 2, 1895, in Boston, after a life of "unsurpassed usefulness to his fellowmen and devotion to his Lord." After graduating from Newton Theological Seminary, Gordon was ordained to the Baptist ministry, in 1863, and six years later was called to pastor the prestigious Clarendon Street Baptist Church of Boston, He became a close friend of Dwight L. Moody and was of great assistance in Moody's evangelistic efforts in Boston. Gordon's literary accomplishments included the editing of the hymnals: *The Service of Song for Baptist Churches* and *The Vestry Hymn and Tune Book*. He was also editor of a monthly periodical, *The Watchword*, as well as author of a series of books called *Quiet Talks*.

When studying the backgrounds behind our enduring hymns such as "My Jesus, I Love Thee," one never ceases to marvel at the workings of God in bringing together the necessary circumstances that make possible the birth and preservation of expressions such as these, which believers in every generation and culture can employ in their praise and adoration of the Almighty.

62   My Sins Are Blotted Out, I Know!

Merrill Dunlop, 1905-   Merrill Dunlop, 1905-

1. What a won-drous mes-sage in God's Word! My sins are blot-ted out,
2. Once my heart was black, but now what joy, My sins are blot-ted out,
3. I shall stand some day be-fore my King, My sins all blot-ted out,

I know! If I trust in His re-deem-ing blood, My sins are
I know! I have peace that noth-ing can de-stroy, My sins are
I know! With the ran-somed host I then shall sing: "My sins are

CHORUS

blot-ted out, I know!
blot-ted out, I know! My sins are blot-ted out, I know!
blot-ted out, I know!"   I know! 195

My sins are blot-ted out, I know! They are bur-ied in the
I know!

depths of the deep-est sea: My sins are blot-ted out, I know!
I know!

© Copyright 1927. Renewal 1955 by Merrill Dunlop. Assigned to Singspiration, Inc. All rights reserved. Used by permission.

My Sins Are Blotted Out, I Know!

Author and Composer—Merrill Dunlop, 1905-
Scripture Reference—Micah 7:18-19

I, even I, am He that blotteth out thy transgressions for mine own sake, and will not remember thy sins.   Isaiah 43:25

Merrill Dunlop was born in Chicago, Illinois, on May 9, 1905. He was converted to Christ in his early teens through the preaching of the late Paul Rader, then pastor of the Moody Memorial Church. Following graduation from the Moody Bible Institute, Dunlop joined Paul Rader's staff at the Chicago Gospel Tabernacle, serving for the next thirty years in the music ministry and in various capacities. Merrill Dunlop has also been active in evangelistic and Bible conference musical ministries in this country as well as around the world to the present time. He gives this account of the writing of this popular gospel hymn:

It was written in a very few minutes, although only after much deliberation, while I was crossing the Atlantic, in 1927, on a liner, *The Leviathan*, and meditating upon the verses in Micah 7:18-19 and upon the great dimensions of the sea—the breadth and depth and what the Bible says about our sins— buried in those depths—removed—blotted out! Then, making it personal, I said: "My sins are blotted out, I know!" The melody came almost simultaneously with the words. I jotted the chorus down aboard the ship, as I walked the deck. Later, in Ireland, I added the words and music to the stanzas. The song was first introduced in Toronto, Canada, by George Dibble in Paul Rader's large Ravina Rink Campaign, when I was the pianist. It "took hold" immediately and quickly spread across America and across the seas. It has been translated into foreign tongues and published in many song and hymnbooks.

196

In campaign meetings, Mr. Dunlop is frequently featured in the writing of a gospel chorus spontaneously, generally within the space of five minutes, while the congregation observes him at work. Titles suggested on the spot by members of the audience are then voted upon by the congregation. When the final vote reveals the winning title, Mr. Dunlop proceeds quickly, writing both words and music. Audiences then learn and sing the new composition with much interest and blessing.

Today, Mr. Dunlop's compositions in gospel songs number several hundred, many of which are well-known, published and sung throughout the English-speaking world. Entire collections of his songs are found in such publications as *Songs of a Christian, Radio Songtime with Merrill Dunlop*, and *Merrill Dunlop's New Gospel Songs*.

*   *   *

"The Christian life that is joyless is a discredit to God and a disgrace to itself."
                                                           Maltbie D. Babcock

Near to the Heart of God

Cleland B. McAfee, 1866-1944   Cleland B. McAfee, 1866-1944

1. There is a place of qui - et rest, Near to the heart of God,
2. There is a place of com - fort sweet, Near to the heart of God,
3. There is a place of full re - lease, Near to the heart of God,

A place where sin can - not mo - lest, Near to the heart of God.
A place where we our Sav - ior meet, Near to the heart of God.
A place where all is joy and peace, Near to the heart of God.

CHORUS

O Je - sus, blest Re - deem - er, Sent from the heart of God,

Hold us who wait be - fore Thee Near to the heart of God.

Near to the Heart of God

Author and Composer—Cleland B. McAfee, 1866-1944

Draw nigh to God, and He will draw nigh to you...   James 4:8

One simple but valid definition of an effective hymn might be: "A spiritual expression that comes from the heart and then reaches the hearts of others." This particular hymn could certainly be cited as a good example of that truth.

"Near to the Heart of God" was written and composed by Cleland B. McAfee, in 1901, while he was pastoring the large First Presbyterian

Church of Chicago, Illinois. He received the news one day that diphtheria had just claimed the lives of his two beloved nieces, and while in his saddened, shocked state, he wrote this hymn, as a comfort for his own soul as well as for the other members of his family. He first sang it with choking voice just outside the darkened, quarantined house of his brother, Howard, the day of the double funeral. The following Sunday, McAfee's choir repeated it as a communion hymn at his own church service. Another brother, Lapsley, was so impressed, with the simple but comforting message of the hymn, that he carried it back to his pastorate, the First Presbyterian Church of Berkeley, California. From that time to the present, it has continued to be a source of great encouragement to believers everywhere.

Cleland Boyd McAfee was born on September 25, 1866, at Ashley, Missouri. He received his theological training at the Union Theological Seminary. Later, he returned to his undergraduate school, Park College in Parkville, Missouri, and served as a teacher and pastor of the college church, from 1881 to 1901. He then served two successful pastorates, the First Presbyterian Church of Chicago and the Lafayette Avenue Presbyterian Church, Brooklyn, New York. From 1912-1930, he was professor of systematic theology at the McCormick Theological Seminary in Chicago. He was known as an eminent theologian, a brilliant speaker, author of a number of books and learned papers, and was honored by his denomination to serve as the elected moderator of the General Assembly of the Presbyterian Church. Yet today, Dr. McAfee is best remembered for this one simple, unassuming, devotional hymn.

198

After his retirement, Dr. McAfee made his home at Jaffrey, New Hampshire, where he remained active with his writing, lecturing, preaching, and teaching until his death on February 4, 1944.

The hymn in its present form first appeared, in 1903, in a magazine called *The Choir Leader*, published by the Lorenz Publishing Company of Dayton, Ohio. It has appeared in nearly every published evangelical hymnal to the present time.

* * *

"When I am with God, my fear is gone
In the great quiet of God.
My troubles are as the pebbles on the road
My joys are like the everlasting hills."
Walter Rauschenbusch: *The Little Gate to God*

"Mid all the traffic of the way,
Turmoil without, within;
Make of my heart a quiet place,
And come and dwell therein."
Unknown

64 Not What These Hands Have Done

AURORA

Horatius Bonar, 1808-1889

Norman Johnson, 1928-1983

1. Not what these hands have done Can save this guilt - y soul;
2. Not what I feel or do Can give me peace with God;
3. Thy work a - lone, O Christ, Can ease this weight of sin;
4. Thy love to me, O God— Not my poor love to Thee—
5. Thy grace a - lone, O God, To me can par - don speak;
6. I bless the Christ of God, I rest on love di - vine;

Not what this toil - ing flesh has borne Can make my spir - it whole.
Not all my prayers and sighs and tears Can bear my aw - ful load.
Thy blood a - lone, O Lamb of God, Can give me peace with - in.
Can rid me of this dark un - rest And set my spir - it free.
Thy pow'r a - lone, O Son of God, Can this sore bond - age break.
And with un - fal - t'ring lip and heart I call this Sav - ior mine!*

199

Tune: AURORA

Music © Copyright 1979 by Singspiration (ASCAP). Division of the Zondervan Corp. All rights reserved. Used by permission.

Not What These Hands Have Done

Author—Horatius Bonar, 1808-1889
Composer—Norman Johnson, 1928-1983
Tune Name—"Aurora"
Meter—SM (66.86)

> Not by works of righteousness which we have done, but according to His mercy He
> saved us, by the washing of regeneration, and renewing of the Holy Ghost; which He
> shed on us abundantly through Jesus Christ our Savior.   Titus 3:5, 6

The history of the Protestant church in Scotland is most interesting and
noteworthy. With the spread of the sixteenth-century, Protestant
Reformation Movement throughout Great Britain and the efforts of reformer
John Knox, 1505-1572, the Presbyterian Church became the established,
government supported and controlled church of Scotland. This church was
strongly dominated by a rigid, Calvinistic system of theology and practice,
believing, for example, that the only acceptable praise to be offered God
must be the Psalms or the exact words taken directly from the Scriptures.

The Church of Scotland did not even allow organs to be used in its "kirks", until 1874, and never published a hymnal, until 1898.

It was not until the evangelical revival began to stir in the nineteenth century and the desire was intensified to have independent churches that a significant change occurred in Scotland's religious climate. By 1840, through the leadership of a Dr. Thomas Chalmers, more than 200 independent churches were established throughout the land. In 1843, a renewed spirit of revolt against the government-controlled, established church began, and this disruption resulted in the separation of the evangelical faction from the established church and the organization of the Free Church of Scotland. After several more defections from the established church, a merger of these dissenting groups resulted in the formation of the United Presbyterian Church. This merged body in turn became united with the Free Church Movement in 1900, with the designation of the United Free Church of Scotland. Shortly, the government released its control over all of the churches, and since 1929, the Scottish churches have been known with the one title, The Church of Scotland. This unified church now uses a common hymnal, *The Church Hymnary*, first compiled in 1898, and later revised in 1927 and again in 1968.

One of the most respected and influential leaders of the 1843 revolt against the established church and the resultant rise of the independent church movement was Horatius Bonar. Bonar became known as an evangelical preacher of great renown as well as the most eminent of all Scottish hymn-writers.

Following his education at the University of Edinburgh and his ordination to the ministry in 1838, Bonar began his pastoral work at the parish church of Kelso, near the English border. Here he labored zealously for twenty-seven years. When the split occurred in the established church, in 1843, Bonar associated himself with the Free Church Movement, and his Kelso congregation became a center of evangelical influence. During this time, Bonar also edited the *Border Watch*, a periodical which did much to foster the Free Church spirit. At the height of his career at Kelso, Horatius Bonar was persuaded to become pastor of the large Chalmers Memorial Church in Edinburgh, a prestigious Free Church, erected in honor of Dr. Thomas Chalmers, the early pioneer and first moderator of this movement. Here Bonar ministered faithfully for another twenty-three years, until his death on July 31, 1889. Several years before his death, Dr. Bonar was honored with the moderatorship of the church General Assembly. It is said that Bonar's death was mourned throughout Christendom as much as that of any man of his generation.

Horatius Bonar was known throughout his ministry as a most able Bible student, especially in the area of eschatology and premillenial prophecy. For twenty-five years, he edited the *Quarterly Journal of Prophecy*, in which he would also include one of his newly written hymn texts. In addition, Bonar was a prolific writer of evangelistic tracts and devotional books as well as more than 600 hymn texts, many of which are still in general use. Several of his important publications include: *Songs for the Wilderness* (1843), *The Bible Hymn Book* (1845), *Hymns, Original and Selected* (1846), *Hymns of Faith and Hope* (1857), *The Song of the New Creation* (1872), *Hymns of the Nativity* (1879), and *Communion Hymns* (1881).

Dr. Bonar was highly respected throughout his life as a man of wide scholarship and culture. It was said of him that "his mind was saturated with the Scriptures, and his heart was possessed by a faith far broader and more generous than the strict Calvinistic creed, to which his intellect gave assent." He loved children, and for them many of his hymns were especially written. He stated that his purpose for writing was "to fill my hymns with the love and light of Christ." His remarkable ministry was characterized by earnest zeal, devotion, and a concern for soul-winning. His many-faceted life was observed by some who said that "he was always visiting," while others said that "he was always preaching," some thought that "he was always writing," and many that "he was always praying." Bonar's wife of forty years, the former Jane Lundie, was also a gifted writer, who penned the beautiful hymn text, "Fade, Fade, Each Earthly Joy."

It is interesting that even though Bonar was a highly-esteemed Free Church preacher and hymn writer, he did not use his own "human composure" hymns with his own worship services, until the very close of his active ministry; since his congregations still insisted on singing only the Psalms. Yet, it was Bonar who encouraged the use of gospel songs, when they were introduced by Dwight L. Moody and Ira Sankey in the Scottish evangelistic crusade meetings. (See "Once for All," No. 72). Bonar actually wrote several gospel songs for Sankey to use during these meetings in Great Britain. Other popular hymns by Horatius Bonar still in use in our hymnals today are "I Heard the Voice of Jesus Say," (*101 Hymn Stories*, No. 35) and the communion hymn, "Here, O My Lord, I See Thee Face to Face."

"Not What These Hands Have Done" first appeared in Bonar's collection, *Hymns of Faith and Hope*, with the title "Salvation Through Christ Alone." It is a clear reflection of his strong, Calvinistic theology that man's only basis for God's favor and salvation rests solely on the finished work of Christ.

The tune, "Aurora," is a relatively new tune to be used with this text. Through the years, numerous tunes have been associated with the short meter (86.86) text. This new tune was composed by Norman Eldon Johnson, a long-time associate with the Singspiration Publishing Company. During the past two decades, this fine musician and man of God made many notable contributions to the cause of evangelical sacred music. Norman was largely responsible for the publication of such hymnals as *Crowning Glory, Great Hymns of the Faith,* and the latest *Praise* hymnal, published by Singspiration in 1979. In his association with John W. Peterson and the Singspiration Company, Norman Johnson also arranged and composed numerous sacred songs and anthems as well as various organ and instrumental collections. Norman stated that it was his desire to compose a new tune for Bonar's fine text that would give a better stress to the proper words than the other existing and borrowed tunes had done. He also related that he named the tune "Aurora" in honor of his first piano teacher in Lindsborg, Kansas—Aurora Nelson, now Mrs. Frank Ross, "a gracious Christian woman who instilled in me a love for sacred music."

After a nine-year struggle with the crippling disease known as Amyotrophic Lateral Sclerosis, Norman joined the heavenly choir on December 19, 1983, while listening to a recording of his favorite choruses from Handel's oratorio, *The Messiah.* The memory and appreciation of Norman Johnson by those of us who knew him well will long be cherished.

* * *

202

NOT TILL THEN
"When this passing world is done,
When has sunk yon glowing sun,
When we stand with Christ in glory,
Looking o'er life's finished story,
Then, Lord, shall I fully know—
Not till then—how much I owe."
Robert McCheyne

CHOOSE THOU FOR ME
"Thy way, not mine, O Lord, however dark it be!
Lead me by Thine own hand, choose out my path for me.
I dare not choose my lot; I would not, if I might;
Choose Thou for me, my God, so shall I walk aright.

"Choose Thou for me my friends, my sickness or my health;
Choose Thou my cares for me, my poverty or wealth.
Not mine, not mine the choice, in things both great or small;
Be Thou my guide, my strength, my wisdom and my all."
Horatius Bonar

65
Now I Belong to Jesus

Norman J. Clayton, 1903-   Norman J. Clayton, 1903-

1. Je - sus my Lord will love me for - ev - er, From Him no pow'r of
2. Once I was lost in sin's deg - ra - da - tion, Je - sus came down to
3. Joy floods my soul, for Je - sus has saved me, Freed me from sin that

e - vil can sev - er; He gave His life to ran - som my soul —
bring me sal - va - tion, Lift - ed me up from sor - row and shame —
long had en - slaved me; His pre - cious blood He gave to re - deem —

CHORUS

Now I be - long to Him! Now I be - long to Je - sus, Je - sus be -

longs to me — Not for the years of time a - lone, But for e - ter - ni - ty.

Copyright 1938 and 1943 by Norman J. Clayton. © Renewed 1966, 1971 by Norman Clayton Publishing Co. (A Div. of Word, Inc.) All rights reserved. International Copyright secured. Used by permission.

Now I Belong to Jesus

Author and Composer—Norman J. Clayton, 1903-

My beloved is mine, and I am His; He pastures His flock among the lilies.
Song of Solomon 2:16

Norman John Clayton, one of the talented and veteran gospel song writers of our times, was born in Brooklyn, New York, on January 22, 1903, the ninth of ten children. His mother was from the Church of England

and became a charter member of the South Brooklyn Gospel Church in the United States in 1898, where she took her children from infancy. Norman was converted at the early age of six years. At the age of twelve he began his life-long ministry as a church organist and accompanist.

Mr. and Mrs. Clayton have two children, both of whom are active in Christian work. For much of his life, Mr. Clayton was involved in the building business as well as the music publishing business. For fifteen years he was the organist with the Word of Life Broadcasts and rallies in New York City. Clayton founded his own publishing company, Gospel Songs, Inc., which later merged with the Rodeheaver Company. Here he worked as a writer and editor. Several of his well-known songs still widely used in evangelical circles today include: "We Shall See His Lovely Face," "He Holds My Hand," "Every Moment of Every Day," and "My Hope Is in the Lord." Mr. Clayton feels that "Now I Belong to Jesus" is still his most widely used song. This inspiring gospel song first appeared in *Word of Life Melodies No. 1*, published in 1943.

Norman Clayton states that he feels it is vitally important that every song he writes be biblically based. With this in mind he has made it a practice to memorize a great deal of Scripture. He tells how it is his usual practice to write the music first before the words. Practically all of his songs are the result of consciously trying to write a song for a particular occasion or on a specific theme. He writes that one of his greatest thrills in life was an occasion when he heard a ten year old deaf girl sing "Now I Belong to Jesus" at a special camp for retarded and handicapped children.

204

This popular gospel song is one that speaks so well to the truth of the mystical union that exists between Christ and the believer—Christ in the believer and the believer in Christ. Who can fathom the mystery of a mortal believer's spirit being united with the divine Christ and yet each retaining his own distinct essence and personality—a glorious relationship that begins for the believer at the moment of genuine response to the call of Christ and one that will last for eternity.

*   *   *

"God is FOR us—that is good.
God is WITH us—that is better.
God is IN us—that is best!"
Unknown

66   O Day of Rest and Gladness

MENDEBRAS

Christopher Wordsworth, 1807-1885

German Folk Song
Lowell Mason, 1792-1872

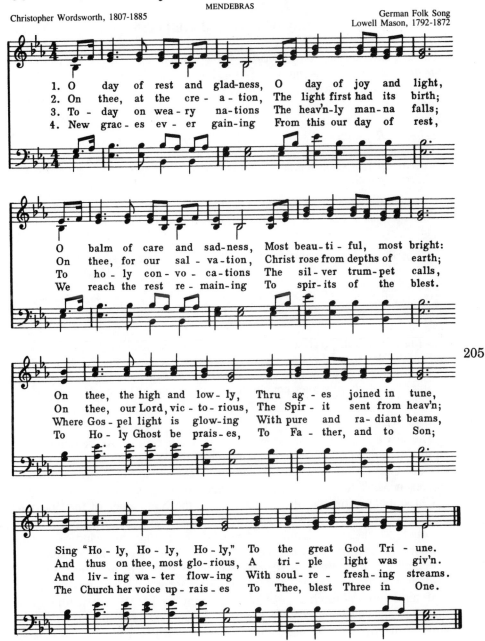

1. O day of rest and glad-ness, O day of joy and light,
2. On thee, at the cre - a - tion, The light first had its birth;
3. To - day on wea - ry na - tions The heav'n-ly man - na falls;
4. New grac - es ev - er gain-ing From this our day of rest,

O balm of care and sad-ness, Most beau-ti - ful, most bright:
On thee, for our sal - va-tion, Christ rose from depths of earth;
To ho - ly con - vo - ca-tions The sil - ver trum-pet calls,
We reach the rest re - main-ing To spir-its of the blest.

205

On thee, the high and low-ly, Thru ag - es joined in tune,
On thee, our Lord, vic - to-rious, The Spir - it sent from heav'n;
Where Gos - pel light is glow-ing With pure and ra - diant beams,
To Ho - ly Ghost be prais-es, To Fa - ther, and to Son;

Sing "Ho - ly, Ho - ly, Ho - ly," To the great God Tri - une.
And thus on thee, most glo-rious, A tri - ple light was giv'n.
And liv - ing wa - ter flow-ing With soul-re - fresh-ing streams.
The Church her voice up - rais - es To Thee, blest Three in One.

O Day of Rest and Gladness

Author—Christopher Wordsworth, 1807-1885
Music—German folk song
Arranger—Lowell Mason, 1792-1872
Tune Name—"Mendebras"
Meter—76.76 Doubled
Scripture Reference—Psalm 118:24

> There remaineth therefore a rest to the people of God. For he that is entered in his rest, he also hath ceased from his own works, as God did from His. Let us labor therefore to enter into that rest...
> Hebrews 4:9, 10, 11

"Sunday is nature's law as well as God's. No individual or nation habitually disregarding it has failed to fall upon disaster and grief."
Daniel Webster

"The Lord's Day is a firm foundation on which to build a six-story week."
The Defender

"O what a blessing is Sunday, interposed between the waves of worldly business like the divine path of the Israelites through the sea."
Samuel Wilberforce

206

"Man needs a day of rest from the cares, toils, and trials of the six days of work in the material realm. He needs to reflect, meditate, contemplate, and to turn his eyes inward, as it were, rather than outward. This has always been true, but surely it is truer now in this strenuous age of the world than ever before."

The Lookout

The nineteenth-century author, Christopher Wordsworth, reminds us in this hymn text of a truth that men have realized through the ages, that even as God rested following His acts of creation, so man, too, needs a day each week for rest and spiritual renewal.

Christopher Wordsworth, a nephew and the biographer of the noted eighteenth-century English poet, William Wordsworth, was born on October 30, 1807, in Lambeth, England. Following his education at Cambridge University, where he received high honors for his academic accomplishments, Wordsworth was eventually elevated, in 1869, to the bishopric of Lincoln, where he labored most successfully in that position, until his death on March 20, 1885. Throughout his life, Wordsworth was known as an outstanding scholar, a tireless worker and a voluminous writer. Among his writings were an important work on the land of Greece, a learned commentary on the entire Bible, and a collection of 127 hymns published, in 1862, in a hymnal called *The Holy Year*. These hymns were written by Wordsworth to illustrate his convictions that hymns should not deal with personal, individual interests, but rather should teach the truths of Scripture and voice the worship of the entire congregation. He also believed that it was the first duty of the hymnwriter to teach sound doctrine to believers, and to reach the unsaved with the gospel. On another occasion he stated, "A church which foregoes the use of hymns in her office of teaching neglects one of the most efficacious instruments for correcting error and for disseminating truth, as well as for ministering comfort and edification."

"O Day of Rest and Gladness" is the first hymn in Wordsworth's, *The Holy Year*, hymnal and the only one still widely used today. This hymn text originally had six stanzas. One of the omitted verses is worthy of interest:

> Thou art a port protected from storms that round us rise;
> A garden intersected with streams of Paradise;
> Thou art a cooling fountain in life's dry, dreary sand;
> From Thee, like Pisgah's mountain, we view our promised land.

Christopher Wordsworth based his hymn text on Psalm 118:24: "This is the day which the Lord hath made; we will rejoice and be glad in it." The hymn was included in the 1868 appendix of the well-known Anglican hymnal, *Hymns Ancient and Modern*.

An important spiritual truth taught and illustrated in this hymn by Christopher Wordsworth is the doctrine of The Trinity. It is interesting to note in the second stanza that the author compares the triune Godhead with three important events that occurred on the first day of the week: The creation of Light (Genesis 1:1), the resurrection of Christ, and the advent of the Holy Spirit. He refers to these events as the "triple light." In the final stanza, Wordsworth addresses each member of the Godhead by name, as the Church raises its perpetual voice to "Thee, blest Three in One."

207

The tune, "Mendebras," is a German folk melody arranged by Lowell Mason, the influential nineteenth-century American composer of church and public school music. Lowell Mason is also the composer of the hymns, "A Charge to Keep I have" (No. 1) and "My Faith Looks Up to Thee" (No. 60) and the arranger of the carol "Joy to the World" (No. 52). Other well-known Mason hymns include: "From Greenland's Icy Mountains" (*101 Hymn Stories*, No. 25), "Nearer My God to Thee" (*ibid.*, No. 61), and "When I Survey the Wondrous Cross" (*ibid.*, No. 100).

* * *

> "Again the Lord's own day is here,
> The day to Christian people dear;
> As, week by week, it bids them tell
> How Jesus rose from death and hell."
> Ascribed to Thomas a Kempis
> Translated by John M. Neale

67

O for a Closer Walk With God

BEATITUDO

William Cowper, 1731-1800

John B. Dykes, 1823-1876

1. O for a clos - er walk with God, A calm and heav'n - ly frame,
2. Where is the bless - ed - ness I knew When first I saw the Lord?
3. Re - turn, O ho - ly Dove, re - turn, Sweet mes - sen - ger of rest;
4. The dear-est i - dol I have known, What - e'er that i - dol be,
5. So shall my walk be close with God, Calm and se - rene my frame;

A light to shine up - on the road That leads me to the Lamb.
Where is the soul - re - fresh - ing view Of Je - sus and His Word?
I hate the sins that made Thee mourn And drove me from my breast.
Help me to tear it from Thy throne And wor - ship on - ly Thee.
So pur - er light shall mark the road That leads me to the Lamb.*

O for a Closer Walk With God

Author—William Cowper, 1731-1800
Composer—John B. Dykes, 1823-1876
Tune Name—"Beatitudo"
Meter—CM (86.86)
Scripture Reference—Genesis 5:24

> Because Thou hast been my help, therefore in the shadow of Thy wings will I rejoice. My soul followeth hard after Thee: Thy right hand upholdeth me.Psalm 63: 7, 8

One of the saddest lives ever lived was that of the author of this hymn text, William Cowper. Early in life, Cowper developed a chronic melancholia and despondency which plagued him till death. In one state of mental torment, he even attempted suicide by drowning in October, 1773. Though Cowper wrote much fine devotional material, he was continually troubled by the lack of assurance of his own salvation. Today, however, his hymns are often referred to as "part of the prized treasures of the Christian Church."

William Cowper (pronounced "koo-per") was born on November 15, 1731, in Great Berkhamstead, England, the son of the chaplain to King

O for a Closer Walk With God

George II. Following a period in his early life when he attempted to study and practice law, Cowper eventually moved to the village of Olney, where he began an association and firm friendship with John Newton, pastor of the Olney Anglican parish church. (See "Glorious Things of Thee Are Spoken," No. 26). In 1799, the combined talents of Newton and Cowper produced the famous *Olney Hymns Hymnal*, one of the most important single contributions made to the field of evangelical hymnody. In this ambitious collection of 349 hymns, sixty-seven were written by Cowper with the remainder by Newton.

During Cowper's residence at Olney, he stayed with a Mrs. Unwin, who remained his devoted friend and guardian till the end of her days. This home is now a very popular museum in Olney, containing interesting relics, books and portraits of Cowper and his friends. Behind the home is the lovely garden where Cowper and Newton met nearly every day to work on their hymns. "O for a Closer Walk With God" is said to have been written on December 9, 1769, during the serious illness of Cowper's dear friend, Mrs. Unwin. In a letter written the following day, referring to this event, Cowper wrote:

> She is the chief of blessings I have met with in my journey since the Lord was pleased to call me. . . . Her illness has been a sharp trial to me. Oh, that it may have a sanctified effect, that I may rejoice to surrender up to the Lord my dearest comforts, the moment He may require them. . . . I began to compose the verses yesterday morning before daybreak but fell asleep at the end of the first two lines: When I awakened, the third and fourth were whispered to my heart in a way which I have often experienced.

The hymn first appeared in *Collection of Psalms and Hymns*, compiled by William Cowper, in 1772. When it was later included in the *Olney Hymns Hymnal*, Book 1, it bore the title "Walking With God," based on Genesis 5:24: "And Enoch walked with God: And he was not; for God took him." "O for a Closer Walk With God" reflects in a most poignant manner the inner struggles of William Cowper's sensitive soul and his earnest desire to experience the inner serenity of God's abiding presence in his life.

Other well-known hymns by William Cowper include: "There Is a Fountain," (*101 Hymn Stories*, No. 95), "God Moves in a Mysterious Way," often described as the finest hymn on God's providence ever written, and "The Spirit Breathes Upon the Word." Not only did Cowper contribute much to hymnody, but he was also one of the most respected secular poets of the eighteenth century. Several of his best-known works include a translation of Homer, a widely acclaimed volume of poems entitled *The Task*, along with his most famous literary poem, "John Gilpin," a happy and mirthful narrative.

The tune, "Beatitudo," was composed by John Bacchus Dykes, one of England's, leading church musicians of the nineteenth century. Dykes was born on March 10, 1823, at Kingston-upon-Hull, England. He received his training at Cambridge University and later was awarded an honorary Doctor of Music degree from Durham University. Dr. Dykes is credited with composing 300 hymn tunes, many of which are still widely used today: "Melita" (See "Eternal Father, Strong to Save," No. 22), "Nicaea" (See "Holy, Holy, Holy," (*101 Hymn Stories*, No. 31), "Vox Dilecti" (See "I Heard the Voice of Jesus Say," (*ibid.*, No. 35) "St. Agnes" (See "Jesus, the Very Thought of Thee," (*ibid.*, No. 49), and "Lux Benigna" (See "Lead, Kindly Light," (*ibid.*, No. 53). The tune "Beatitudo" was originally composed by John Dykes for the hymn text "How Bright These Glorious Spirits Shine," which appeared in the 1875 edition of the *Hymns Ancient and Modern* hymnal. "Beatitudo" was a word coined by Cicero, meaning "the condition of blessedness."

* * *

"God often visits us, but most of the time we are not at home."

Unknown

210

"Lord, teach us how to pray aright
With reverence and with fear;
Though dust and ashes in Thy sight,
We may, we must draw near.

"God of all grace, we bring to Thee
A broken contrite heart;
Give, what Thine eye delights to see,
Truth in the inward part.

"Faith is the only sacrifice
That can for sin atone;
To cast our hopes, to fix our eyes,
On Christ, on Christ alone.

"Give these, and then Thy will be done;
Thus, strengthen'd with all might,
We, through Thy Spirit and Thy Son
Shall pray, and pray aright."

James Montgomery

68

O Happy Day

Philip Doddridge, 1702-1751

Edward F. Rimbault, 1816-1876

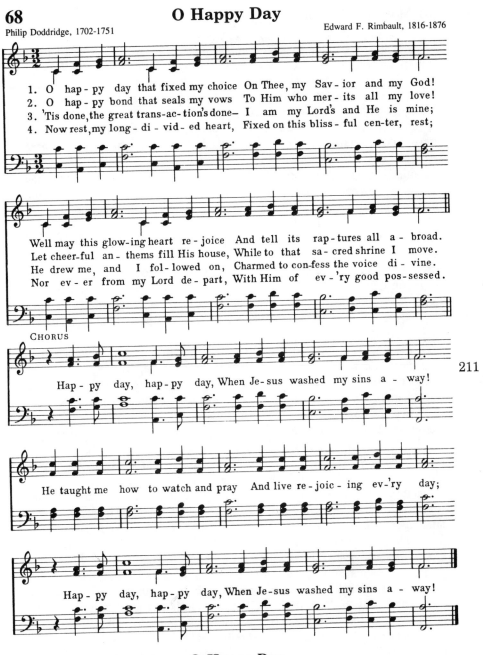

1. O hap-py day that fixed my choice On Thee, my Sav-ior and my God!
2. O hap-py bond that seals my vows To Him who mer-its all my love!
3. 'Tis done, the great trans-ac-tion's done— I am my Lord's and He is mine;
4. Now rest, my long-di-vid-ed heart, Fixed on this bliss-ful cen-ter, rest;

Well may this glow-ing heart re-joice And tell its rap-tures all a-broad.
Let cheer-ful an-thems fill His house, While to that sa-cred shrine I move.
He drew me, and I fol-lowed on, Charmed to con-fess the voice di-vine.
Nor ev-er from my Lord de-part, With Him of ev-'ry good pos-sessed.

CHORUS

Hap-py day, hap-py day, When Je-sus washed my sins a-way!

211

He taught me how to watch and pray And live re-joic-ing ev-'ry day;

Hap-py day, hap-py day, When Je-sus washed my sins a-way!

O Happy Day

Author—Philip Doddridge, 1702-1751
Composer—Edward F. Rimbault, 1816-1876
Scripture Reference—2 Chronicles 15:15

Behold, God is my salvation; I will trust, and not be afraid: For the Lord Jehovah is my strength and my song; He also is become my salvation.   Isaiah 12:2

Along with Charles Wesley, Philip Doddridge is generally ranked as one of England's, finest, eighteenth-century hymn writers. He was also a friend and admirer of Isaac Watts, whose hymns by this time had greatly revived congregational singing in England. This friendship between these two spiritual leaders continued until Watts' death in 1748.

Philip Doddridge was born on June 26, 1702, in London, England, the youngest of twenty children. Physically, he was such a delicate child that his life was despaired of almost from birth, and poor health plagued him throughout all of his life. His parents died when he was only a young boy, but kind friends cared for him and helped with his schooling. His unusual talents as a student were soon recognized, and the Duchess of Bedford offered to send him to Cambridge, if he would become a minister of the Anglican Church upon graduation. This, however, Doddridge declined to do, and, instead, he entered a non-conformist seminary and eventually became one of the most influential, evangelical, independent church leaders of England.

At the age of twenty-seven, Doddridge began a fruitful, twenty-two-year pastorate at the Castle Hill Congregational Chapel in Northampton, England. Here he also directed a theological training school, where he trained approximately two hundred young men for a ministry in independent churches. Doddridge did most of the teaching in the school, conducting classes in Hebrew, Greek, mathematics, philosophy, Bible and theology. He became known as a brilliant scholar and was honored for his accomplishments with a Doctor of Divinity degree from Aberdeen University, in 1736. Doddridge was also a voluminous writer. Several of his most notable works included his famous theological treatise, "The Rise and Progress of Religion in the Soul," which was translated into seven languages. He also wrote a commentary on the New Testament, called the *Family Exposition*, which was equally well-received. However, Doddridge was best known as the author of approximately 400 hymn texts. Nearly all of his hymns were written as summaries to his sermons. He would then teach these new hymns with the customary practice of that day, which was to "line out" the hymn—that is to repeat them from the pulpit line-by-line with the congregation responding in like fashion.

None of Doddridge's hymns was published during his own lifetime, but manuscript copies were widely circulated among the non-conformist congregations throughout England. In 1755, four years after his death, a long-time friend, Job Orton, published a collection of these hymns for the first time in a hymnal called *Doddridge's Hymns, Founded on Various Texts in the Holy Scriptures*.

O Happy Day

At the age of forty-eight and at the height of his ministry, Doddridge developed a severe condition of tuberculosis. A number of devoted friends collected funds to send him to Lisbon, Portugal, hoping to prolong his life with a more favorable climate. The action proved too late, however, and Doddridge died on October 26, 1751, and was buried in the English cemetery in Lisbon. At the news of his home-going, he was widely mourned throughout England. Doddridge's extensive accomplishments, combined with godly character, won for him the highest esteem of Christian leaders and thinkers of England, regardless of church or creed.

"O Happy Day," a text which expresses so aptly the sense of joy in a personal relationship with God, is Doddridge's best-known hymn today. It was originally entitled "Rejoicing in Our Covenant Engagement to God" and was based on 2 Chronicles 15:15:

And all Judah rejoiced at the oath: for they had sworn with all their heart, and sought Him with their whole desire; and He was found of them: and the Lord gave them rest round about.

One of the verses omitted in most hymnals is worthy of interest:

High Heav'n that heard the solemn vow,
That vow renewed shall daily hear;
Till in life's latest hour I bow,
And bless in death a bond so dear.

213

The hymn first appeared without the refrain in the 1755 collection of Doddridge's writings, published posthumously.

The tune for these lyrics, often cited as an example of one not equal in quality to the text, did not appear for nearly one hundred years after the text. The refrain melody was added and adapted from a popular song by Edward F. Rimbault entitled "Happy Land." The music for the verses was probably the product of various anonymous musicians. The present complete tune first appeared in *The Wesleyan Sacred Harp* by William McDonald, in 1854, set to another hymn text, but with the same refrain, "Happy Day, Happy Day."

The composer, Edward Francis Rimbault, was born on June 13, 1816, in London, England. He served as an organist in a number of London churches and was recognized as a noted musicologist and scholar. He received honorary Doctorate of Music degrees from several schools, including Harvard University in the United States. He did a great deal of publishing, including music of many kinds—madrigals, ballads, and sacred.

"O Happy Day" has been widely used in various church circles. It has been employed on numerous occasions by the British royalty for confirmation services of their court children. The hymn has also been given much use as a dedication hymn for services of Christian baptism, especially by the Methodist and Baptist denominations.

69   O Perfect Love

O PERFECT LOVE — SANDRINGHAM

Dorothy B. Gurney, 1858-1932

Joseph Barnby, 1839-1896

1. O per - fect Love, all hu - man thought trans - cend - ing,
2. O per - fect Life, be Thou their full as - sur - ance
3. Grant them the joy which bright - ens earth - ly sor - row;

Low - ly we kneel in prayer be - fore Thy throne,
Of ten - der char - i - ty and stead - fast faith,
Grant them the peace which calms all earth - ly strife,

That theirs may be the love which knows no end - ing,
Of pa - tient hope, and qui - et, brave en - dur - ance,
And to life's day the glo - rious un - known mor - row

Whom Thou for - ev - er - more dost join in one.
With child - like trust that fears nor pain nor death.
That dawns up - on e - ter - nal love and life. A - men.

O Perfect Love

Author—Dorothy B. Gurney, 1858-1932
Composer—Joseph Barnby, 1839-1896
Tune Name—"O Perfect Love" and "Sandringham"

For this cause shall a man leave his father and mother, and shall be joined unto his wife, and they two shall be one flesh.   Ephesians 5:31

This hymn has often been called one of the finest and most impressive wedding hymns in the English language. It was written in 1883 by an English woman named Dorothy B. (Blomfield) Gurney, who wrote only this one hymn text throughout her lifetime. Mrs. Gurney wrote the text especially for her older sister's wedding. The author has stated that the writing of the hymn "was no effort whatever after the initial idea had come to me of the two-fold aspect of perfect union—love and life—and I have always felt that God helped me write it." The text first appeared in the Anglican Church hymnal, *Hymns Ancient and Modern*, Supplement, published in 1889.

Dorothy Gurney was visiting her soon-to-be-married sister in the lovely, English Lake region of Windermere, the land of William Wordsworth and many other romantic poets, when the sister complained that, for her forthcoming wedding, she could not find appropriate words for one of her favorite hymn tunes known as "Strength and Stay" by John B. Dykes. Mrs. Gurney has left the following account of the writing of this text:

215

We were all singing hymns one Sunday evening and had just finished "Strength and Stay," a special favorite with my sister, when someone remarked what a pity it was that the words should be unsuitable for a wedding. My sister, turning suddenly to me, said: "What is the use of a sister who composes poetry, if she cannot write me new words to this tune?" I picked up a hymn book and said: "Well, if no one will disturb me I will go into the library and see what I can do." After about fifteen minutes I came back with the text, "O Perfect Love," and there and then we all sang it to the tune of "Strength and Stay." It went perfectly, and my sister was delighted, saying that it must be sung at her wedding. For two or three years it was sung privately at many London weddings, and then it found its way into the hymnals.

Dorothy Frances Gurney was born on October 4, 1858, in London, England. She grew up in the atmosphere of a devout Anglican Church parsonage marked by refinement and culture. Her father, Rev. Frederick G. Blomfield, was a rector of a London parish, while her grandfather had been a distinguished bishop of London. Dorothy displayed literary gifts early in life with the writing of two volumes of verse as well as a devotional work titled *A Little Book of Quiet*. One of her best known poems is "God's Garden," from which these lines are often quoted:

Dorothy married Gerald Gurney, a former actor who became an ordained minister in the Anglican Church. However, in 1919, the Rev. and Mrs. Gurney both left the Anglican Church and became Roman Catholics.

The tune, known in some hymnals as "O Perfect Love" and in others as "Sandringham," was composed by Joseph Barnby, one of England's most distinguished church musicians of the nineteenth century. His church choirs in London were widely known for their excellence. At the St. Ann's Soho Church, where he served as organist and choir director from 1871-76, Barnby began the annual singing festivals of J. S. Bach's passion music. Joseph Barnby is also credited with writing 246 hymn tunes, all of which were published in one volume, one year after his death. In addition, he composed an oratorio as well as numerous liturgical anthems. Barnby also edited five important hymnals, the most noted of which was *The Hymnary*, published in 1872. In 1892, Joseph Barnby was knighted by the Queen of England for his many musical contributions to English culture.

In 1898, Joseph Barnby composed a special anthem based on Dorothy Gurney's text for the marriage ceremony of the Duke and Duchess of Fife. The present hymn tune is really an adaptation from that anthem. "Sandringham" first appeared as a hymn tune in John Stainer's *The Church Hymnary*, published in 1898. "Sandringham" is named after the English royal family's residence, which is located in Norfolk. The tune has been used for many, other fine hymn texts, including "We Would See Jesus" by Anna B. Warner and "I Am the Lord's! O Joy Beyond Expression" by Lucy A. Bennett. In 1954, when the Second Assembly of the World Council of Churches met at Evanston, Illinois, this tune was chosen by the Hymnal Committee to introduce a new, award-winning hymn text for that special occasion.

Joseph Barnby is also the composer of the tune "Laudes Domini," used for the hymn "May Jesus Christ Be Praised" (*101 Hymn Stories*, No. 57), and the tune "Merrial," used for the hymn "Now the Day Is Over" (*ibid.*, No. 63).

*   *   *

"God has set the type of marriage everywhere throughout the creation. . . . Every creature seeks its perfection in another. . . . The very heavens and earth picture it to us."

Martin Luther

70   O Sacred Head, Now Wounded

PASSION CHORALE

Attr. to Bernard of Clairvaux, 1091-1153
Trans. by Paul Gerhardt, 1607-1676
Trans. by James W. Alexander, 1804-1859

Hans Leo Hassler, 1564-1612
Har. by Johann Sebastian Bach, 1685-1750

1. O sa - cred Head, now wound - ed, With grief and shame weighed down,
2. What Thou, my Lord, hast suf - fered Was all for sin - ners' gain:
3. What lan-guage shall I bor - row To thank Thee, dear - est Friend,

Now scorn-ful - ly sur - round - ed With thorns Thy on - ly crown,
Mine, mine was the trans-gres - sion, But Thine the dead - ly pain.
For this Thy dy - ing sor - row, Thy pit - y with - out end?

How art Thou pale with an - guish, With sore a - buse and scorn!
Lo, here I fall, my Sav - ior! 'Tis I de - serve Thy place;
O make me Thine for - ev - er! And, should I faint - ing be,

217

How does that vis - age lan - guish Which once was bright as morn!
Look on me with Thy fa - vor, Vouch-safe to me Thy grace.
Lord, let me nev - er, nev - er Out - live my love to Thee!

O Sacred Head, Now Wounded

Author—Attributed to Bernard of Clairvaux, 1091-1153
Translated into German by Paul Gerhardt, 1607-1676
Translated into English by James W. Alexander, 1804-1859
Music—Hans Leo Hassler, 1564-1612
Harmonized by Johann Sebastian Bach, 1685-1750
Tune Name—"Passion Chorale"
Meter—76.76 Doubled

> And when they had plaited a crown of thorns, they put it upon His head, and a reed in His right hand; and they bowed the knee before Him, and mocked Him, saying, 'Hail, King of the Jews!' And they spit upon Him, and took the reed, and smote Him on the head. Matthew 27:29, 30

The text of this deeply-moving hymn is thought to have its roots in twelfth-century monastic life. It has long been attributed to Saint Bernard, abbot of the monastery of Clairvaux, France. Recent research, however, has raised some questions as to whether this was actually the work of Saint Bernard or possibly the writings of a later medieval author, Arnulf von Loewen.

218   Bernard was born to a noble family at Fontaine-in-Burgundy, France; his father was a knight and his mother a person of radiant goodness. While in his early twenties, Bernard chose the life of a monk at the monastery of Citeaux, France. It is generally agreed that Bernard of Clairvaux became one of the finest and most influential church leaders of that period. He is said to have represented the best of monastic life in his time. The emphasis of his ministry was a life of holiness, simplicity, devotion, prayer, preaching, and ministering to the physical and spiritual needs of mankind. In the sixteenth century, Martin Luther wrote of Bernard that "he was the best monk that ever lived, whom I admire beyond all the rest put together." It has also generally been believed that Bernard wrote another long poem entitled, *Dulcis Jesus Memorial* ("Joyful Rhythm on the Name of Jesus"), from which Edward Caswall in the nineteenth century translated portions of the lines for his well-known hymn text, "Jesus, the Very Thought of Thee" (*101 Hymn Stories*, No. 49).

"O Sacred Head, Now Wounded" is taken from a lengthy, medieval poem *Rhythmica Oratio*, in seven parts, with each part addressing various members of Christ's body as He suffered on the cross: His feet, knees, hands, side, breast, heart, and face. This hymn text is from the seventh portion of the poem and was originally titled "Salve Caput Cruentatum." The German translation by Paul Gerhardt first appeared in 1656 in the German hymnal, *Praxis Pietatis Melica*. Here it was titled "O Haupt voll Blut Wunden" ("To the Suffering Face of Jesus Christ"). The hymn text first appeared in English, in 1830, in the hymnal, *The Christian Lyre*, after James W. Alexander, a Presbyterian minister, had translated Paul Gerhardt's free German translation.

Paul Gerhardt was born at Grafenheinchen, Saxony, Germany, on March 12, 1607, and eventually was ordained to the German Reformed Church ministry. His life was a tragic one, beginning with much suffering in his early life during the Thirty Years' War (1618-1648), and later he experienced the early loss of his wife and four children, who died in early childhood. Gerhardt also became the center of much theological and political controversy during the rule of Frederick William I, Elector of Saxony, when Gerhardt refused to assent to the edict of the ruler, that forbade free discussion of the differences between the Lutheran and Calvinist Reformed Churches. Yet today, Paul Gerhardt and the Lutheran pastor, Martin Rinkart, (See "Now Thank We All Our God," (*101 Hymn Stories*, No. 62) are recognized as the foremost, German hymnists of the seventeenth century. Paul Gerhardt is credited with writing 132 hymn texts during his life. His texts are said to be a reflection of inner spiritual wealth, many of them written "under circumstances which would have made most men cry rather than sing." Gerhardt's hymns represent a transition from pure objective faith to a more subjective note in hymnody, containing an emotional warmth that often was lacking in the earlier Lutheran hymns. Catherine Winkworth, noted nineteenth-century English hymn translator, has written this concerning Paul Gerhardt: "The religious song of Saxony finds its purest and sweetest expression in his writing."

219

James Waddell Alexander was born at Hopewell, Virginia, on March 13, 1804. He received his seminary training at Princeton Theological Seminary and later taught church history there for several years. Following his ordination, Alexander pastored several large Presbyterian churches in New Jersey and New York. He always maintained a keen interest in hymnology, especially in translating the earlier Latin and German texts. A number of these translations were published posthumously, in 1861, in a book titled *The Breaking Crucible and Other Translations*.

The tune, "Passion Chorale," was originally a German love song ("My Heart is Distracted by a Gentle Maid") in Hans Leo Hassler's collection, *Lustgarten Neuer Deutscher Gessang*, of 1601. Hassler is generally considered to be one of the finest German composers of the late Renaissance, in both secular and sacred music. The tune first appeared with Gerhardt's text in the *Praxis Pietatis Melica*, published by Johann Cruger, in 1644. It has been associated with this text both in German and in English ever since. The *Praxis Pietatis Melica* is recognized as the most influential and widely used German hymnal of the seventeenth century. Within one hundred years after its initial publication, nearly fifty editions of the hymnal had been printed.

The harmonization of this tune is by the German master-composer, Johann Sabastian Bach, undoubtedly the greatest church musician of history. Bach was not only a superb musician (to study traditional harmony today is still to study the writings of Bach), but also a devout Christian, who insisted that "the aim and final reason of all music should be nothing else but the glory of God and the refreshment of the spirit." Many of Bach's compositions began with the inscription, "Jesus, help me!" and at their close, "To God alone be the praise." It would appear that Bach was especially fond of this melody, since he used the chorale five times throughout his well-known *St. Matthew Passion*, composed in 1729. The present musical version of this hymn is really a combination of various harmonizations of this melody employed by Bach.

This classic hymn has shown in three tongues—Latin, German and English—and in three confessions—Roman, Lutheran and Reformed—with equal effect, the dying love of our Savior and our boundless indebtedness to Him.

Philip Schaff

*   *   *

220   "Alexander, Caesar, Charlemagne, and I myself have founded empires; but upon what do these creations of our genius depend? Upon force. Jesus alone founded His empire upon love; and to this very day millions would gladly die for Him."

Napoleon

"Thorns crowned His blessed head,
Blood stained His every tread;
Cross laden, on He sped —
    For Me!

"Pierced through His hands and feet,
Three hours o'er Him did beat;
Pierce rays of noontide heat —
    For Me!

"In thought and word and deed,
Thy will to do; oh, lead my feet;
E'en though they bleed —
    To Thee!"

Selected

71 On Jordan's Stormy Banks

PROMISED LAND

Samuel Stennett, 1727-1795

American Melody
Adapted by Rigdon M. McIntosh, 1836-1899

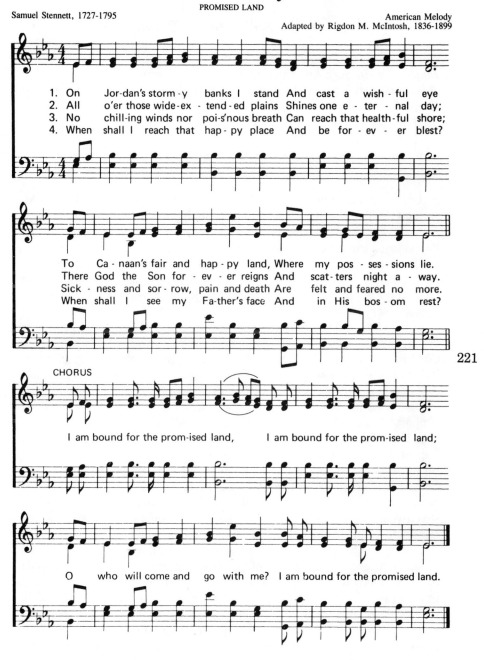

1. On Jor-dan's storm-y banks I stand And cast a wish-ful eye
2. All o'er those wide-ex - tend-ed plains Shines one e - ter - nal day;
3. No chill-ing winds nor poi-s'nous breath Can reach that health-ful shore;
4. When shall I reach that hap - py place And be for - ev - er blest?

To Ca - naan's fair and hap - py land, Where my pos - ses - sions lie.
There God the Son for - ev - er reigns And scat-ters night a - way.
Sick - ness and sor - row, pain and death Are felt and feared no more.
When shall I see my Fa-ther's face And in His bos - om rest?

221

CHORUS

I am bound for the prom-ised land, I am bound for the prom-ised land;

O who will come and go with me? I am bound for the promised land.

On Jordan's Stormy Banks

Author—Samuel Stennett, 1727-1795
Music—Traditional American melody
Adapted by Rigdon M. McIntosh, 1836-1899
Tune Name—"Promised Land"
Meter—CM (86.86)

> If in this life only we have hope in Christ, we are of all men most miserable.
> 1 Corinthians 15:19

Anticipation has always been an important characteristic of God's people. In the Old Testament, it was Israel's anticipation of the promised land, Canaan. For the New Testament believer, it is the glorious hope of one day sharing eternity with our Savior and Lord.

This hymn text, written by an English Baptist minister, Samuel Stennett, first appeared in John Rippon's *Selection of Hymns*, in 1787, with the title "Heaven Anticipated." It has since been a joyous favorite with evangelical people everywhere.

Samuel Stennett was one of the most respected and influential preachers among the Dissenting or non-conformist groups of his time. He was highly esteemed by all religious groups and classes of people; it was said that he was even a personal friend of the reigning monarch, King George III. Not only was Stennett known as an outstanding evangelical preacher, but he also used his influence among the statesmen of the time in vigorous support of social reforms and religious freedom.

Samuel Stennett was born, in 1727, in Exeter, England, the son of a Baptist minister. Later, his father received a call to pastor the Baptist Church on Little Wild Street, London, and at the age of twenty, young Samuel became his father's assistant there. Upon his father's death, in 1758, Samuel became the pastor and continued this ministry, until his own death thirty-seven years later. Among his influential parishioners was John Howard, the noted English philanthropist and prison reformer.

Throughout his ministry, Stennett also authored thirty-nine hymns, most of which he contributed to one of the most important evangelical hymnals of the eighteenth century, John Rippon's *Selection of Hymns*, published in 1787 (See *101 Hymn Stories*, No. 32). Stennett's two most popular hymns still in usage are "Majestic Sweetness Sits Enthroned" (*ibid.*, No. 56) and "On Jordan's Stormy Banks." In 1763, the University of Aberdeen conferred the Doctor of Divinity degree upon Samuel Stennett, in recognition of his accomplishments.

The tune, "Promised Land," is one of the many traditional melodies used in the United States during the early part of the nineteenth century.

There are several secular songs from this time that closely resemble the "Promised Land" melody. Its first appearance as a hymn tune can be traced back to 1835 in a hymnal called *Southern Harmony*, where it is shown with shaped notes. Later, a noted Southern musician named Rigdon M. McIntosh altered the tune by changing the tonality from minor to major as well as by adding the refrain. The hymn was first published in its present form, in 1895, in a hymnal called *The Gospel Light*, edited by H. R. Christie.

Samuel Stennett completed his faithful and effective ministry for God and reached "Canaan's fair and happy land" on August 24, 1795.

* * *

"The hope of heaven under troubles is like the wind and sails to the soul."
Samuel Rutherford

"The joys of heaven are not the joys of passive contemplation, of dreamy remembrance, of perfect repose; but they are described thus, 'They rest not day or night...His servants serve Him and see His face.'"
Alexander MacLaren

"In heaven, to be even the least is a great thing, where all will be great; for all shall be called the children of God."
Thomas a Kempis

223

NEARER HOME
"One sweetly solemn thought comes to me o'er and o'er:
I am nearer my home today than I ever have been before.

"Nearer my Father's house, where the many mansions be;
Nearer the great white throne, nearer the crystal sea.

"Nearer the bound of life, where we lay our burden down;
Nearer leaving the cross; nearer gaining the crown.

"But lying darkly between, winding down through the night,
Is the silent, unknown stream, that leads at last to the light.

"Oh, if my mortal feet have almost gained the brink;
If it be I am nearer home, even today, than I think!

"Father, perfect my trust; let my spirit feel in death,
That her feet are firmly set on the rock of a living faith!"
Phoebe Cary

72
Once for All

Philip P. Bliss, 1838-1876

Philip P. Bliss, 1838-1876

1. Free from the law— O hap-py con - di - tion! Je - sus hath bled,
2. Now are we free — there's no con-dem - na - tion! Je - sus pro - vides
3. Chil-dren of God— O glo-ri - ous call - ing! Sure-ly His grace

and there is re - mis-sion; Cursed by the law and bruised by the fall—
a per-fect sal - va - tion;"Come un - to Me—" O hear His sweet call!
will keep us from fall-ing; Pass - ing from death to life at His call,

Chorus

Grace hath re-deemed us once for all.
Come— and He saves us once for all.
Bless - ed sal - va - tion— once for all.

Once for all— O sin - ner, re -

224

ceive it! Once for all— O broth-er, be - lieve it! Cling to the

cross, the bur-den will fall— Christ hath re-deemed us once for all!

Once For All

Author and Composer—Philip P. Bliss, 1838-1876
Scripture Reference—Hebrews 10:10

For by grace are ye saved through faith; and that not of yourselves, It is the gift of God—not of works, lest any man should boast. Ephesians 2:8, 9

In his book, *Memoirs and Reminiscenses*, George C. Stebbins, also a noted gospel songwriter (See "Saved by Grace," No. 76 and "Ye Must Be Born Again," (No. 101) states that this hymn is conceded to be the clearest statement of the doctrine of grace, in distinction from the law, to be found in all of hymnody. It is said that, at the time of Moody and Sankey's first evangelistic visit to Scotland, in 1873, the singing of this hymn had more to do than anything else with breaking down the prejudice that existed against American gospel hymns up to that time. Its teaching was scriptural and in perfect accord with the teachings of the Scottish divines, who prided themselves on their doctrinal scholarship and purity. The Presbyterians in Scotland had long insisted that only the Psalms should be sung in church, and then without any accompaniment.

Ira D. Sankey, in his book, *My Life and the Story of the Gospel Hymns*, relates the following account of his use of this hymn while conducting a meeting in Edinburgh, Scotland, upon seeing the noted Scottish preacher, Horatius Bonar in the audience: (See "Not What These Hands Have Done," No. 64).

Of all men in Scotland, he was the one concerning whose decision I was most solicitous. He was indeed my ideal hymnwriter, the prince among the hymnists of his day and generation. Yet, he would never sing one of his beautiful hymns in his own congregation, because he ministered in a church that believed in the use of the Psalms only.

With fear and trembling, I announced as a solo, the song, "Free From the Law, O Happy Condition. . . ." Feeling that the singing might prove only as an entertainment and not a spiritual blessing, I requested the whole congregation to join me in a word of prayer, asking God to bless the truth about to be sung. In my prayer my anxiety was relieved. Believing and rejoicing in the glorious truth contained in the song, I sang it through to the end.

At the close of Mr. Moody's address, Dr. Bonar turned toward me with a smile on his venerable face, and reaching out his hand, he said, "Well, Mr. Sankey, you sang the gospel tonight." And thus the way was opened for the ministry of sacred song in Scotland.

"Once for All" first appeared in Bliss's *Sunshine for Sunday School* collection, published in 1873, and again in his *Gospel Songs* of 1875, which he did in collaboration with Ira D. Sankey. Bliss wrote this text after meditating upon the truth of Hebrews 10:10: "By the which will we are sanctified through the offering of the body of Jesus Christ once for all."

George C. Stebbins gives this further tribute to Philip P. Bliss, who along with Ira D. Sankey, has been called the "Father of Gospel Music."

> He occupied a pre-eminence that still stands unrivalled. There has been no writer since his time who has shown such a grasp of the fundamental truths of the gospel, nor such a gift for putting them into poetic and singable form as he. In all of his hymns, there was manifest a happy blending of the poet and musician, and along with it a rare judgment and deep spiritual insight into the needs of presenting the saving truths of Scripture in clear and singable form.

> So versatile were his talents, that his gifts as a singer and leader were little less than those he possessed as a writer of hymns. He had a voice of rare quality and splendid volume, a baritone of extraordinary range and evenness throughout, and a perfect method of voice production and control. . . . He was six feet tall, and of commanding stature, with features as perfect in form, and eyes that were large and kindly in expression. He sang without ostentation, playing his own accompaniment. . . . His leading was also without display or any attempt at attracting attention to himself.

226   Philip P. Bliss was born in Clearfield County, Pennsylvania, on July 9, 1838. As a young man, he moved to Chicago and became involved in the evangelistic ministries of Dwight L. Moody and Ira Sankey. He became one of the most prolific, gospel song writers of this time, before his tragic death in a train accident at Ashtabula, Ohio, on December 29, 1876, when only thirty-eight years of age. (See "My Redeemer," (*101 Hymn Stories*, No. 59).

Several of the Philip P. Bliss gospel song favorites still widely used in evangelical circles today include: "Let the Lower Lights Be Burning" (No. 55), "Hold the Fort" (*101 Hymn Stories*, No. 30), "I Gave My Life for Thee" (*ibid.*, No. 34), "It Is Well With My Soul" (*ibid.*, No. 44), "Jesus Loves Even Me" (*ibid.*, No. 46), and "My Redeemer" (*ibid.*, No. 59).

*   *   *

GRACE ALONE
"Not saved are we by trying, from self can come no aid;
'Tis on the blood relying, once for our ransom paid.
'Tis looking unto Jesus, the holy one and just;
'Tis His grace that saves me—it is not 'try' but trust!"
Anonymous

73 Our Great Savior

HYFRYDOL

J. Wilbur Chapman, 1859-1918

Rowland W. Prichard, 1811-1887
Arr. by Robert Harkness, 1880-1961

1. Je - sus! what a Friend for sin - ners! Je - sus! Lov - er of my soul;
2. Je - sus! what a Strength in weak-ness! Let me hide my - self in Him;
3. Je - sus! what a Help in sor - row! While the bil - lows o'er me roll;
4. Je - sus! what a Guide and Keep - er! While the tem-pest still is high;
5. Je - sus! I do now re - ceive Him, More than all in Him I find;

Friends may fail me, foes as - sail me, He, my Sav - ior, makes me whole.
Tempt - ed, tried, and some-times fail - ing, He, my Strength, my vic - t'ry wins.
E - ven when my heart is break-ing, He, my Com - fort, helps my soul.
Storms a - bout me, night o'er-takes me, He, my Pi - lot, hears my cry.
He hath grant - ed me for - give - ness, I am His, and He is mine.

CHORUS

Hal - le - lu - jah! what a Sav - ior! Hal - le - lu - jah! what a Friend!

Sav - ing, help-ing, keep-ing, lov - ing, He is with me to the end.

227

Copyright 1910. Renewal 1938 by Hope Publishing Co., Carol Stream, IL 60188. All rights reserved. Used by permission.

Our Great Savior

Author—J. Wilbur Chapman, 1859-1918
Composer—Rowland W. Prichard, 1811-1887
Arranged by Robert Harkness, 1880-1961
Tune Name—*"Hyfrydol"*
Meter—87.87 Doubled

> ...For we have heard Him ourselves, and know that this is indeed the Christ, the Savior
> of the world.   John 4:42

Through the centuries, individuals who have known and been impressed with Christ have tried valiantly to present His portrait both with brush and pen. Yet the noblest efforts of artists and poets seem feeble and inadequate. Isaac Watts, in his hymn "Join All the Glorious Names," reached this same conclusion:

> Join all the glorious names of wisdom, love, and pow'r,
> That ever mortals knew, that angels ever bore:
> All are too poor to speak His worth,
> Too poor to set my Savior forth.

228

Evangelist J. Wilbur Chapman, too, has provided a worthy text extolling various attributes of Christ as they relate to our personal lives: "Friend of sinners," "Lover of my soul," "Strength in weakness," "My victory, help in sorrow, comfort, guide, keeper, pilot." Finally, after reviewing all of what Christ means to a believer, one must respond with Chapman's refrain: "Hallelujah! what a Savior! Hallelujah! what a Friend!"

J. Wilbur Chapman was born in Richmond, Indiana, on June 17, 1859. He received his graduate training at the Lane Theological Seminary and later was ordained to the Presbyterian Church ministry. For twenty years, he served Presbyterian churches in New York and Philadelphia. Then he felt called of God to an evangelistic, Bible Conference ministry and traveled extensively around the world for more than ten years. During this time he was assisted for several years by the well-known singer and song leader, Charles M. Alexander. Chapman was later appointed as the first director of the Winona Lake Bible Conference in Winona Lake, Indiana, and was influential in starting similar conferences at Montreat, North Carolina and Stony Brook, New York. In 1917, he was honored by his denomination by being elected moderator of the General Assembly of the Presbyterian Church, U.S.A. J. Wilbur Chapman also authored eight books as well as a number of hymn texts, including the still popular hymn "One Day."

The tune, "Hyfrydol," is a jubilant Welsh melody that has been widely used for a number of different hymn texts with this same meter. The composer, Rowland W. Prichard, was born in North Wales, on January 14, 1811. He was well-known in his community of Balo, Wales as a choir director and amateur musician. A number of his hymn tunes were published in Welsh periodicals throughout his lifetime. "Hyfrydol" was composed by Prichard around 1830, when he was less than twenty years of age. The name in Welsh means "good cheer." The tune was first published, in 1844, in Prichard's publication, *Cyfailly Cantorion* (The Singer's Friend), which contained most of his tunes. It is interesting to note that the entire melody of this tune with the exception of one note, lies within the first five-note range of the scale.

Robert Harkness, who harmonized the "Hyfrydol" tune, was born in Bendigo, Australia, on March 2, 1880. When the Torrey-Alexander evangelistic team visited that country, in 1902, they persuaded Harkness to join them as their pianist. For six years he toured extensively with this team and later became associated with J. Wilbur Chapman in his evangelistic and Bible conference ministries. Robert Harkness was recognized as one of the finest gospel pianists of his day. He has composed more than two thousand gospel songs, including such favorites as: "In Jesus" (No. 44), "No Longer Lonely," "Why Should He Love Me So?," "Thine, Lord," "Only Believe and Live," and "When I See My Savior Hanging on Calvary."

"Our Great Savior" was first published in its present form, in 1910, in *Alexander's Gospel Songs*, No. 2, published by the Revell Company. It has continued to be a widely used hymn in evangelical circles.

*　　*　　*

"At the name of Jesus, every knee shall bow,
Every tongue confess Him, King of glory now;
'Tis the Father's pleasure, we should call Him Lord,
Who, from the beginning, was the mighty Word.

"Humbled for a season, to receive a name
From the lips of sinners, unto whom He came.
Faithfully He bore it, spotless to the last;
Brought it back victorious, when from death He passed...

"Name Him, brothers, name Him with love strong as death,
But with awe and wonder, and with bated breath;
He is God the Savior, He is Christ the Lord;
Ever to be worshipped, trusted and adored."

Caroline Maria Noel

74 Room at the Cross for You

Ira F. Stanphill, 1914-1994

Ira F. Stanphill, 1914-1994

1. The cross up-on which Je-sus died Is a shel-ter in which we can hide; And its grace so free is suf-fi-cient for me, And deep is its foun-tain— as wide as the sea.

2. Tho mil-lions have found Him a friend And have turned from the sins they have sinned, The Sav-ior still waits to o-pen the gates And wel-come a sin-ner be-fore it's too late.

3. The hand of my Sav-ior is strong, And the love of my Sav-ior is long; Through sun-shine or rain, through loss or in gain, The blood flows from Cal-v'ry to cleanse ev-'ry stain.

CHORUS

There's room at the cross for you, There's room at the cross for you; Tho mil-lions have come, There's still room for one—Yes, there's room at the cross for you.

230

© Copyright 1946. Renewal 1974 by I. Stanphill. Assigned Singspiration (ASCAP). Division of the Zondervan Corp. All rights reserved. Used by permission.

Room at the Cross for You

Author and Composer—Ira F. Stanphill, 1914-1994

> But God commendeth His love toward us, in that, while we were yet sinners, Christ died for us. **Romans 5:8**

The name of Ira F. Stanphill has become generally well-known in evangelical churches as the author and composer of such popular gospel songs as "Room at the Cross for You," "I Know Who Holds Tomorrow," "Mansion Over the Hilltop," "Follow Me," "Supper Time," "Happiness Is the Lord," and many others. Altogether Mr. Stanphill has written more than 600 gospel songs with well over 400 published in songbooks and sheet music.

Ira F. Stanphill was born on February 14, 1914, at Bellview, New Mexico. His parents were musical people and always active in church work. After traveling by covered wagon from Arkansas to New Mexico, where they homesteaded government land, the family moved to Oklahoma and later to Kansas, where they settled in Coffeyville. Here Ira received his high school and college education. He was converted to Christ at the age of twelve and was called to the Christian ministry, while attending the Assembly of God church. Even though he had only a year of piano instruction, Ira's natural musical ability soon made him proficient in piano, organ, ukelele, and the accordion. At the age of seventeen, Ira wrote his first song for his church youth group, and, for several years, he traveled as a musical assistant with other evangelists. On his twenty-second birthday, Stanphill began his own preaching ministry in a revival meeting in Arcadia, Kansas. Since then, he has served Assembly of God pastorates in Florida, Pennsylvania, and Texas. As a singing evangelist, Ira Stanphill has preached the gospel all over the United States as well as in forty other nations.

One of Mr. Stanphill's unique practices (as part of a public service) is to write a new gospel song from suggested titles received from the congregation. "Some are good," he says, "some bad, some indifferent." Some he sings—in his full baritone voice—"once, and some, a thousand times." "Room at the Cross" was written in 1946, as a result of a suggested title at one of his meetings. Although he did not write this song during the service, Ira Stanphill tells that upon returning home and cleaning out the scraps of paper from his pocket, he became impressed with this title and quickly wrote both words and music. This song, like many other Stanphill favorites, has been published in several foreign languages, including Spanish, German, and Italian, and has been recorded by numerous Christian artists. "Room at the Cross" has also been used by the nationally-aired Revival Time Broadcast as the closing theme for many years. Only eternity will reveal the number of individuals who have been influenced

231

to accept Christ, through this gospel song that began as a title on a piece of scrap paper.

Mr. Stanphill writes regarding some of the highlights throughout his fruitful ministry for God:

> One of the greatest events of my life was hearing one of my songs sung by six lepers, in Liberia. I was thrilled to know that, despite their condition, they had hope in their hearts.

He also relates how "Room at the Cross" was used in a tent meeting in Germany some years ago, while Al Garr, an artist for Supreme Records, was singing its message. A man, passing the tent on his way to commit suicide, heard the song and was so attracted to it, that he entered the tent and was converted to Christ.

Rev. Mr. Stanphill shares this philosophy for writing gospel songs:

> The basic reason I have written songs is that I love God and Christ has loved me. Most of my songs are the outgrowth of real experiences with Christ. I think they appeal to people, because I have had trials, heartaches, and sorrow in my own life and I know what I write about.

232 Ira F. Stanphill formerly pastored the Rosen Heights Assemblies of God Church in Fort Worth, Texas. For the past several years, Mr. Stanphill has been active in an itinerant music ministry.

* * *

"All my theology is reduced to this narrow compass—Jesus Christ came into the world to save sinners."

Archibald Alexander

"Go to dark Gethsemane, ye that feel the tempter's power;
Your Redeemer's conflict see, watch with Him one bitter hour.
Turn not from His griefs away, learn of Jesus Christ to pray.

"See Him at the judgment hall, beaten, bound, reviled, arraigned;
See Him meekly bearing all, love to man His soul sustained.
Shun not suffering, shame or loss, learn of Christ to bear the cross.

"Calvary's mournful mountain climb, there adoring at His feet;
Mark that miracle of time, God's own sacrifice complete:
"It is finished!" hear Him cry; learn of Jesus Christ to die."

James Montgomery

75 Satisfied

Clara Tear Williams, 1858-1937

Ralph E. Hudson, 1843-1901

1. All my life long I had pant-ed For a draught, from some clear spring,
2. Feed-ing on the husks a-round me, Till my strength was al-most gone,
3. Poor I was, and sought for rich-es, Something that would sat-is-fy,
4. Well of wa-ter, ev-er spring-ing, Bread of life so rich and free,

That I hoped would quench the burn-ing Of the thirst I felt with-in.
Longed my soul for some-thing bet-ter, On-ly still to hun-ger on.
But the dust I gath-ered round me On-ly mocked my soul's sad cry.
Un-told wealth that nev-er fail-eth, My Re-deem-er is to me.

CHORUS

Hal-le-lu-jah! I have found Him Whom my soul so long has craved!   233

Je-sus sat-is-fies my long-ings—Thru His blood I now am saved.

Satisfied

Author—Clara Tear Williams, 1858-1937
Composer—Ralph E. Hudson, 1843-1901

For He satisfieth the longing soul, and filleth the hungry soul with goodness.
                                                                    Psalm 107:9

The author, Clara Tear Williams, has given the following description of the writing of this inspirational testimony hymn:

About 1875, I was helping in meetings in Troy, Ohio, where Professor R. E. Hudson conducted the singing, when, just before retiring one night, he asked me to write a song for a book he was preparing to publish. Before sleeping, I wrote "Satisfied." In the morning, he composed the music.

In his book, *Songs That Lift the Heart*, George Beverly Shea (See "I'd Rather Have Jesus," No. 42) gives the following account regarding the author of this hymn:

My father, the Reverend A. J. Shea, and I were on an afternoon shopping trip for Mother, as I recall. When we came out of a store in Houghton, New York, where we had recently moved from Winchester, Ontario, we met a tall, elderly woman making her way slowly up the street. She was walking in that slow, mincing step older people sometimes do, cautious not to lose balance.

Dad tipped his hat and said good-day to her as we passed. She stopped and looked up to see who was speaking. Smiling sweetly, she returned his greeting.

"Do you know who that was, son?" he asked me on up the way. I turned and watched as she continued her careful progress. Though a distinguished woman (whom I would now describe as looking a lot like Whistler's Mother)—I had no idea who she was.

234

"That," said Dad, "was Mrs. Clara Tear Williams. She writes hymns." There was a near reverence in his voice, and though I was only eight years old, I was duly impressed. Already, I was fascinated by music and anyone who was involved in it. . . .

When Dad and I got home that afternoon, I told Mother about meeting Mrs. Williams, the hymnwriter. She smiled knowingly and nodded her head. Then she went to the piano bench and found a hymnal that contained one of Clara Tear Williams' compositions.

She explained that Mrs.Williams—a Wesleyan Methodist like us—had written the words, but that the music had been written by Ralph E. Hudson, an Ohio publisher who also was an evangelistic singer.

A few years later, when I was in my teens and began to sing solos, I memorized the hymn that Mother played that day and sang it. It was entitled "Satisfied."

The composer of this hymn, Ralph E. Hudson, was born on July 9, 1843, in Napoleon, Ohio. Following his discharge from the Union Army and the Civil War in 1864, he taught music at Mount Vernon College, Alliance, Ohio, for five years. He became licensed to preach in the Methodist Episcopal Church and was active in evangelistic work. He was also known as a singer, songwriter, and compiler, establishing his own publishing company at Alliance, Ohio. A strong prohibitionist, Hudson wrote several temperance songs and published *The Temperance Songster*, in 1886. Several of his hymnal collections include *Salvation Echoes* (1882), *Gems of Gospel Song* (1884), *Songs of Peace, Love and Joy* (1885), and *Songs of the Ransomed* (1887), all of which were later combined into one volume, titled *Quartette*.

Other gospel hymns for which Ralph Hudson has supplied music include: "Blessed Be the Name," "At the Cross," "A Glorious Church," and "I'll Live for Him" (words only).

Clara Tear Williams' text with Ralph Hudson's music appeared in the first printing of *Gems of Gospel Song* (1881), compiled by E. A. Hoffman, J. H. Tenney, and Ralph E. Hudson. It is still widely sung today.

* * *

"Three things make us happy and content: the seeing eye, the hearing ear, and the responsive heart."

Missionary Digest

"Have your heart right with Christ, and He will visit you often, and so turn weekdays into Sundays, meals into sacraments, homes into temples, and earth into heaven."

Charles Haddon Spurgeon

235

> "I have tasted heaven's manna,
> And I want no other bread.
> In green pastures I am dwelling,
> And my hung'ring soul is fed.
>
> "At the living fount of waters,
> I have quenched my thirst for aye.
> I am living in God's glory,
> And my sins are washed away."
> Avis B. Christiansen

76 Saved by Grace

Fanny J. Crosby, 1820-1915

George C. Stebbins, 1846-1945

1. Some day the sil - ver cord will break, And I no more as now shall sing;
2. Some day my earth- ly house will fall— I can-not tell how soon 'twill be;
3. Some day, when fades the gold-en sun Be-neath the ros - y - tint - ed west,
4. Some day— till then I'll watch and wait, My lamp all trimmed and burn-ing bright,

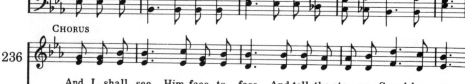

But O the joy when I shall wake With-in the pal-ace of the King!
But this I know— my All in All Has now a place in heav'n for me.
My bless-ed Lord will say, "Well done!" And I shall en-ter in - to rest.
That when my Sav - ior opes the gate, My soul to Him may take its flight.

CHORUS

236

And I shall see Him face to face, And tell the sto-ry— Saved by grace;

And I shall see Him face to face, And tell the sto-ry— Saved by grace.

Arr. © Copyright 1968 by Singspiration, Inc. All rights reserved. Used by permission.

Saved by Grace

Author—Fanny J. Crosby, 1820-1915
Composer—George C. Stebbins, 1846-1945

As for me, I will behold Thy face in righteousness: I shall be satisfied when I awake with Thy likeness.

Psalm 17:15

When one reflects on the phenomenal rise of the evangelical movement in the latter quarter of the nineteenth and the early years of the twentieth centuries, three spiritual stalwarts stand out as the most influential: Evangelist Dwight L. Moody, musician Ira D. Sankey, and hymn writer Fanny J. Crosby. In his later years, Sankey himself once remarked that the success of the Moody-Sankey evangelistic campaigns was due, more than any other human factor, to the use of Fanny Crosby's hymns.

In the period of 1870 to her death in 1915, it is estimated that Fanny Crosby wrote between 8,000 and 9,000 gospel hymn texts, more than any other, known hymn writer. The majority of her lasting favorites were written in her mid-life during the decade of the 1870's. These include such popular hymns still found in our hymnals as "Safe in the Arms of Jesus," "Blessed Assurance," "Pass Me Not, O Gentle Savior," "Jesus, Keep Me Near the Cross," "I Am Thine, O Lord," "All the Way My Savior Leads Me," "Close to Thee," "Praise Him, Praise Him!" "To God Be the Glory," and "Rescue the Perishing." Fanny Crosby's favorite motto was, "I think life is not too long, and therefore I determine that many people will read a song who would not read a sermon."

"Saved by Grace" was one of the choice, later hymns written by Fanny Crosby, in 1891, when she was seventy-one years of age. It became one of the most widely used hymns, during the closing years of the Moody-Sankey evangelistic ministry. It was prompted by a tract, read to Fanny Crosby containing the final message of a pastor friend, who had recently died. The statement which greatly moved the aging, blind poetess was: "If each of us is faithful to the grace which is given us by Christ, that same grace which teaches us how to live will also teach us how to die."

Fanny Crosby completed the poem in a matter of minutes under a great sense of "divine inspiration." She titled her new poem "Some Day" and often referred to it as her "heart's song." After completing the poem, Fanny sent it to her publisher, the Biglow-Main Company, and received her customary two-dollar check. The publisher put the poem in the files and nothing more was heard of it for the next three years.

It was the summer of 1894, and Fanny Crosby was attending the Christian Worker's Conference in Northfield, Massachusetts, a ministry that Mr. Moody had established in 1879. When it was learned that the noted poetess, Fanny Crosby, was on the grounds, there was a request for her to address the group. At first she firmly declined, saying that she could not speak to such an array of talent. Finally, however, she relented and, in the midst of her remarks, quoted her "heart's song"—the poem "Some Day." When she finished there was not a dry eye in the auditorium.

That evening, Ira Sankey asked Fanny where and when she had written those beautiful words. She told him that she had submitted it to the Biglow and Main Publishers, three years earlier, but that no one had seen fit to set it to music. She further stated that she had now decided to stow it away in her memory, to use when she was invited to speak at occasions such as today, and added, "I don't intend to let any of you singers have it either," meaning that she did not want it set to music, lest it become too well-known and less desirable for her own individual speaking use. However, a reporter of the *London Christian Paper* had been in attendance at the meeting and was much impressed with Fanny Crosby's poem. Not knowing of her desire to keep the poem exclusive, he had taken the words in shorthand, and soon it was printed in his English periodical. Shortly, Ira Sankey saw the verses in print. He contacted George Stebbins and showed him the verses that Fanny had quoted at the Bible conference meeting. Evidently, Mr. Sankey felt at liberty to ask Stebbins to compose music for the text, since it was now in print. A short time later, Mr. Stebbins completed the appropriate music and also added the chorus to the stanzas.

"Saved by Grace" became one of the personal favorites of both Moody and Sankey, during this latter period of their ministry, and they used the song at nearly every service. It is stated that a typical scene at one of these meetings was the sight of "old Moody" sitting on the platform with a far-off look in his eyes, while tears ran copiously down his ruddy, whiskered cheeks, whenever the song was sung. Mr. Moody loved to hear a large audience sing the song, especially if the hymn could be divided between the choir and the audience, with the choir singing the phrase "and I shall see Him face to face" and the audience responding with "and tell the story, saved by grace."

Then on the morning of August 13, 1908, as Ira Sankey drifted off into a coma, it is reported that he did so, singing these lines:

Some day the silver cord will break, and I no more as now shall sing,
But, oh, the joy when I shall wake within the palace of the King.

By nightfall of that day, Ira D. Sankey experienced the truth of the last song he ever sang.

George Cole Stebbins is another influential name in the development of the early gospel song movement. He served as a respected music director of several, large Baptist churches in the East, and later he became closely involved with such evangelists as D. L. Moody, George F. Pentecost, and Major Whittle. After the tragic death of Philip P. Bliss, in 1876, Stebbins, along with James McGranahan, assisted Ira Sankey in the task of editing and completing the 3rd, 4th, 5th, and 6th editions of the important *Gospel Hymn* series.

Fanny Crosby developed a very close relationship with George Stebbins, and the two collaborated on many other songs, including the familiar invitation hymn, "Jesus Is Calling." Fanny often said that she valued

Stebbins as one of her most devout and precious friends. "If ever there was a man of high honor and culture of character, it is Mr. Stebbins. He has filled up every nook of my life with his goodness."

George Stebbins, too, thought highly of Fanny Crosby. In his autobiography of 1924, he wrote, "There was probably no writer in her day who appealed more to the valued experiences of the Christian life or who expressed, more sympathetically, the deep longings of the heart than did Fanny Crosby."

George Stebbins is also the composer of: "Have Thine Own Way, Lord" (No. 32), "Ye Must Be Born Again" (No. 101), "There Is a Green Hill Far Away" (*101 Hymn Stories*, No. 96), "Jesus, I Come," "Take Time to Be Holy," "Savior, Breathe an Evening Blessing," and many others.

The following are a few scattered highlights in the life of Fanny Crosby, often called the "Queen of Gospel Hymnody:"

Born in Southeast, New York, on March 24, 1820, she died in Bridgeport, Connecticut on February 12, 1915, having lived ninety-five years.

Blinded when six weeks old through an improper medical treatment. She was able, however, to distinguish between day and night. She never considered blindness a handicap but rather a blessing and always insisted that blind people can accomplish almost everything sighted persons can.

Lived a normal, happy childhood. She wrote, "I could climb a tree like a squirrel and ride a horse bareback."

239

Early in life, she began memorizing the Bible and eventually could repeat, by rote, the entire Pentateuch, all four Gospels, many of the Psalms, all of Proverbs, as well as the entire books of Ruth and Song of Solomon. She stated at the close of her life, "The Holy Book has nurtured my entire life."

Spent twelve years as a pupil in the New York Institution for the Blind and served as a teacher there from 1847-1858, teaching language and history.

Known for her musical abilities as well as a talent for writing poetry. She had a fine soprano voice as well as being accomplished in playing the guitar, harp, piano, and organ. Was also well-versed in the great classics of music. Wrote some tunes for her texts but generally did not want them used, for she felt that they were too complicated for ordinary people to sing.

Married a blind musician and teacher from the school, Alexander Van Alstyne, in 1858. Very little is told of this marital relationship or of Mr. Van Alstyne other than that he was known as a very capable organist in the New York area. The Van Alstynes had a child born the following year, who evidently died in early infancy. This event was something that Fanny Crosby would never discuss with anyone throughout her life.

Fanny Crosby was very small in appearance, less than five feet tall, and she weighed no more than one hundred pounds. She was said to have been a physically unattractive person—a long face, prominent front teeth with a gap between them, thick, wavy hair parted in the middle and pulled backward in curls that hung to the shoulders, and always the dark, rectangular glasses obscuring her sightless eyes. Yet, when she spoke, it is said that there was an unusual charisma about her, as her face lit up with an expression that gave her great charm and attractiveness.

Though always devout and religious from childhood, on November 20, 1850, Fanny Crosby had a dramatic conversion experience at a Methodist revival meeting. "My very soul was flooded with celestial light. . . for the first time I realized that I had been trying to hold the world in one hand and the Lord in the other." Years later, when speaking of her November conversion experience, she said: "The Lord planted a star in my life and no cloud has ever obscured its light."

Though she had written a great deal of poetry as well as a number of secular songs in her early life, it was not until 1865 that Fanny Crosby wrote her first gospel song, through the encouragement of William B. Bradbury, one of the most prolific hymn writers of that period. From that time on, Fanny felt that writing gospel hymn texts was her particular mission in life.

In addition to being a hymnwriter, Fanny Crosby thought of herself as a home mission worker, generally spending several days each week in the missions of New York's bowery district. She always referred to these derelicts as "her boys." Of her mission work, she said, "It is the most wonderful work in the world, and it gives such an opportunity for love. That is all people want—love."

240

Fanny Crosby was always eager to hear any reports regarding personal conversions as a result of the use of her hymns. It was her continual prayer that God would allow her to be the means of leading a million souls to Christ during her lifetime.

"Aunt Fanny" always had a special love for children, and even in her old age when asked to speak in a church service, she generally included a special children's sermon.

Though partial to the Methodist Church, Fanny Crosby was a friend of all believers who "loved Jesus and accepted the Scriptures." She frequently attended the Plymouth Congregational Church in Brooklyn to hear Henry Ward Beecher, her favorite preacher. She also liked to visit the Fifth Avenue Presbyterian Church and the Trinity Episcopal Church, especially when the dynamic Phillips Brooks was guest speaker.

Fanny Crosby was considered to be a very jovial person by those who knew her, noted for her quick wit and humor. Her sermons and speeches were characterized with funny stories and whimsical anecdotes. She often stated that the best way to chide or to criticize was through making people laugh at themselves.

In her later years, Fanny Crosby was in great demand as a speaker and guest lecturer throughout the country. She generally traveled alone for these engagements. A typical introduction of her was with such titles as "the Protestant saint," and "the most wonderful person living."

Other hymns by Fanny Crosby include: "All the Way My Savior Leads Me" (*101 Hymn Stories*, No. 5), "Blessed Assurance" (*ibid.*, No. 11), "My Savior First of All" (*ibid.*, No. 60), and "Rescue the Perishing" (*ibid.*, No. 76).

* * *

"Grace is but glory begun, and glory is but grace perfected."
Jonathan Edwards

I MET THE MASTER FACE TO FACE

"I had walked life's path with an easy tread
Had followed where comfort and pleasure led;
And then one day in a quiet place
I met the Master, face to face.

"With station and rank and wealth for a goal
Much thought for the body, but none for the soul;
I had thought to win in life's mad race,
When I met the Master, face to face.

"I had built my castles and reared them high,
Till their towers pierced the blue of the sky,
I had vowed to rule with an iron mace,
When I met the Master, face to face.

"I met Him and knew Him, and blushed to see
That eyes full of sorrow were turned on me;
And I faltered, and fell at His feet that day,
While all my castles melted away.

"Melted and vanished, and in their place
I saw nought else but my Master's face;
And I cried aloud: "Oh, make me meet
To follow the path of Thy wounded feet."

"And now my thoughts are for the souls of men,
I've lost my life, to find it again.
E'er since that day in a quiet place
I met the Master, face to face."
Author Unknown

241

77 Shepherd of Eager Youth

ITALIAN HYMN

Clement of Alexandria, c. 170-c.220
Trans. by Henry Martyn Dexter, 1821-1890

Felice De Giardini, 1716-1796

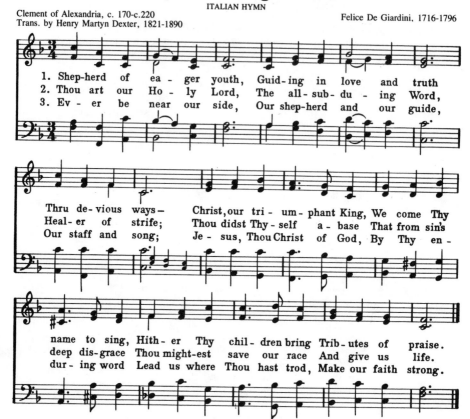

1. Shep-herd of ea - ger youth, Guid-ing in love and truth
2. Thou art our Ho - ly Lord, The all - sub- du - ing Word,
3. Ev - er be near our side, Our shep-herd and our guide,

Thru de-vious ways— Christ, our tri - um - phant King, We come Thy
Heal- er of strife; Thou didst Thy - self a - base That from sin's
Our staff and song; Je - sus, Thou Christ of God, By Thy en -

name to sing, Hith- er Thy chil - dren bring Trib-utes of praise.
deep dis-grace Thou might-est save our race And give us life.
dur - ing word Lead us where Thou hast trod, Make our faith strong.

Shepherd of Eager Youth

Author—Clement of Alexandria, c. 170-c. 220
English Translation—Henry Martyn Dexter, 1821-1890
Composer—Felice de Giardini, 1716-1796
Name of Tune—"Italian Hymn"
Meter—664.6664

Remember now thy Creator in the days of thy youth, while the evil days come not, nor the years draw nigh, when thou shalt say, I have no pleasure in them.

Ecclesiastes 12:1

The inclusion of this hymn is important to any understanding of hymnody since it represents the oldest Christian hymn whose authorship is known. Clement of Alexandria wrote this hymn text in the Greek language some time between A.D. 202 and the time of his death in A.D. 220.

Historical records indicate that the early Christians began using songs with New Testament scriptures and truths, in addition to the existing Jewish Psalms and Canticles, very early in the first century. However, few of these early hymns have been preserved. Typical New Testament expressions included:

The Song of Mary—"The Magnificat"—Luke 1:46-55
The Song of Zacharias—"The Benedictus"—Luke 1:68-79
The Song of Simeon—"The Nunc Dimittis"—Luke 2:29-32
The Song of the Angels—"Gloria in Excelsis Deo"—Luke 2:14

Other portions of New Testament scripture that probably were sung by the early Christians included: Ephesians 5:14, 1 Timothy 3:16, 4:15, 16; 2 Timothy 2:11-13; and Titus 3:4. "Shepherd of Eager Youth" is one of the few first or second-century hymns whose authorship can be determined with any degree of certainty. It is known, therefore, as the oldest of all Christian hymn texts.

Clement of Alexandria was born Titus Flavius Clement in Athens in A.D. 170. He became converted to Christianity under Pantaeus, the founder of the catechetical school of Alexandria. In A.D. 190, Clement succeeded Pantaeus as the director of this school and became known as a distinguished scholar, teacher, and preacher of the gospel. Several of his noted students were Origen, regarded to be one of the outstanding scholars in the early church, and Alexander, later Bishop of Jerusalem. In A.D. 202, Clement fled Alexandria at the beginning of the nine-year persecution of the Christians by Roman Emperor, Septimus Severus. Little is known of Clement's later life except that he died a martyr's death in A.D. 220. Another interesting writing by Clement is a letter, he wrote to a friend, describing the spirit of these early Christians: 243

We cultivate our fields, praising. We sail the seas, humming. Our lives are filled with prayers and praises and Scripture reading before meals and before bed, and even during the night. By this means, we unite ourselves to the heavenly choir.

"Shepherd of Eager Youth" in the original Greek could literally be translated "Tamer of Steeds Unbridled." It was evidently used as a hymn of Christian instruction for new young converts from heathenism, the thought being that it was the church's responsibility to break the wills of the youth and to train them diligently, in order to make them usable for the Kingdom of God. Clement is also known for three books that he wrote entitled *The Tutor*, which contained instructions to new Christians. The first volume relates *How God Trains His Own*; the second deals with *Rules* of Daily Living: and the third volume describes the *True Beauty of the Spirit*. In this book, Clement especially deplores extravagance of dress in both men and women. "Shepherd of Eager Youth" is thought to have been one of two poems that were appended to *The Tutor*, with one of the poems titled "A Hymn to the Savior."

The English translator of this text was a New England, Congregational minister named Henry Martyn Dexter. Dexter was recognized as an able preacher and a careful scholar who devoted much of his life to the early history of Congregationalism. He was a graduate of Yale and Andover Divinity School, and he pastored several churches in the East. Dexter first used the text, in 1846, as part of a sermon based on the theme in Deuteronomy 32:7—"Remember the Days of Old...." It was first published in 1849, in *The Congregationalist*, a publication that Dexter later served as editor for twenty-three years. Its first appearance for congregational usage was in the *Hymns for the Church of Christ* by Hedge and Huntington, published in 1853. Dexter's translation is generally considered to be not too literal or true to the original Greek but rather a very spirited and interesting paraphrase of the hymn's intent and still a very usable text for youth to sing today.

The tune, "Italian Hymn," is generally more familiar with the hymn text "Come, Thou Almighty King," for which it was originally composed by Felice de Giardini, in 1769 (*101 Hymn Stories*, No. 14). This Italian composer was born in Turin, Italy, on April 12, 1716. He moved to London, England, where he became a popular violinist in London's operatic circles. Later, Giardini spent time in Moscow, Russia, as an operatic conductor, and died there, in 1796. In some hymnals this tune is called the "Moscow Tune," presumably for the city in which this composer died.

244

*   *   *

"The bulwark of religious training is vital if the line is to be held against the forces of corruption, crime, and disloyalty. I believe men imbued with spiritual values do not betray their country. I believe that children reared in homes in which morality is taught and lived rarely become delinquents."

J. Edgar Hoover

78 Standing on the Promises

R. Kelso Carter, 1849-1928

R. Kelso Carter, 1849-1928

1. Stand-ing on the prom-is-es of Christ my King, Thru e-ter-nal
2. Stand-ing on the prom-is-es that can-not fail, When the howl-ing
3. Stand-ing on the prom-is-es of Christ the Lord, Bound to Him e-
4. Stand-ing on the prom-is-es I can-not fall, Lis-t'ning ev-'ry

a-ges let His prais-es ring; Glo-ry in the high-est I will
storms of doubt and fear as-sail, By the liv-ing word of God I
ter-nal-ly by love's strong cord, O-ver-com-ing dai-ly with the
mo-ment to the Spir-it's call, Rest-ing in my Sav-ior as my

CHORUS

shout and sing, Stand-ing on the prom-is-es of God. Stand - -
shall pre-vail, Stand-ing on the prom-is-es of God. Stand-ing on the
Spir-it's sword, Stand-ing on the prom-is-es of God.
all in all, Stand-ing on the prom-is-es of God.

ing, stand - - ing, Stand-ing on the
prom-is-es, stand-ing on the prom-is-es, Stand-ing on the

prom-is-es of God my Sav-ior; Stand - - ing,
Stand-ing on the prom-is-es,

245

stand - - ing,   I'm stand-ing on the prom-is-es of   God.
stand-ing on the prom-is-es,

Standing on the Promises

Author and Composer—R. Kelso Carter, 1849-1928

For all the promises of God in Him are yea, and in Him Amen, unto the glory of God by us.
                                                                 2 Corinthians 1:20

A believer's stability for this life as well as his confidence for eternity rests solely on the written promises of God's Word. How meaningful, then, are scriptural promises such as these:

When thou passest through the waters, I will be with thee...Isaiah 43:2

The Lord is nigh unto them that are of a broken heart; and saveth such as be of a contrite spirit. Psalm 34:18

Cast thy burden upon the Lord, and He shall sustain thee. Psalm 55:22

Whereby are given unto us exceeding great and precious promises: that by these ye might be partakers of the divine nature, having escaped the corruption that is in the world through lust. 2 Peter 1:4

It is this reminder of a Christian's daily dependence upon the promises of God that has made this straight-forward, rhythmical gospel hymn a favorite with God's people for the past century.

Russell Kelso Carter was born on November 18, 1849, at Baltimore, Maryland, and died on August 23, 1928 at Catonsville, Maryland. During his student days, he was known as an outstanding athlete. In 1887, he was ordained into the Methodist ministry and became an active leader in the Holiness, camp meeting movement. Throughout his entire life, Carter was known as a most interesting, versatile individual. In addition to being a Methodist minister, he was a professor of chemistry, natural science, civil engineering, and mathematics for a number of years at the Pennsylvania Military Academy. He was also a sheep rancher in California for a period of time, a publisher of a number of textbooks in his various teaching disciplines, as well as the author of several novels, and an assistant in the compilation of the Christian and Missionary Alliance hymnal, *Hymns of the Christian Life* (1891) a hymnal in which he contributed sixty-eight original tunes and fifty-two poems. Then in his later years, he decided to study medicine and become a practicing physician in Baltimore, Maryland.

"Standing on the Promises" was written and composed, in 1886, while Carter was serving as a professor in the Pennsylvania Military Academy, a school in which he had been a member of the first graduating class, in 1867. Phil Kerr, in his book *Music in Evangelism*, suggests that the rhythmic martial tone of the hymn's music possibly reflects Mr. Carter's military academy experience. The hymn was first published in the same year that it was written, 1866, in the hymnal, *Songs of Perfect Love*, compiled by John K. Sweney and Carter. The hymn originally consisted of five stanzas. The third stanza, which is omitted from most of our hymnals, is as follows:

> Standing on the promises I now can see
> Perfect, present cleansing in the blood for me;
> Standing in the liberty where Christ makes free,
> Standing on the promises of God.

This hymn has been widely used in the great evangelistic crusades 247 throughout the past century. It is still included in many evangelical hymnals published today, although there is a growing tendency to replace the original tune with new music considered more appropriate for the text.

* * *

> "Little faith will bring us to heaven,
> But great faith will bring heaven to
> us."
>   Unknown

> "Faith, mighty faith the promise sees
> And rests on that alone;
> Laughs at impossibilities,
> And says it shall be done."
>   Charles Wesley

Still, Still With Thee

CONSOLATION

Harriet B. Stowe, 1812-1896

Felix Mendelssohn, 1809-1847

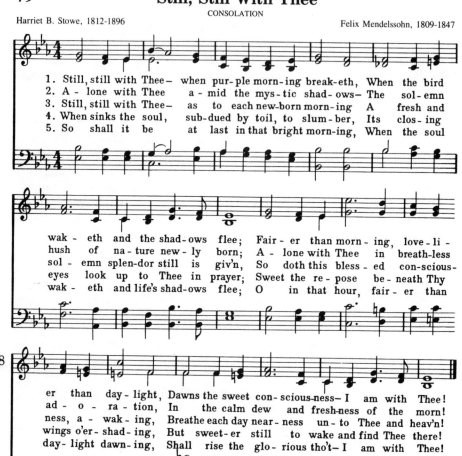

1. Still, still with Thee— when pur-ple morn-ing break-eth, When the bird
2. A - lone with Thee a - mid the mys-tic shad-ows— The sol-emn
3. Still, still with Thee— as to each new-born morn-ing A fresh and
4. When sinks the soul, sub-dued by toil, to slum-ber, Its clos-ing
5. So shall it be at last in that bright morn-ing, When the soul

wak - eth and the shad-ows flee; Fair - er than morn - ing, love-li -
hush of na - ture new - ly born; A - lone with Thee in breath-less
sol - emn splen-dor still is giv'n, So doth this bless - ed con-scious-
eyes look up to Thee in prayer; Sweet the re - pose be - neath Thy
wak - eth and life's shad-ows flee; O in that hour, fair - er than

er than day-light, Dawns the sweet con-scious-ness— I am with Thee!
ad - o - ra-tion, In the calm dew and fresh-ness of the morn!
ness, a - wak-ing, Breathe each day near-ness un - to Thee and heav'n!
wings o'er-shad-ing, But sweet-er still to wake and find Thee there!
day-light dawn-ing, Shall rise the glo-rious tho't— I am with Thee!

Still, Still With Thee

Author—Harriet Beecher Stowe, 1812-1896
Composer—Felix Mendelssohn, 1809-1847
Tune Name—"Consolation"
Meter—11 10. 11 10.
Scripture Reference—Psalm 139:17, 18

> My voice shalt Thou hear in the morning, O Lord; in the morning will I direct my prayer unto Thee, and will look up. Psalm 5:3

Harriet Beecher Stowe was born into the eminent, New England, Congregational Beecher family on June 14, 1812, in Litchfield, Connecticut. Her father was the noted clergyman, Dr. Lyman Beecher, and one of her brothers was the still-more-famous minister, Henry Ward Beecher, often referred to as one of our country's ablest preachers. In 1832, Harriet moved with her family to Cincinnati, Ohio, where her father had become president of Lane Theological Seminary. While here, she and her family often helped the runaway slaves escape to Canada through the underground railroad. In 1836, she married a teacher of languages and biblical literature in the seminary, Professor Calvin E. Stowe. Later, the couple moved to Maine, where Mr. Stowe taught at the Andover Theological Seminary. It was here that Mrs. Stowe published her famous novel, *Uncle Tom's Cabin*. It first appeared, in serial form, in the Washington *National Era* paper, in 1851, and in the following year, it appeared as a complete book, reaching sales of more than a million copies as well as being translated into more than twenty languages. This book has generally been recognized as one of the strong influences that ushered in the Civil War against slavery. Altogether Mrs. Stowe wrote approximately forty books, all mainly concerned with various social conditions and problems of her time. She also had a volume of religious poems published in 1867.

Throughout her life, Mrs. Stowe was known as an avid abolitionist as well as a saintly, godly woman. In 1853, she even traveled to Europe for the purpose of arousing the women there in the fight against world-wide slavery. Harriet dated her conversion experience to her early teen years, after hearing one of her father's sermons. She gives this account of that event:

249

> As soon as my father came home and was seated in his study, I went up to him and fell in his arms, saying, "Father, I have given myself to Jesus, and He has taken me." I never shall forget the expression on his face as he looked down into my earnest childish eyes; it was so sweet, so gentle, and like sunlight breaking out upon a landscape. "Is it so?" he said, holding me silently to his heart, as I felt the hot tears on my head. "Then has a new flower blossomed in the kingdom this day."

In later years, in looking back over many of the difficulties she had experienced in her busy life of raising six children, along with her other pursuits, Harriet wrote, "I thank God there is one thing running through all of them, from the time I was thirteen years old, and that is the intense unwavering sense of Christ's educating, guiding presence, and care."

In 1855, Harriet was introduced as a hymn writer when her brother, Henry Ward Beecher, included three of her poems in his new hymnal, *Plymouth Collection of Hymns and Tunes*. "Still, Still With Thee" was originally titled "Resting in God" and was written by Mrs. Stowe two years earlier, while meditating on Psalm 139:17, 18, especially on the phrase "When I awake, I am still with Thee." It is said that Mrs. Stowe generally arose at four-thirty in the morning to enjoy the coming of dawn, the singing of the birds, and the over-shadowing presence of her God. It is commonly agreed by hymnists today, that for sheer poetic beauty, there is probably not a single American lyric that can excel "Still, Still With Thee." It is Mrs. Stowe's only hymn text that has survived to the present time, however. Harriet Beecher Stowe died in Hartford, Connecticut, on July 1, 1896.

The tune for this text, "Consolation," is based on Melody Number Three, Book Two of *Songs Without Words* by Felix Mendelssohn. Mendelssohn, considered to be one of the master composers of all time, was born a Jew in Hamburg, Germany, on February 3, 1809. At the age of eleven, he professed Christianity. Throughout his life, he was a great admirer of J. S. Bach. In 1829, he conducted a performance of Bach's *St. Matthew Passion*, the first performance of this monumental work since Bach's death in 1750. Mendelssohn was a prolific composer of musical works throughout his brief lifetime. These compositions included symphonies, overtures, chamber music, concertos, organ, piano, and vocal works as well as two popular oratorios, the *St. Paul* and the *Elijah*. Felix Mendelssohn is also credited with developing modern conducting techniques and was himself an influential director, particularly of large festivals. Mendelssohn also founded the well-known Leipzig Conservatory of Music, which is still highly respected in Germany and throughout the world.

Felix Mendelssohn has contributed the music for the Christmas carol "Hark! the Herald Angels Sing" (No. 31) and the harmonization of the "Munich" tune for the hymn "O Word of God Incarnate" (*101 Hymn Stories*, No. 71).

*   *   *

"Grace—the outward expression of the inward harmony of the soul"

Hazlitt

"The grace of the spirit comes only from heaven, and lights up the whole bodily presence."

Charles Haddon Spurgeon

80 Surely Goodness and Mercy

John W. Peterson, 1921-
Alfred B. Smith, 1916-

John W. Peterson, 1921-
Alfred B. Smith, 1916-

1. A pil-grim was I, and a-wan-d'ring, In the cold night of
2. He re-stor-eth my soul when I'm wea-ry, He giv-eth me
3. When I walk thru the dark lone-some val-ley, My Sav-ior will

sin I did roam, When Je-sus the kind Shep-herd found me, And
strength day by day; He leads me be-side the still wa-ters, He
walk with me there; And safe-ly His great hand will lead me To the

CHORUS

now I am on my way home.
guards me each step of the way. Sure-ly good-ness and mer-cy shall
man-sions He's gone to pre-pare.

251

fol-low me All the days, all the days of my life; Sure-ly good-ness

and mer-cy shall fol-low me All the days, all the days of my life.

May be omitted until final chorus:

And I shall dwell in the house of the Lord for-ev-er, And I shall feast at the

ta-ble spread for me; Sure-ly good-ness and mer-cy shall fol-low me

All the days, all the days of my life, All the days, all the days of my life.

© Copyright 1958 by Singspiration, Inc. All rights reserved. Used by permission.

Surely Goodness and Mercy

252

Authors and Composers—John W. Peterson, 1921-
Alfred B. Smith, 1916-
Scripture Reference—Psalm 23

> Hear me, O Lord; for Thy lovingkindness is good. Turn unto me according to the
> multitude of Thy tender mercies. Psalm 69:16

The beloved words of Psalm 23 have undoubtedly provided greater comfort and encouragement to God's people through the years than any other portion of Scripture. In times of deep need, how these tender words from the Psalmist David minister so meaningfully to our wounded spirits. This Psalm has also formed the textual basis for more sacred music than any other scriptural setting. A contemporary version of this text, written in 1958 by John W. Peterson and Alfred B. Smith, has since become a favorite in our evangelical hymnals.

Charles Haddon Spurgeon, known as the "Prince of Preachers" of the past century, labored for more than twenty years on his unrivaled commentary of the Psalms, a seven-volume work entitled *The Treasury of David*. "Only those who have meditated profoundly upon the Psalms," wrote Spurgeon, "can have any adequate conception of the wealth they contain." Here are just a few of the comments that Mr. Spurgeon made about the 23rd Psalm:

No man has a right to consider himself the Lord's sheep, unless his nature has been renewed, for the scriptural description of unconverted men does not picture them as sheep, but as wolves or goats. A sheep is an object of property, not a wild animal. It is well to know, as certainly as David did, that we belong to the Lord. There is a tone of confidence about this sentence—The Lord is my Shepherd. The sweetest word of the whole is that monosyllable, ''my.'' He does not say, ''The Lord is the shepherd of the world at large, and leadeth forth the multitude as his flock.'' If He is a shepherd to no one else, He is a shepherd to me. He cares for me, watches over me, and preserves me. The words are in the present tense. Whatever be the believer's position, he is even now under the pastoral care of Jehovah. (In one-volume edition entitled *Spurgeon on the Psalms*, page 107. Kregel Publications.)

John W. Peterson recalls the events associated with the writing of this hymn:

One day while improvising at the piano in my Montrose, Pennsylvania studio, Albert B. Smith, with whom I was associated at the time, walked in. For no particular reason that I can remember, we started to develop a new song. I would come up with a thought, then Al. In a short time ''Surely Goodness and Mercy'' was born. I had never worked with another writer in such a manner to compose a song. Later Al and I wrote two or three other numbers like that.

Alfred B. Smith remembers more about the initial inspiration for the song. He adds this humorous touch:

253

It was written after receiving a letter from one of the descendants of P. P. Bliss telling of Bliss's first, country school teacher, named Miss Murphy, whom he dearly loved. It told of her teaching the class (before they could read or write) to memorize the 23rd Psalm. When the part ''surely goodness and mercy'' was reached, little Philip thought it said ''surely good Miss Murphy shall follow me all the days of my life.'' This little incident focused our thoughts on the phrase which became the heart and title of the song.

The name of John Willard Peterson has become especially well-known in evangelical circles, since the days of World War II. He is often called the ''dean of contemporary gospel song writers.'' Mr. Peterson was born in Lindsborg, Kansas, on November 1, 1921, into a musical Swedish family. During World War II, he served in the Air Force as a pilot in Asia. Following the war, he received his musical training at the Moody Bible Institute and the American Conservatory of Music. He has since received honorary doctorate degrees from the Western Conservative Baptist Seminary and from John Brown University, in recognition of his contributions to gospel music. John Peterson has composed more than 1200 gospel songs and has supplied church choirs with more than twenty-five cantatas and musicals, which have sold in excess of six million copies.

Mr. Peterson is also the composer of the missionary hymn ''So Send

I You" (*101 Hymn Stories*, No. 82). Other John Peterson favorites now found in many contemporary hymnals include: "All Glory to Jesus," "Come, Holy Spirit," "Jesus Is Coming Again," "God's Final Call," "No One Understands Like Jesus," "Shepherd of Love," "Over the Sunset Mountains," "It Took a Miracle," "Heaven Came Down," and "Spring of Living Water."

Alfred Barney Smith, the co-author and composer of this hymn, is also a well-known name in the field of gospel hymnody. Mr. Smith was born on November 8, 1916, at Midland Park, New Jersey. His education included the Moody Bible Institute and later the Juilliard School of Music. In 1943, he was graduated from Wheaton College. While a student at Wheaton, he served as the concertmaster of the Wheaton College Symphony Orchestra. Later, Smith founded and served as president of the Singspiration Publishing Company until 1962, editing and publishing many gospel songbook collections and hymnals, including the popular *Inspiring Hymns*. In 1972, Mr. Smith began another music company, the Encore Publications, editing another fine evangelical hymnal, *Living Hymns*. Altogether, Alfred B. Smith has written approximately 500 gospel songs and choruses, including such favorites as "For God So Loved the World" and "With Eternity's Values in View."

254 Composers like John W. Peterson and Alfred B. Smith are often asked their method of writing songs. Do the lyrics come first or the music? Do composers generally write in the heat of inspiration or is the song the result of much tedious work? Both of these men state that there does not seem to be any set pattern or iron-clad rule for writing gospel music. Songs come at different times and in all different ways—some quickly while others are the result of much hard work. We give thanks for the combined talents of these two fine gospel song writers and their delightful setting of the beloved 23rd Psalm.

*   *   *

"The Lord is my Shepherd, He makes me repose
Where the pastures in beauty are growing;
He leads me afar from the world and its woes,
Where in peace the still waters are flowing."
John Knox

81 Sweet By and By

Sanford F. Bennett, 1836-1898

Joseph P. Webster, 1819-1875

1. There's a land that is fair-er than day, And by faith we can
2. We shall sing on that beau-ti-ful shore The me-lo-di-ous
3. To our boun-ti-ful Fa-ther a-bove We will of-fer our

see it a-far, For the Fa-ther waits o-ver the way To pre-
songs of the blest; And our spir-its shall sor-row no more— Not a
trib-ute of praise, For the glo-ri-ous gift of His love And the

CHORUS

pare us a dwell-ing-place there.
sigh for the bless-ing of rest.
bless-ings that hal-low our days.

In the sweet by and
In the sweet

255

by, We shall meet on that beau-ti-ful shore; In the
by and by, by and by,

sweet by and by, We shall meet on that beau-ti-ful shore.
In the sweet by and by,

Sweet By and By

Author—Sanford F. Bennett, 1836-1898
Composer—Joseph P. Webster, 1819-1875

> In my Father's house are many mansions: if it were not so, I would have told you.
> I go to prepare a place for you. And if I go and prepare a place for you, I will come
> again, and receive you unto myself; that where I am, there ye may be also.John 14:2, 3

This simple gospel hymn has been a sentimental favorite with many of
God's people, especially as a comforting funeral hymn, since it first appeared, in 1868, in a hymnal entitled *The Signet Ring, a New Collection
of Music and Hymns, Composed for Sabbath Schools*, compiled by Joseph
P. Webster.

Following the close of the Civil War, Sanford Bennett, the author,
returned to Elkhorn, Wisconsin, where he became the proprietor of the
local drugstore, while also studying medicine. Joseph Webster, the
composer, was a music teacher and was recognized as the town's leading
musician. These two gentlemen met often in Bennett's drugstore for friendly
discussions. Bennett tells this story of how Webster, violin under his arm,
dropped in to see him one quiet winter afternoon:

> Mr. Webster, like many musicians, was of an exceeding nervous and sensitive
> nature, and subject to periods of depression, in which he looked upon the dark
> side of all things in life. I had learned his peculiarities so well, that on meeting
> him I could tell at a glance if he was melancholy, and had found that I could
> rouse him by giving him a new song on which to work.

> He came into my place of business, walked down to the stove, and turned
> his back on me without speaking. I was at my desk writing. Turning to him
> I said, "Webster, what is the matter now?" "It's no matter," he replied, "it
> will be all right by and by." The idea came to me like a flash of sunlight,
> and I replied, "The Sweet By and By! Why would not that make a good hymn?"
> "Maybe it would," said he indifferently. Turning to my desk, I penned the
> words as fast as I could write. I handed the words to Webster. As he read,
> his eyes kindled, and stepping to the desk, he began writing the notes. Taking
> his violin, he played the melody and then jotted down the notes of the chorus.
> It was not over thirty minutes from the time I took my pen to write the words
> before two friends with Webster and myself were singing the hymn.

Sanford Fillmore Bennett had a varied and illustrious career. He was
born at Eden, New York, on June 21, 1836, and died on June 12, 1898,
in Richmond, Indiana. He was converted at a Methodist revival meeting,
but later in life he declared himself a Universalist. Bennett was educated

at the University of Michigan and later served briefly as the superintendent of schools in Richmond, Illinois, before moving to Elkhorn, Wisconsin, to become the associate editor of a weekly newspaper, *The Independent*. During the Civil War Bennett served as a second lieutenant in the Fortieth Wisconsin Volunteers. It was after the war that he returned to Elkhorn, became proprietor of the local drugstore, and studied medicine at the Rush Medical College, from which he graduated, in 1874. Dr. Bennett practiced medicine for the next twenty-two years. Throughout his lifetime, he also wrote a considerable amount of both prose and verse, with his first poems appearing in the *Waukegan Gazette* in the early 1850's. "Sweet By and By" is Bennett's only hymn text still in use, however.

Joseph Philbrick Webster was recognized as a talented musician in his day. He studied music with Lowell Mason in Boston, Massachusetts, and spent several years in New York and Connecticut, teaching music and giving concerts. He was said to have been proficient in playing the flute, violin, and piano. Because of his strong anti-slavery convictions, Webster moved to Elkhorn, Wisconsin, shortly before the outbreak of the war. He is credited with more than one thousand musical compositions, with his most popular song being "Lorena," a secular number. Webster was the compiler of a Sunday school hymnal, *The Signet Ring*, in which "Sweet By and By" first appeared, in 1868. Joseph P. Webster died on January 18, 1875, at the age of fifty-six.

Today visitors to Elkhorn, Wisconsin, may visit the Webster House and see the authentic, nineteenth-century home of the composer of this hymn and view the violin that was first used to play the melody of this beloved gospel hymn.

*   *   *

"I have been dying for twenty years, now I am going to live."
James Drummond Burns: *His Last Words*

"To look upon the soul as going on from strength to strength, to consider that it is to shine forever with new accessions of glory, and brighten to all eternity; that it will be still adding virtue to virtue, and knowledge to knowledge—carries in it something wonderfully agreeable to that ambition which is natural to the mind of men."
Joseph Addison

82   Sweet Hour of Prayer

SWEET HOUR

William W. Walford, 1772-1850   William B. Bradbury, 1816-1868

1. Sweet hour of prayer, sweet hour of prayer, That calls me from a world of care
2. Sweet hour of prayer, sweet hour of prayer, Thy wings shall my pe - ti - tion bear
3. Sweet hour of prayer, sweet hour of prayer, May I thy con - so - la - tion share,

Fine

And bids me at my Fa-ther's throne Make all my wants and wish- es known!
To Him whose truth and faith-ful-ness En- gage the wait - ing soul to bless;
Till from Mount Pis-gah's loft - y height I view my home and take my flight:

D.S.– And oft es- caped the tempt-er's snare By thy re - turn, sweet hour of prayer.
D.S.– I'll cast on Him my ev - 'ry care, And wait for thee, sweet hour of prayer.
D.S.– And shout, while pass-ing thru the air, "Fare-well, fare-well, sweet hour of prayer!"

D.S.

258

In sea-sons of dis-tress and grief My soul has oft - en found re- lief,
And since He bids me seek His face, Be- lieve His Word and trust His grace,
This robe of flesh I'll drop, and rise To seize the ev - er - last- ing prize,

Sweet Hour of Prayer

Author—William W. Walford, 1772-1850
Composer—William B. Bradbury, 1816-1868
Tune Name—"Sweet Hour"
Meter—88.88 Doubled

> Praying always with all prayer and supplication in the Spirit, and watching thereunto with all perseverance and supplication for all saints.   Ephesians 6:18

> "Between the humble and contrite heart and the majesty of heaven there are no barriers; the only password is prayer."   Hosea Ballou

> "And Satan trembles when he sees the weakest saint upon his knees."   William Cowper

Sweet Hour of Prayer

"Prayers are heard in heaven very much in proportion to our faith. Little faith will get very great mercies, but great faith still greater."

Charles Haddon Spurgeon

Through the ages, devout believers have recognized the necessity of maintaining intimate relations with God through His ordained channel of prayer. It has often been said that prayer is as basic to spiritual life as breathing is to our natural lives. Or, as others have stated: "Prayer is exhaling the spirit of man and inhaling the Spirit of God" (Edwin Keith). And, "Prayer is not merely an occasional impulse to which we respond when we are in trouble; prayer is a life attitude" (Walter A. Mueller, *The ABC's of Prayer*).

For more than a century "Sweet Hour of Prayer" has been one of our most familiar and beloved hymns, reminding Christians of the importance of daily communion with God. The text is thought to have been written, in 1842, by William W. Walford, an obscure and blind lay preacher and owner of a small trinket shop in the village of Coleshill, Warwickshire, England. The traditional account generally associated with the origin of this hymn is that one day a Coleshill Congregational clergyman, Thomas Salmon, stopped at Walford's shop for a visit with his blind friend. William Walford had just completed a new poem on the subject of prayer and is said to have requested Salmon to notate it for him. Then, three years later, Salmon visited the United States and showed this poem to the editor of the *New York Observer*. The poem first appeared in the September 13, 1845 issue. It was here that Salmon described the poem as the product of a blind, fellow-clergyman named Walford in Warwickshire, England. The text first occurred in a hymnal, in 1859, in a Baptist edition of *Church Melodies*, compiled by Thomas Hastings and Robert Turnbull.

The tune, "Sweet Hour," was composed for this text by the noted American composer of early gospel music, William Batchelder Bradbury, in 1861. This was the year that the text and Bradbury's tune first appeared together in a hymnal collection, the *Golden Chain*. Lifted on the wings of this melody, the prayer poem was soon sung around the world.

William B. Bradbury has contributed the music to many of our gospel hymns still widely sung today. These include "Depth of Mercy" (No. 20), "Even Me" (No. 23), and "The Solid Rock" (No. 87) as well as "He Leadeth Me" (*101 Hymn Stories*, No. 28), "Jesus Loves Me" (*ibid.*, No. 47), and "Just As I Am" (*ibid.*, No. 52).

In recent years there has been uncertainty raised about the authorship of this text. William J. Reynolds in his book *Hymns of Our Faith*, 1964, has done considerable research and has been unable to establish with certainty that a blind William W. Walford ever lived in Coleshill, England at the time when this text was written. Mr. Reynolds believes that the real author was a Rev. William Walford, a Congregational minister, who was president of the Homerton Academy in England and the author of several books, including one entitled *The Manner of Prayer*, the text of which has many similarities to the hymn's text. Reynolds raises the possibility that Thomas Salmon in his enthusiasm for the text could have exaggerated some of his data when presenting the poem to the editor of the *New York Observer* publication. Mr. Reynolds further suggests that it is possible that the "blind" William W. Walford of Coleshill and the Rev. Walford of Homerton could be one and the same individual.

Regardless of the identity of the author of this text, we must conclude that "Sweet Hour of Prayer" has been greatly used of God for many years to challenge believers with this basic truth—whenever we spend time in communion with God, it becomes a sweet and meaningful hour in our lives.

* * *

"There is no sweeter time than this, the hour we spend with Jesus;
To taste with Him, eternal bliss, the hour we spend with Jesus."

Unknown

"O Thou, by whom we come to God, the life, the truth, the way
The path of prayer Thyself has trod, Lord, teach us how to pray."

James Montgomery

260 THE VOID BETWEEN INTENT AND PERFORMANCE
"We sing 'Sweet Hour of Prayer'—
and content ourselves with a few minutes of prayer
each day, if even that much.
We sing 'Onward, Christian Soldiers'—
and wait to be pushed into the Lord's service.
We sing 'O For a Thousand Tongues'—
without rightly using the tongue we have.
We sing 'Blest Be the Tie That Binds'—
and let the least little offense sever it.
We sing 'Serve the Lord With Gladness'—
and gripe about all we have to do.
We sing 'I Love to Tell the Story'—
and never mention it all year to our friends and
associates.
We sing 'Cast Thy Burden on the Lord'—
and worry ourselves into nervous breakdowns.
We sing 'The Whole Wide World for Jesus'—
and never invite our next-door neighbors to church.
We sing 'Throw Out the Life Line'—
and content ourselves with throwing out a fishing line
on Sunday."

Unknown

83   Sweet Peace, the Gift of God's Love

Peter P. Bilhorn, 1865-1936   Peter P. Bilhorn, 1865-1936

1. There comes to my heart one sweet strain, A glad and a joy-ous re-frain;
2. Thru Christ on the cross peace was made, My debt by His death was all paid;
3. When Je-sus as Lord I had crowned, My heart with this peace did a-bound;
4. In Je-sus for peace I a-bide, And as I keep close to His side,

I sing it a-gain and a-gain— Sweet peace, the gift of God's love.
No oth-er foun-da-tion is laid For peace, the gift of God's love.
In Him the rich bless-ing I found— Sweet peace, the gift of God's love.
There's noth-ing but peace doth be-tide— Sweet peace, the gift of God's love.

CHORUS

Peace, peace, sweet peace! Won-der-ful gift from a-bove! (a-bove!) O

won-der-ful, won-der-ful peace! Sweet peace, the gift of God's love!

261

Sweet Peace, the Gift of God's Love

Author and Composer—Peter P. Bilhorn, 1865-1936

Great peace have they which love Thy law; and nothing shall offend them.
Psalm 119:165

The quest for inner calm and peace has been a universal struggle for mankind throughout the ages. Even for those who profess to be followers of the "Prince of Peace," it is difficult to realize with consistency that "God's ways are always higher than our ways and His thoughts than our thoughts." It becomes normal living much of the time to experience undue anxiety about our plans without ever consulting Him for His perfect will. If only we could learn this simple lesson:

'Tis far, far better to let Him choose the way that we should take,
If only we thus leave our life with Him, He will guide without mistake.

Peter P. Bilhorn, noted gospel musician and soul-winner, relates the following account concerning the writing of this hymn:

I had been invited to sing one afternoon in the Ocean Grove, New Jersey Camp-meeting. I sang one of my early songs, "I Will Sing the Wondrous Story." At the close of the service a friend, Mrs. Ida Stoddard Demerast, said, "Mr. Bilhorn, I wish you would write a song to suit my voice as well as 'I Will Sing the Wondrous Story' seems to suit your voice." I asked, "What shall it be?" She replied, "Oh, any sweet piece," which suggested the title and which I penciled in my notebook. In the twilight hour, at the home of S. T. Gordon, while seated at the piano, the music came to me, but I had no words except the title.

The following winter, a call came from D. L. Moody, asking me to join Major Whittle in a meeting in the State of Iowa. We left Chicago together. When nearing Wheaton, Illinois, the engine gave a shrill whistle of warning, which always gives a person a feeling of apprehension of someone in danger. In this case our fears were not unfounded. The train came to a sudden stop and backed up a distance of about three hundred feet. We found, lying in a ditch, beside a telegraph pole, the mangled body of an old lady, which they carried across the street into a cottage, leaving a pool of blood where she had lain. Major Whittle, placing one hand on my shoulder said, "Do you know that is all Jesus Christ left on this earth? His body rose for our justification, but His blood was left to atone for our sins!" I replied, "Yes, Major, and that is what gives me sweet peace, just to know for certain that His blood atones for my sins." When we had returned to the train, the thought of the song came to me again and the words were written.

Peter P. Bilhorn was born in Mendota, Illinois, in 1865. With the death of his father, Peter was forced to leave school at the age of eight to help support his mother and family. At the age of fifteen, he moved with his family to Chicago, where his voice became a great attraction in German concert halls and among his worldly comrades in the taverns. At the age of twenty, Peter was converted to Christ at one of the meetings conducted by Dr. George Pentecost and musician George Stebbins. Following his conversion, Bilhorn was greatly used of God in various forms of Christian service, including personal soul-winning. It is estimated that he wrote approximately 2,000 gospel songs. (See "I Will Sing the Wondrous Story"

Sweet Peace, the Gift of God's Love

101 Hymn Stories, No. 39). Bilhorn's evangelistic ministry carried him into all the states of the union and to Great Britain as well as to other foreign countries. He became widely-known for his evangelistic song-leading ability and preceded Homer Rodeheaver as Billy Sunday's song leader, prior to 1908. The Bilhorn Publishing Company and the folding organ company which he started, also met with considerable success. Peter Bilhorn's published works include: *Crowning Glory*, No. 1, and 2, *Soul-Winning Songs, Choice Songs, Hymns of Heavenly Harmony, Sunshine Songs, Songs of Peace and Power, Century Gospel Hymns, Songs for Male Choruses*, vol. 1 and 2, *Sacred and Secular Selections for Ladies' Voices*, and three books of choir anthems.

"Sweet Peace, the Gift of God's Love" first appeared in the hymnal *Crowning Glory*, No. 1, published, in 1888, by the Bilhorn Publishing Company.

* * *

"Thou hast touched me and I have been translated into Thy peace."
St. Augustine: *Confessions*, Book 10, Chapter 27

"Drop Thy still dews of quietness till all our striving cease;
Take from our souls the strain and stress,
And let our ordered lives confess
The beauty of Thy Peace."
John Greenleaf Whittier

263

JESUS! JESUS! JESUS!
"To many, Jesus Christ is only a grand subject for a painting, a heroic theme for a pen, a beautiful form for a statue, or a thought for a song.
But to those who have heard His voice, who have felt His pardon, who have received His benediction,
He is music—light—joy—hope and salvation—a Friend who never forsakes, lifting you up when others try to put you down.
There is no name like His. It is more inspiring than Caesar's, more musical than Beethoven's, more eloquent than Demosthenes', more patient than Lincoln's.
The name of Jesus throbs with all life, weeps with all pathos, groans with all pains, stoops with all love.
I struggle for a metaphor with which to express Jesus. He is not like the bursting forth of an orchestra. That is too loud and it might be out of tune.
He is not like the sea when lashed by a storm, that is too boisterous.
He is not like a mountain canopied with snow, that is too solitary and remote.
He is the Lily of the Valley; the Rose of Sharon; a gale of sweet spices from Heaven. He is our home."
Source Unknown

84 Take the Name of Jesus With You

Lydia Baxter, 1809-1874

William H. Doane, 1832-1915

1. Take the name of Je-sus with you, Child of sor-row and of woe;
2. Take the name of Je-sus ev - er, As a shield from ev-'ry snare;
3. O the pre-cious name of Je - sus! How it thrills our souls with joy,
4. At the name of Je-sus bow-ing, Fall-ing pros-trate at His feet,

It will joy and com-fort give you— Take it, then,wher-e'er you go.
If temp - ta-tions round you gath - er, Breathe that ho - ly name in prayer.
When His lov-ing arms re - ceive us And His songs our tongues em-ploy!
King of kings in heav'n we'll crown Him When our jour-ney is com-plete.

CHORUS

264

Pre-cious name, O how sweet! Hope of earth and joy of heav'n;
precious name, how sweet!

Pre-cious name, O how sweet! Hope of earth and joy of heav'n.
precious name, how sweet!

Take the Name of Jesus With You

Author—Lydia Baxter, 1809-1874
Composer—William H. Doane, 1832-1915

And whatsoever ye do in word or deed, do all in the name of the Lord Jesus, giving
thanks to God and the Father by Him.   Colossians 3:17

Take the Name of Jesus With You

Despite being a bed-ridden invalid for much of her life, Lydia Baxter was known as a zealous Christian worker. She was born on September 8, 1809, in Petersburg, New York. Shortly after her conversion as a young person, she and her sister were personally responsible for establishing a Baptist church in her home town of Petersburg, New York. After her marriage, she moved with her husband to New York City, where she continued her Christian service. Her home was known as a gathering place for preachers, evangelists, and Christian workers, who came to her for inspiration and advice. Her friends used to say that a visit to her sickroom was not so much to give her encouragement and comfort as to receive some buoyancy for their own spirits.

Mrs. Baxter was also an avid student of the Bible and loved to discuss the significance of scriptural names with her friends. "You recall," she often said, "that when Esau was born, Jacob had hold of Esau's heel, as if he were trying to pull his twin brother back, so he could be born first. Consequently he was named Jacob, which means 'supplanter.' Isaac means 'laughter,' for when Abraham and Sarah learned that, at their advanced age, they were to become parents, they laughed out loud, thinking it was impossible as well as incredible. As for the names of the twelve sons of Jacob, after whom most of the twelve tribes of Israel took their names, they were named for the strange events surrounding their birth, as well as the rivalries which existed between the wives of husband-father Jacob."

Mrs. Baxter would often inform her friends that Samuel means "asked of God," Hannah-"grace," Sarah-"princess," and Naomi-"pleasantness." But the name that meant everything to Lydia Baxter was the name of "Jesus." Whenever she was questioned about her cheery disposition despite her physical difficulties, she would reply, "I have a very special armor. I have the name of Jesus. When the tempter tries to make me blue or despondent, I mention the name of Jesus, and he can't get through to me anymore. The name Jesus means 'Savior' and it comes from the same Hebrew root from which the names of Joshua and Joash come."

"Take the Name of Jesus With You" is said to have been written by Mrs. Baxter on her sick-bed just four years before her death on June 22, 1874, in New York City. Although she wrote a number of other gospel hymn texts, this is her only hymn still in common usage. Mrs. Baxter also had a collection of devotional poems published in 1855, entitled *Gems by the Wayside*.

William H. Doane composed the music for this text shortly after Mrs. Baxter wrote it, and the hymn was first published in the hymnal, *Pure Gold*, edited by Doane and Robert Lowry, in 1871. This hymn was widely used, during the Moody-Sankey evangelistic campaigns, in the latter quarter of the nineteenth century. It is still a most popular and usable hymn with evangelical congregations everywhere.

William Howard Doane, composer of this music, was born in Preston, Connecticut, on February 3, 1832. Following his conversion as a senior in high school, he became an active, Baptist lay-worker. Early in his life, he began a life-long association with the J. A. Fay and Company, manufacturers of woodworking machinery. In 1860, Doane moved with this firm to Cincinnati, Ohio, and later became its president. While serving in this capacity, Mr. Doane was credited with more than seventy inventions. William Doane spent the remainder of his life in Cincinnati, where he increasingly became a respected and beloved civic and church leader. For more than twenty-five years, he was superintendent of the Sunday school of the Mount Auburn Baptist Church. Doane wrote and published music merely as an avocation. Yet he composed more than twenty-two hundred hymn tunes as well as editing and publishing more than forty collections, in addition to numerous Christmas cantatas. In 1875, William Doane received an honorary Doctor of Music degree from Denison University in Granville, Ohio, in recognition of his many musical accomplishments. Doane collaborated with Fanny Crosby in producing many of the popular gospel hymns still widely sung today: "To God Be the Glory," "Near the Cross," "Will Jesus Find Us Watching?" "Pass Me Not," "I Am Thine, O Lord," "'Tis the Blessed Hour of Prayer," and "Rescue the Perishing" (*101 Hymn Stories*, No. 76). Mr. Doane has also supplied the music for Elizabeth Prentiss' hymn text, "More Love to Thee" (No. 58).

266

Despite William Doane's huge financial success, he was always known as a humble and active Christian lay-worker as well as a generous benefactor. He donated the pipe organ in the Cincinnati Y.M.C.A. hall as well as providing the finances for the construction of the Doane Memorial Music Building at the Moody Bible Institute in Chicago.

William H. Doane, a man mightily used of God, died on December 24, 1915, at South Orange, New Jersey.

* * *

"The name of Jesus is the one lever that lifts the world."

Anonymous

"The name of Christ—the one great word—well worth all the languages in earth or heaven."

Samuel Bailey

85 Thanks to God!

TACK, O GUD

August Ludvig Storm, 1862-1914
Trans. by Carl E. Backstrom, 1901-

John Alfred Hultman, 1861-1942
Arr. by Norman Johnson, 1928-1983

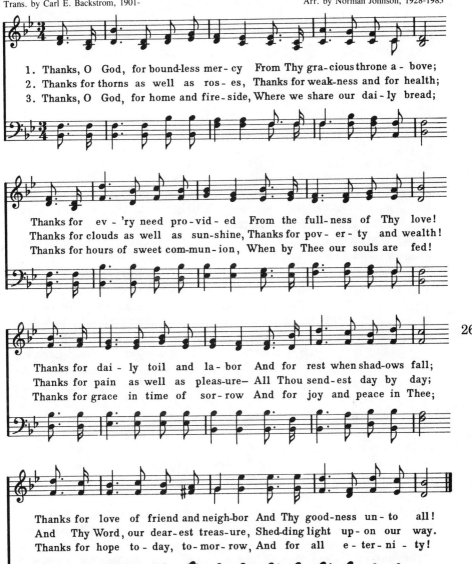

1. Thanks, O God, for bound-less mer-cy   From Thy gra-cious throne a-bove;
2. Thanks for thorns as well as ros-es, Thanks for weak-ness and for health;
3. Thanks, O God, for home and fire-side, Where we share our dai-ly bread;

Thanks for ev-'ry need pro-vid-ed From the full-ness of Thy love!
Thanks for clouds as well as sun-shine, Thanks for pov-er-ty and wealth!
Thanks for hours of sweet com-mun-ion, When by Thee our souls are fed!

267

Thanks for dai-ly toil and la-bor And for rest when shad-ows fall!
Thanks for pain as well as pleas-ure— All Thou send-est day by day;
Thanks for grace in time of sor-row And for joy and peace in Thee;

Thanks for love of friend and neigh-bor And Thy good-ness un-to all!
And   Thy Word, our dear-est treas-ure, Shed-ding light up-on our way.
Thanks for hope to-day, to-mor-row, And for all e-ter-ni-ty!

Arr. © Copyright 1966, 1968 by Singspiration, Inc. all rights reserved. Used by permission.

Thanks to God!

Author—August Ludvig Storm, 1862-1914
Translated into English by Carl E. Backstrom, 1901-
Composer—John Alfred Hultman, 1861-1942
Arranger—Norman E. Johnson, 1928-1983
Tune Name—"Tack, O Gud"
Meter—87.87 Doubled

> Giving thanks always for all things unto God and the Father in the name of our Lord Jesus Christ.
>
> Ephesians 5:20

This typically delightful song is another from the Swedish heritage. As is true with so many of these songs, there is a warmth of text and a folk-like quality about the music that appeals to believers of every nationality. "Thanks to God!" is one of the most popular of these Swedish songs that have found their way into many evangelical hymnals in recent times. For example: "More Secure Is No One Ever" (No. 59), "He the Pearly Gates Will Open" (No. 34), and "Day By Day" (*101 Hymn Stories*, No. 17).

The author, August Ludvig Storm, was born in October, 1862, in Motala, Sweden. He lived most of his life in Stockholm. As a young man he was converted to Christ in a Salvation Army meeting. Soon he joined the Salvation Army Corps and in time became one of its leading officers. He wrote this hymn's text for the Army publication, *Stridsropet (The War Cry)*, on December 5, 1891. The original Swedish version had four stanzas, with each verse beginning with the word *tack* "thanks", having a total of thirty-two "thanks" in all. The gratitude expressed to God ranges from the "dark and dreary fall" to the "pleasant, balmy springtime," "pain" as well as "pleasure," "thorns" as well as "roses." Storm's text later appeared in the *Swedish Salvation Army* songbook with a Welsh tune. It wasn't until 1910, however, when J. A. Hultman included the text with his own tune in the publication *Solskenssonger* that the hymn became really popular, both in Sweden and in America.

At the age of thirty-seven, August Storm suffered a back ailment that left him crippled for life. He continued, however, to administer his Salvation Army duties until his death. A year before his death on July 1, 1914, he wrote another poem in which he thanked God for the years of calm and quiet as well as the years of pain. After his funeral, the Swedish *War Cry* wrote the following about August Storm: "It was a delight to listen to his powerful, thoughtful, and well-articulated sermons. And the numerous verses that flowed from his pen are the best that have ever appeared in the Army's publications."

The composer, John Alfred Hultman, was born in Sweden on July 6, 1861, and he died in California on August 7, 1942. He migrated to this country with his family as a young boy and settled in Iowa. Early in life, young Hultman gave evidence of unusual musical ability and a fine voice. For more than sixty years, he divided his time between Sweden and the United States, concertizing the gospel in his own distinctive manner. His informal, inspirational singing ministered to large gatherings everywhere. Hultman's biographer, Nils Lund, has written: "He was a gospel troubadour, and the common people heard him gladly." Hultman was known as the "Sunshine Singer" because of his musical style as well as his cheerful personality. But J. A. Hultman was more than a singer. At various times throughout his life he pastored Mission Covenant Churches, taught at North Park College in Chicago, Illinois, was a church organist, a manufacturer of pianos, a composer of more than five hundred songs, and a publisher of numerous hymnal collections. At the age of eighty-one, the "Sunshine Singer" died as he had lived—singing the simple gospel message in concert at the Covenant Church of Burbank, California.

The original translator, Carl Ernest Backstrom, has pastored Evangelical Mission Covenant churches in Nebraska, Iowa, and Ohio. He translated this text especially for the *Covenant Hymnal*, published in 1931. Although Backstrom omitted stanza three from the original Swedish, he did incorporate many of its ideas into the present translated verses.

The arranger and further translator of this hymn was Norman E. Johnson, a long-time associate with the Singspiration Publishing Company and church music director in the Evangelical Covenant denomination. Mr. Johnson also contributed the music for the hymn text "Not What These Hands Have Done" (See No. 64).

269

"My God, I thank Thee who hast made the earth so bright,
So full of splendor and of joy, beauty and light;
So many glorious things are here, noble and right.

"I thank Thee too, that Thou has made joy to abound,
So many gentle thoughts and deeds circling us round,
That, in the darkest spot of earth, some love is found.

"I thank Thee more, that all our joy is touched with pain,
That shadows fall on brightest hours, that thorns remain;
So that earth's bliss may be our guide, and not our chain.

"I thank Thee, Lord, that Thou has kept the best in store;
We have enough, but not too much to long for more—
A yearning for a deeper peace, not known before."
Adelaide A. Procter

86 The Love of God

Frederick M. Lehman, 1868-1953

Frederick M.. Lehman, 1868-1953

1. The love of God is great-er far Than tongue or pen can ev - er
2. When years of time shall pass a - way And earth-ly thrones and kingdoms
3. Could we with ink the o - cean fill And were the skies of parch-ment

tell, It goes be - yond the high-est star And reach-es to the low -est
fall, When men, who here re-fuse to pray, On rocks and hills and mountains
made, Were ev -'ry stalk on earth a quill And ev -'ry man a scribe by

hell; The guilt- y pair, bowed down with care, God gave His Son to
call, God's love so sure shall still en - dure, All mea - sure - less and
trade, To write the love of God a - bove Would drain the o - cean

win: His err - ing child He rec-on - ciled And par -doned from his sin.
strong: Re-deem-ing grace to Ad-am's race— The saints' and an - gels' song.
dry, Nor could the scroll con-tain the whole Tho stretched from sky to sky.

CHORUS

O love of God, how rich and pure! How mea-sure - less and strong!

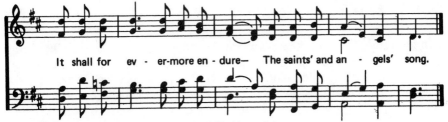

It shall for ev - er-more en - dure— The saints' and an - gels' song.

Copyright 1917. Renewed 1945 by Nazarene Publishing House. Used by permission.

The Love of God

Author and Composer—Frederick M. Lehman, 1868-1953

> . . . Yea, I have loved thee with an everlasting love: therefore with lovingkindness have
> I drawn thee.   Jeremiah 31:3

This beloved gospel song has its roots in a Jewish poem, written in Germany in the eleventh century. Frederick M. Lehman, the twentieth-century author and composer, wrote a pamphlet, in 1948, entitled "History of the Song, *The Love of God.*" Portions of Mr. Lehman's account are as follows:

> While at campmeeting in a mid-western state, some fifty years ago in our early ministry, an evangelist climaxed his message by quoting the last stanza of this song. The profound depths of the lines moved us to preserve the words for future generations.
> Not until we had come to California did this urge find fulfillment, and that at a time when circumstances forced us to hard manual labor. One day, during short intervals of inattention to our work, we picked up a scrap of paper and, seated upon an empty lemon box pushed against the wall, with a stub pencil, added the (first) two stanzas and chorus of the song.
> . . . Since the lines (3rd stanza from the Jewish poem) had been found penciled on the wall of a patient's room in an insane asylum after he had been carried to his grave, the general opinion was that this inmate had written the epic in moments of sanity.
> The key-stanza (third verse) under question as to its authorship was written nearly one thousand years ago by a Jewish songwriter, and put on the scorepage by F. M. Lehman, a Gentile songwriter, in 1917.

The Jewish poem, *Hadamut*, in the Aramaic language, has ninety couplets. The poem itself is in the form of an acrostic, with the author's name woven into the concluding verses. It was composed, in the year 1096, by Rabbi Mayer, son of Isaac Nehorai, who was a cantor in the city of Worms, Germany. The poem may be broken down into two parts. In the first section, the poet praises God as the ruler of the world, the One who created all things, including the angels, to serve Him. The poet also includes the creation of the children of Israel as God's special portion. In the second section, the writer describes the polemic between the nations of the world and the chosen Jewish people. He describes how these people have been persecuted and even killed, throughout the ages, for the sanctity of God's Holy Name. The poem tells how the nations of the world have attempted to influence the Jewish people to leave their religion and to cooperate with the non-Jewish majority. This the Jews have refused to do, however, believing with absolute conviction, that though this world may be one of hatred and destruction, the world to come will vindicate them, and then all the nations of the world will know that God has chosen Israel for His eternal glory.

The *Hadamut* poem also speaks of a certain miracle, which happened, about which the poet comments. There are three opinions as to the contents of this miracle. The first opinion is that the miracle was the giving of the Ten Commandments on Mount Sinai. Incidentally, it is for this reason that the poem is still read on the first day of the Feast of Shavuot (Fall Harvest—Festival of Weeks, begun seven weeks after Passover) before the reading of the Ten Commandments. The second opinion simply states that we really cannot know with certainty, from the references, what the actual miracle was. The third opinion believes that the miracle took place in the city of Worms, home of the rabbi-poet. It is thought that there was a medieval, German priest who once spoke evil of the Jewish community. The king called upon the Jews of the city to produce a representative to argue and defend themselves against the priest. If the Jewish spokesman was successful, then the Jewish community would be spared mass genocide. But if the anti-Jewish priest proved successful, then all of the Jewish community of Worms would be put to death. The story has a happy ending, as the Jewish representative was successful in the defense of their faith, and the community of Worms was spared.

272

Throughout the poem, the theme of God's eternal love and concern for His people is evident. One section of this poem, from which the present third stanza of "The Love of God" was evidently adapted, reads as follows:

Were the sky of parchment made,
A quill each reed, each twig and blade,
Could we with ink the oceans fill,
Were every man a scribe of skill,
The marvelous story
Of God's great glory
Would still remain untold;
For He, most high
The earth and sky
Created alone of old.

Frederick Martin Lehman pastored Nazarene churches, throughout his ministry in Indiana and Illinois, before moving to Kansas City, in 1911, where he became involved in starting the Nazarene Publishing House. His later years were lived in California, where he died at Pasadena in 1953. Throughout his ministry, Frederick Lehman wrote numerous poems and songs, including the publishing of five volumes of *Songs That Are Different*. "The Love of God" first appeared in Volume Two of that series, in 1919, although the copyright was obtained two years earlier. The harmonization of this gospel song was accomplished by Mr. Lehman's daughter, Claudia (Mrs. W. W. Mays, 1892-1973), who also was associated with the Nazarene Publishing House as its secretary for a period of time.

"The Love of God" has been widely used during the past several decades as a special number by numerous gospel musicians. It is presently being included in many of the newer evangelical hymnals as a worthy congregational hymn.

*   *   *

GOD, THOU ART LOVE

"If I forget,
    Yet God remembers! If these hands of mine
Cease from their clinging, yet the hands divine
    Hold me so firmly that I cannot fall;
And if sometimes I am too tired to call
    For Him to help me, then He reads the prayer
Unspoken in my heart, and lifts my care.

"God, Thou art love! I build my faith on that.
    I know Thee who has kept my path, and made
Light for me in the darkness, tempering sorrow
    So that it reached me like a solemn joy;
It were too strange that I should doubt Thy love."
                     Robert Browning

273

(The author is indebted to the following for their assistance with this hymn story: Leon Rowland, Professor of Old Testament. Grand Rapids Baptist Seminary, for research information from the *Encyclopedia Judaica*, copyright Jerusalem, Keter Publishing, 1973 and the *Neir Netiv Encyclopedia*, printed in Israel, 1968. Also Professor J. Harold Moyer, Music Department of Bethel College and co-editor of *Exploring the Mennonite Hymnal: Handbook*, published by the Faith and Life Press, North Newton, Kansas, 1983. Also, Mr. Ken Bible, Lillenas Publishing Company, for making available the 1948 leaflet by Frederick M. Lehman.)

87

The Solid Rock

SOLID ROCK

Edward Mote, 1797-1874

William B. Bradbury, 1816-1868

1. My hope is built on noth-ing less Than Je-sus' blood and right-eous-ness;
2. When dark-ness veils His love-ly face, I rest on His un-chang-ing grace;
3. His oath, His cov-e-nant, His blood Sup-port me in the whelm-ing flood;
4. When He shall come with trum-pet sound, O may I then in Him be found,

I dare not trust the sweet-est frame, But whol-ly lean on Je-sus' name.
In ev-'ry high and storm-y gale My an-chor holds with-in the veil.
When all a-round my soul gives way, He then is all my hope and stay.
Dressed in His right-eous-ness a-lone, Fault-less to stand be-fore the throne.

REFRAIN

On Christ, the sol-id Rock, I stand— All oth-er ground is

sink-ing sand, All oth-er ground is sink-ing sand.

The Solid Rock

Author—Edward Mote, 1797-1874
Composer—William B. Bradbury, 1816-1868
Tune Name—"Solid Rock"
Meter—88.88 with refrain

For other foundation can no man lay than that is laid, which is Jesus Christ.

1 Corinthians 3:11

Many of our gospel hymns are criticized by theologians as being too subjective and experiential, or for stating one's assurance of salvation and eternal life entirely upon a personal experience—i.e. "You ask me how I know He lives, He lives within my heart" (No. 33). The "Solid Rock" text, however, is quite different in this respect. Note the believer's basis of faith as expressed in this text: Jesus' blood, His righteousness, His unchanging grace, His oath and covenant. Truly, when one has such objective truth upon which to build a life and future hope, "all other ground is sinking sand."

The personal life of this hymn's author is most interesting. Edward Mote was born on January 21, 1797, of very poor, ungodly parents, in London, England. His parents were keepers of an inn or public house in London. In writing of his youth, Mote said, "My Sundays were spent in the streets. So ignorant was I that I did not know that there was a God." He further states that the school he attended did not even allow a Bible to be seen, much less taught. As a youth, Mote was apprenticed to a cabinetmaker and eventually became known as a successful craftsman of that trade. At the age of sixteen, he was taken by his master to hear the esteemed preacher, John Hyatt, of the Tottenham Court Chapel. Here young Edward was genuinely converted to Christ. He later settled at Southwark, a suburb of London, where he became known as a successful cabinetmaker and a devoted churchman.

At the age of fifty-five, Edward Mote realized a life-long dream. Largely through his personal efforts, a building for a Baptist congregation was built in the village of Horsham, Sussex, England. The church members, out of gratitude to Mote, offered him the deed to the property. He refused their offer, saying: "I do not want the chapel; I only want the pulpit, and when I cease to preach Christ, then turn me out of that." Here Mote ministered faithfully for the next twenty-one years until forced to resign because of poor health, one year before he died on November 13, 1874. Just prior to his death, he said: "The truths I have been preaching, I am now living upon, and they do very well to die upon." Edward Mote lies buried in the churchyard of the Horsham church. Near the pulpit in the church is a tablet with this inscription:

275

In loving memory of Mr. Edward Mote, who fell asleep in Jesus November 13th, 1874, aged 77 years. For 26 years the beloved pastor of this church, preaching Christ and Him crucified, as all the sinner can need, and all the saint desire.

Edward Mote wrote more than one hundred hymn texts throughout his life. Many of these were included in his collection entitled *Hymns of Praise, A New Selection of Gospel Hymns, Combining All the Excellencies of Our Spiritual Poets, With Many Originals*, published in 1836.

The "Solid Rock" text was written in 1834, and Mote titled it, "The

Gracious Experience of a Christian.'' The completed hymn text originally consisted of six stanzas. Expressions from portions of these two omitted verses are interesting to observe:

> My hope is built on nothing less than Jesus' blood and righteousness; 'Midst all the hell I feel within, on His completed work I lean.
> I trust His righteous character, His council, promise, and His power;
> His honor and His name's at stake, to save me from the burning lake.

The following account was given to one of the local newspapers by Edward Mote regarding the writing of his hymn:

> One morning it came into my mind as I went to labor, to write an hymn on the "Gracious Experience of a Christian." As I went up Holborn I had the chorus, "On Christ the solid rock I stand, all other ground is sinking sand."
>
> In the day, I had the first four verses complete, and wrote them off. On the Sabbath following, I met Brother King as I came out of the Lisle Street Meeting...who informed me that his wife was very ill, and asked me to call and see her. I had an early tea and called afterwards. He said that it was his usual custom to sing a hymn, read a portion, and engage in prayer, before he went to the meeting. He looked for his hymnbook, but could find it nowhere. I said, "I have some verses in my pocket; if you like, we could sing them." We did, and his wife enjoyed them so much that after the service he asked me, as a favor, to leave a copy of them for his wife. I went home, and by the fireside composed the last two verses, wrote them off, and took them to Sister King. As these verses so met the dying woman's case, my attention to them was the more arrested, and I had a thousand of them printed for distribution. I sent one to the *Spiritual Magazine*, without my initials, which appeared some time after this. Brother Rees, of Crown Street, Soho, brought out an edition of hymns, in 1836, and this hymn was in it. David Denham introduced it, in 1837, with Rees' name given as the author.

In his *Hymns of Praise* collection of 1836, Edward Mote included this hymn and reclaimed its authorship under the title, *"The Immutable Basis of a Sinner's Hope."*

The music for Mote's text was composed, in 1863, by William Batchelder Bradbury,, one of the foremost composers of early, American gospel music. It first appeared in his collection, *The Devotional Hymn and Tune Book*, published in 1864, by the American Baptist Publication Society. This was the only, new Baptist hymnal to appear in our country during the Civil War years.

William Bradbury is also the composer for these hymns: "Depth of Mercy" (No. 20), "Even Me" (No. 23), "Sweet Hour of Prayer" (No 82), as well as "He Leadeth Me" (*101 Hymn Stories*, No. 28), "Jesus Loves

Me'' (*ibid.*, No. 47), and "Just As I Am" (*ibid.*, No. 52). Other well-known gospel hymns for which Bradbury has contributed the music include: "'Tis Midnight—and on Olive's Brow," "Savior, Like a Shepherd Lead Us," and "There Is No Name So Sweet on Earth."

Some song leaders today prefer to use the "Melita" tune (generally used with the navy hymn text, "Eternal (Almighty) Father, Strong to Save"—See No. 22) with the "Solid Rock" text, rather than Bradbury's more rhythmic music, feeling that the intensity of the "Melita" melodic line is more compatible with the strength of the lyrics. Interchanging different tunes with comparable meters and familiar texts is a musical practice that occasionally provides a refreshing change for any congregation.

* * *

"Life with Christ is an endless hope; without Him a hopeless end."
Anonymous

THE CHRIST
"He is a path, if any be misled;
He is a robe, if any naked be;
If any chance to hunger, He is bread;
If any be a bondman, He is free;
If any be but weak, how strong is He!
To dead men life He is; to sick souls health;
To blind men, sight, and to the needy, wealth;
A pleasure without loss, a treasure without stealth."
Giles Fletcher, Jr. 1588-1623

277

88

The Strife Is O'er

VICTORY

Latin Hymn, c. 1695
Trans. by Francis Pott, 1832-1909

Giovanni P. da Palestrina, c. 1525-1594
Adapted by William H. Monk, 1823-1889

Organ

1. The strife is o'er— the bat - tle done, The vic - to - ry of life is
2. The pow'rs of death have done their worst, But Christ their le - gions hath dis -
3. The three sad days have quick - ly sped, He ris - es glo - rious from the
4. He closed the yawn - ing gates of hell, The bars from heav'n's high por - tals
5. Lord, by the stripes which wound-ed Thee, From death's dread sting Thy serv - ants

won; The song of tri - umph has be - gun: Al - le - lu - ia!
persed; Let shouts of ho - ly joy out - burst: Al - le - lu - ia!
dead; All glo - ry to our ris - en Head! Al - le - lu - ia!
fell; Let hymns of praise His tri - umphs tell: Al - le - lu - ia!
free, That we may live and sing to Thee: Al - le - lu - ia!

D.S.

The Strife is O'er

Text—An anonymous Latin hymn from approximately 1695
English Translation—Francis Pott, 1832-1909
Composer—Giovanni P. da Palestrina, c. 1525-1594
Adapted by William H. Monk, 1823-1889
Tune Name—"Victory"
Meter—888.4 with Alleluias

O death, where is thy sting? O grave, where is thy victory? The sting of death is sin;
and the strength of sin is the law. But thanks be to God, which giveth us the victory
through our Lord Jesus Christ.　　　　　　　1 Corinthians 15:55, 56, 57

This inspiring, Easter hymn text first appeared anonymously in a Jesuit
collection, *Symphonia Sirenum,* published in Cologne, Germany,
in 1695.

The joyous music of the great, sixteenth-century Catholic composer, Palestrina, no doubt accounts for the continuous popularity of this hymn.

It was more than 150 years after its writing before this hymn was used by English-speaking churches. In 1859, the translation was made by Francis Pott, an Anglican minister, to be included in his publication, *Hymns Fitted to the Order of Common Prayer*. Then it was revised and used in the historic Anglican hymnal, *Hymns Ancient and Modern*, published in 1861.

The tune, "Victory," is an adaptation from the "Gloria Patri" of the "Magnificat Tertii Toni," contained in the work titled *Magnificat Octo Tonorum*, which Palestrina had published in 1591. The musical arrangement that Dr. William H. Monk made for this text first appeared in the 1861 edition of *Hymns Ancient and Modern*. In making this musical adaptation from Palestrina's work, Dr. Monk used the first two phrases, repeated the first phrase and added original alleluias for the beginning and the end. ("Alleluia" is a Latin form of the Hebrew "Hallelujah," which means "praise the Lord!"). The text and this music have enjoyed a lasting association to the present time. It is interesting to note the interplay between the statements of fact contained in the first half of each stanza, related to the resurrection, and the personal response to these factual truths as expressed in the last half of each verse, concluding with the jubilant "Alleluia!"

Francis Pott was born on December 29, 1832, in London, England. Following his education at Oxford University and ordination by the Church of England in 1856, for twenty-five years, he served the parish church at Northill, Bedfordshire. Rev. Mr. Pott always maintained a strong interest in hymnology throughout his ministry. He was a member of the original committee that prepared the prestigious Anglican hymnal, *Hymns Ancient and Modern* (1861). Following his retirement from the ministry due to deafness, Pott devoted his energies to research and the translating of Latin and Syriac hymns. In 1898, he published another collection, *The Free Rhythm Psalter*.

Giovanni Pierluigi da Palestrina was born, in or about 1525, in a town called Palestrina, twenty miles outside of Rome. The exact date of birth is unknown, due to a fire in the archives of his native town, in the year 1577. In 1551, Palestrina came to Rome to become organist and director of the Julian Choir, the performing choir at St. Peter's Church in the Vatican. The ruling pontiff, Pope Marcellus, died unexpectedly shortly after Palestrina assumed his new position. It is said that Palestrina was so moved by this event that he desired to write a perfect mass in honor of his beloved pope. This he did, and to this day, the Pope Marcellus mass has been considered the ultimate or standard for all Catholic masses. Palestrina's beautiful a cappella style of choral writing has made the sixteenth century known as the "golden age of choral polyphony." Among

279

Palestrina's many works are approximately one hundred masses, two hundred motets, hymns, offertories, and other liturgical materials. His complete works, contained in thirty-three volumes, were published by Brietkopt and Hartel between 1862 and 1903.

William Henry Monk was born on March 16, 1823, in London, England. He was the music editor for the first three editions of the historic, Anglican hymnal, *Hymns Ancient and Modern* (1861, 1875, 1889). In addition to his work as editor of this hymnal, considered by hymnologists to be one of the most important hymnals ever published, William Monk was also choir director and organist at King's College, London. He was awarded an honorary, Doctorate of Music degree from Durham University, in 1882, in recognition of his many musical accomplishments, including some fifty original tunes to the *Hymns Ancient and Modern* hymnals. Dr. Monk has contributed such tunes as "Eventide" (See "Abide with Me," *101 Hymn Stories*, No. 2) and "Coronae" (See "Look, Ye Saints! the Sight Is Glorious," *ibid.*, No. 55).

*　　*　　*

"I know that my Redeemer lives:
What comfort this sweet sentence gives!
He lives, He lives, who once was dead;
He lives, my everlasting Head.

"He lives, my kind, wise, constant Friend
Who still will keep me to the end;
He lives, and while He lives I'll sing;
Jesus, my Prophet, Priest, and King.

"He lives my mansion to prepare,
And He will bring me safely there;
He lives, all glory to His Name!
Jesus, unchangeably the same!"

Samuel Medley

"Jesus lives! thy terrors now can, O death, no more appall us;
Jesus lives! by this we know thou, O grave, canst not enthrall us.

"Jesus lives! our hearts know well naught from us His love shall sever;
Life, nor death, nor powers of hell tear us from His keeping ever.

"Jesus lives! to Him the throne over all the world is given;
May we go where He has gone, rest and reign with Him in heaven."

Christian Furchtegott Gellert
Translated by Frances Elizabeth Cox

280

89   There's a Wideness in God's Mercy

WELLESLEY

Frederick W. Faber, 1814-1863   Lizzie S. Tourjee, 1858-1913

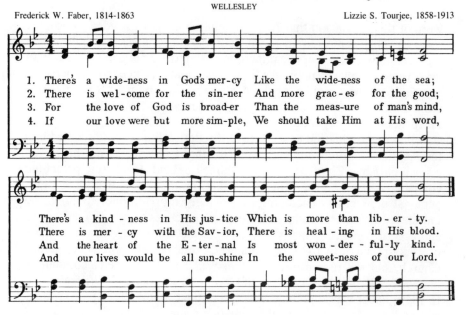

1. There's a wide-ness in God's mer-cy Like the wide-ness of the sea;
2. There is wel-come for the sin-ner And more grac-es for the good;
3. For the love of God is broad-er Than the meas-ure of man's mind,
4. If our love were but more sim-ple, We should take Him at His word,

There's a kind - ness in His jus-tice Which is more than lib - er - ty.
There is mer - cy with the Sav-ior, There is heal - ing in His blood.
And the heart of the E - ter - nal Is most won - der - ful-ly kind.
And our lives would be all sun-shine In the sweet-ness of our Lord.

Arr. © Copyright 1968 by Singspiration, Inc. All rights reserved. Used by permission.

There's a Wideness in God's Mercy   281

Author—Frederick W. Faber, 1814-1863
Composer—Lizzie S. Tourjee, 1858-1913
Tune Name—"Wellesley"
Meter—87.87

> But Thou, O Lord, art a God full of compassion, and gracious, longsuffering, and plenteous in mercy and truth.   Psalm 86:15

Frederick William Faber was born on June 28, 1814, in Calverley, Yorkshire, England. He was raised as a strict Calvinist, strongly opposed to the teachings of the Roman Catholic Church. In 1838, he published a work titled, *The Ancient Things of the Church of England*, vindicating the Church of England as opposed to the Roman Church, declaring the Catholic Church to be unscriptural and guilty of adding falsehood to the sacraments.

During the time of Faber's education at Oxford University, however, he came under the teachings and practices of the Oxford or Tractarian Movement, which exerted a powerful influence upon the Anglican Church, during the mid-1800's. The leaders of this new movement, such as John Henry Newman (See "Lead, Kindly Light," *101 Hymn Stories*, No. 53), were of the persuasion that Anglican church services needed to become more liturgical and ceremonial. Much of this concern was due to the growing strength of the evangelical faction, within the Anglican Church, with its greater emphasis upon the individual and his need of a personal conversion experience. Also the concern of the Oxford Movement was the indifferent and careless worship conducted in many of the more independent congregations of that time.

Following graduation from Oxford, Frederick Faber was ordained into the Anglican Church ministry, and, for the next three years, he served a small parish at Elton, Huntingdonshire, England. His strong preaching contributed to a moral reformation in that community. However, with his personal convictions becoming increasingly more Roman Catholic, he introduced into his ministry such ritualistic practices as private confessions and acts of penance. Finally, Faber went the whole way to which these practices pointed. In 1845, he renounced Protestantism, joined the Roman Church, and was re-baptized as Father Wilfred. He founded a community known as "Brothers of the Will of God" and later as the "Wilfridians." In 1849, Faber was appointed Superior of the Catholic Brompton Oratory in London, where he spent the remaining years of his life.

Frederick Faber wrote many devotional and theological books, but he is best remembered today for the 150 hymn texts, that were written by him and published, after he became a Catholic. He worked tirelessly in writing hymn materials that would express the universal Catholic faith and which could be used by the people for their own devotional purposes. Faber had long realized the great influence that hymnsinging had in Protestant circles and was determined to provide materials for the Catholic Church in the same manner. His collections of hymn texts included: *Hymns*, published in 1849, *Jesus and Mary—Catholic Hymns for Singing and Reading*, published in 1849, and again in 1852, *Oratory Hymns*, published in 1854, and another edition of *Hymns*, published in 1862. Frederick Faber's most popular hymn today, sung by both Protestant and Catholic congregations, is "Faith of Our Fathers" (*101 Hymn Stories*, No. 22). In 1854, the Pope honored Faber with an honorary, Doctor of Divinity degree in recognition of his accomplishments to Catholicism.

Throughout his ministry both as an Anglican and as a Roman Catholic priest, Frederick Faber was recognized as a man of personal charm and an eloquent preacher with a great gift of persuasive influence. He died on September 26, 1863, in London, England, at the early age of forty-nine.

"There's a Wideness in God's Mercy" is part of a thirteen-verse poem written by Frederick Faber entitled *Come to Jesus*. It began with the words, "Souls of men, why will ye scatter like a crowd of frightened sheep? Foolish hearts, why will ye wander from a love so true and deep?" The text was first published in Faber's collection *Hymns*, in 1862. The present hymn version uses only stanzas 4, 6, 8 and 12. One of the omitted verses is worthy of interest:

> But we make His love two narrow with false limits of our own;
> And we magnify His strictness with a zeal he will not own.

There are some meaningful spiritual concepts expressed in Faber's text that are worthy of our contemplation, such as the line, "There's a kindness in His justice which is more than liberty." The final stanza is also a beautiful expression of truth:

> If our lives were but more simple, we should take Him at His word;
> And our lives would be all sunshine in the sweetness of our Lord.

The tune, "Wellesley," was composed by a teen-age girl, Lizzie S. Tourjee, for her high school graduation exercise. Her father, Dr. Eben Tourjee, founder of the New England Conservatory of Music, named the tune for Wellesley College, which his daughter later attended. While serving as one of the editors for the *Hymnal of the Methodist Episcopal Church*, Dr. Tourjee had the "Wellesley" tune included with this text in the 1878 publication. Although other tunes have been associated with Frederick Faber's text, the "Wellesley" tune has been the one most commonly used, especially in American hymnals.

283

*   *   *

"Among the attributes of God, although they are all equal, mercy shines with even more brilliancy than justice."

Miguel Cervantes

90 Thy Word Have I Hid in My Heart

Ernest O. Sellers, 1869-1952

Ernest O. Sellers, 1869-1952

1. Thy Word is a lamp to my feet, A light to my path al - way,
2. For - ev - er, O Lord, is Thy Word Es - tab-lished and fixed on high;
3. At morn-ing, at noon and at night I ev - er will give Thee praise;
4. Thru Him whom Thy Word hath fore-told, The Sav - ior and Morn-ing Star,

To guide and to save me from sin And show me the heav'n-ly way.
Thy faith - ful - ness un - to all men A - bid - eth for - ev - er nigh.
For Thou art my por - tion, O Lord, And shall be thru all my days!
Sal - va - tion and peace have been bro't To those who have strayed a - far.

CHORUS

Thy Word have I hid in my heart, (in my heart,) That I might not

sin a-gainst Thee; (a - gainst Thee;) That I might not sin, that

I might not sin, Thy Word have I hid in my heart.

Thy Word Have I Hid in My Heart

Text—Adapted by Ernest O. Sellers, 1869-1952
Music—Ernest O. Sellers, 1869-1952
Scripture Reference—Psalm 119

...the words that I speak unto you, they are spirit, and they are life. John 6:63

"The Bible is God's chart for you to steer by, to keep you from the bottom of the sea, and to show you where the harbor is, and how to reach it without running on rocks and bars."

Henry Ward Beecher

"Other books were given for our information;
The Bible was given for our transformation."

The Defender

"The Bible differs from all other books. To grow in one's understanding of its meaning, one must live its teaching."

Unknown

"Nobody ever outgrows the Scriptures; the Book widens and deepens with our years."

Charles Haddon Spurgeon

"Sin will keep you from this Book. This Book will keep you from sin."

Dwight L. Moody

"No Christian nation can be considered great which ignores the sacred book."

Fanny Crosby

This familiar gospel hymn is a paraphrase of portions of Psalm 119, a Scripture selection containing 176 verses, the majority of which speak pointedly regarding the importance of knowing and obeying the written words of God.

Stanza one of this hymn is based on verse 105:

Thy word is a lamp unto my feet, and a light unto my path.

Stanza two is based on verses 89 and 90:

Forever, O Lord, Thy Word is settled in heaven. Thy faithfulness is unto all generations: Thou hast established the earth, and it abideth.

Stanza three is based on verses 164, 62, and 44:

Seven times a day do I praise Thee, because of Thy righteous judgments. At midnight, I will rise to give thanks unto Thee, because of Thy righteous judgments. So shall I keep Thy law continually forever and ever.

Stanza four is based on verse 41:

Let Thy mercies come also unto me, O Lord, even Thy salvation, according to Thy word.

The refrain is taken directly from verse 11:

Thy word have I hid in mine heart, that I might not sin against Thee.

Ernest Orlando Sellers, author and composer of this hymn, was born on October 29, 1869, at Hastings, Michigan. Following high school, he was eventually appointed city engineer and superintendent of public works in Lansing, Michigan. After his conversion experience in the Lansing Y.M.C.A., Sellers resigned from this position and enrolled as a student at the Moody Bible Institute, in 1895. Following graduation, Mr. Sellers served as a Y.M.C.A. secretary throughout the country. From 1908 to 1919, Sellers once again became associated with the Moody Bible Institute as an assistant to Daniel B. Towner, the first director of the school's music department. Sellers was also active in evangelistic work during this time, directing singing for such well-known evangelists as Reuben A. Torrey, Gypsy Smith, A. C. Dixon, and J. Wilbur Chapman. During the early years of World War I, Sellers served with the armed forces overseas as a special Y.M.C.A. representative. In 1919, Mr. Sellers accepted the position as director of the Music Department of the Baptist Bible Institute of New Orleans, now known as the New Orleans Baptist Theological Seminary. Here he remained until his retirement, in 1945. He was a highly respected teacher, the author of numerous articles and poems, and the composer of a number of hymn tunes, including the still popular hymn "Wonderful, Wonderful Jesus!" Among Mr. Sellers' published works are: *Personal Evangelism* (1923), *How to Improve Church Music* (1928), *Elements of Music Notation and Conducting* (1938), *Worship, Why and How* (1941), and *Evangelism in Service and Song* (1946)—a most interesting little book in which the author shares first-hand insights into the lives of some of the well-known evangelists and singers of his time, including Dwight L. Moody, Billy Sunday, Ira Sankey, Charles Alexander, and others.

286

"Thy Word Have I Hid in My Heart" was written and composed by Ernest O. Sellers, in 1908. Its first publication was in the *Ideal Song and Hymn Book*, compiled by Daniel B. Towner, in 1909. It is still one of the hymns most frequently sung by young and old alike concerning the believer's relationship to the Scriptures.

91 'Tis So Sweet to Trust in Jesus

Louisa M. R. Stead, c. 1850-1917

William J. Kirkpatrick, 1838-1921

1. 'Tis so sweet to trust in Je-sus, Just to take Him at His word,
2. O how sweet to trust in Je-sus, Just to trust His cleans-ing blood,
3. Yes, 'tis sweet to trust in Je-sus, Just from sin and self to cease,
4. I'm so glad I learned to trust Thee, Pre-cious Je-sus, Sav-ior, Friend;

Just to rest up-on His prom-ise, Just to know, "Thus saith the Lord."
Just in sim-ple faith to plunge me 'Neath the heal-ing, cleans-ing flood!
Just from Je-sus sim-ply tak-ing Life and rest and joy and peace.
And I know that Thou art with me, Wilt be with me to the end.

CHORUS

Je-sus, Je-sus, how I trust Him! How I've proved Him o'er and o'er!

287

Je-sus, Je-sus, pre-cious Je-sus! O for grace to trust Him more!

'Tis So Sweet to Trust in Jesus

Author—Louisa M. R. Stead, c. 1850-1917
Composer—William J. Kirkpatrick, 1838-1921

That ye should be to the praise of His glory, who first trusted in Christ. In whom ye also trusted, after that ye heard the word of truth, the gospel of your salvation: in whom also after that ye believed, ye were sealed with that Holy Spirit of promise.

Ephesians 1:12, 13

It has been said that a believer must learn to exercise such a strong trust in God's providence during the good days of life that, when the despairing times with their accompanying doubts come, which surely they do to all, trusting Jesus continues to be the normal pattern of living. Or, "You will not doubt in the dark, if you have truly learned to trust in the light."

"'Tis So Sweet to Trust in Jesus" was written by a most remarkable woman, Louisa M. R. Stead, out of one of her darkest hours—the tragic drowning of her husband.

Louisa Stead was born about 1850, at Dover, England. As a youngster she felt the call of God upon her life for missionary service. She arrived in America in 1871, and she lived for a time in Cincinnati, Ohio. In 1875, Louisa married a Mr. Stead, and to this union was born a daughter, Lily. When the child was four years of age, the family decided one day to enjoy the sunny beach at Long Island Sound, New York. While eating their picnic lunch, they suddenly heard cries of help and spotted a drowning boy in the sea. Mr. Stead charged into the water. As often happens, however, the struggling boy pulled his rescuer under the water with him, and both drowned before the terrified eyes of wife and daughter. Out of her "why?" struggle with God during the ensuing days flowed these meaningful words from the soul of Louisa Stead:

288

'Tis so sweet to trust in Jesus, just to take Him at His word;
Just to rest upon His promise; just to know, 'Thus saith the Lord.'

A short time later, Mrs. Stead and her daughter left for South Africa, where Louisa worked diligently as a missionary in the Cape Colony for the next fifteen years. Here she married Robert Wodehouse, a native of South Africa. In 1895, Louisa's failing health made it necessary for the family to return to America for her recuperation, during which time Mr. Wodehouse pastored a local Methodist church. By 1900, Louisa's health had improved sufficiently for the family to return once more to a Methodist missionary station at Umtali, in Southern Rhodesia. Something of her same life-long trust in God can be learned from a communique Louisa sent back shortly after their arrival:

In connection with this whole mission there are glorious possibilities, but one cannot, in the face of the peculiar difficulties, help say, "Who is sufficient for these things?" But with simple confidence and trust we may and do say, "Our sufficiency is of God."

After ten years of further service, ill health again forced Louisa to retire. Her daughter, Lily, who had become Mrs. D. A. Carson, continued to serve for many additional years in this mission field of Southern Rhodesia. After several years of prolonged illness, Louisa Stead Wodehouse died on January 18, 1917, at her home in Penkridge, near the Mutambara Mission, about fifty miles from Umtali. After her death, a fellow missionary wrote concerning the continued use of "'Tis So Sweet to Trust in Jesus":

> We miss her very much, but her influence goes on as our five thousand native Christians continually sing this hymn in their native tongue.

The composer of the music, William James Kirkpatrick, is another of the influential nineteenth-century composers and publishers who did much to promote the cause of early gospel music. He spent his entire life in the Philadelphia area, where he served as music director in various Methodist churches in addition to managing a furniture business for a time, as well as composing and compiling a great deal of gospel music. Kirkpatrick is said to have compiled one hundred gospel song books, with total sales running into the millions. Several of the still popular hymns for which he composed the music include: "Lead Me to Calvary," "Jesus Saves!" "He Hideth My Soul," "We Have an Anchor," "Stepping in the Light," "O to Be Like Thee," "Redeemed," and "When Love Shines In." William Kirkpatrick composed this tune especially for Mrs. Stead's text with the hymn first appearing, in 1882, in the collection *Songs of Triumph*, compiled by John R. Sweney and Wm. J. Kirkpatrick. Mr. Kirkpatrick also served as president of the Praise Publishing Company, Philadelphia, which published many of his works. He died suddenly on September 29, 1921, at Germantown, Pennsylvania, while working on this new hymn text, also based on the theme of trust:

289

> Just as Thou wilt, Lord, this is my cry;
> Just as Thou wilt, to live or to die.
> I am Thy servant; Thou knowest best,
> Just as Thou wilt, Lord, labor or rest.

*   *   *

> "O Child of God, wait patiently,
> When dark thy path may be;
> And let thy faith lean trustingly,
> On Him who cares for thee;
> And though the clouds hang drearily
> Upon the brow of night,
> Yet in the morning, joy will come
> And fill thy soul with light!"
> Unknown

92 Trust and Obey

John H. Sammis, 1846-1919

Daniel B. Towner, 1850-1919

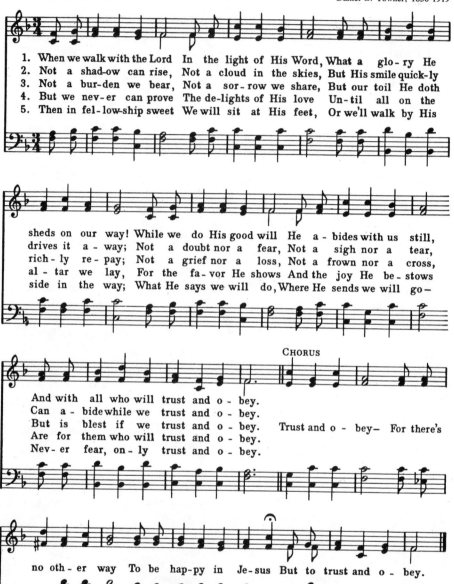

1. When we walk with the Lord In the light of His Word, What a glo-ry He
2. Not a shad-ow can rise, Not a cloud in the skies, But His smile quick-ly
3. Not a bur-den we bear, Not a sor-row we share, But our toil He doth
4. But we nev-er can prove The de-lights of His love Un-til all on the
5. Then in fel-low-ship sweet We will sit at His feet, Or we'll walk by His

sheds on our way! While we do His good will He a-bides with us still,
drives it a-way; Not a doubt nor a fear, Not a sigh nor a tear,
rich-ly re-pay; Not a grief nor a loss, Not a frown nor a cross,
al-tar we lay, For the fa-vor He shows And the joy He be-stows
side in the way; What He says we will do, Where He sends we will go—

CHORUS

And with all who will trust and o-bey.
Can a-bide while we trust and o-bey.
But is blest if we trust and o-bey.   Trust and o-bey— For there's
Are for them who will trust and o-bey.
Nev-er fear, on-ly trust and o-bey.

no oth-er way To be hap-py in Je-sus But to trust and o-bey.

Trust and Obey

Author—John H. Sammis, 1836-1919
Composer—Daniel B. Towner, 1850-1919

And Samuel said, Hath the Lord as great delight in burnt offerings and sacrifices, as in obeying the voice of the Lord? Behold, to obey is better than sacrifice, and to hearken than the fat of rams.   1 Samuel 15:22

This favorite gospel hymn has long been cited as a choice example of a balanced biblical view of a believer's faith in Christ and the resultant good works that should then be evident. We begin with implicit trust in His, finished redemptive work and then spend our lives seeking to obey Him and to fulfil His revealed will in our daily living. Evangelist D. L. Moody once gave this formula for successful Christian living:

> The blood alone makes us safe-
> The Word alone makes us sure-
> But obedience alone makes us happy.

The inspiration for this hymn came, in 1886, during an occasion when Daniel B. Towner was leading music for Mr. Moody in Brockton, Massachusetts. Towner, the composer, has left the following account:

> Mr. Moody was conducting a series of meetings in Brockton, Massachusetts, and I had the pleasure of singing for him there. One night a young man rose in a testimony meeting and said, "I am not quite sure—but I am going to trust, and I am going to obey." I just jotted that sentence down, and sent it with the little story to the Rev. J. H. Sammis, a Presbyterian minister. He wrote the hymn, and the tune was born.

Upon receiving Mr. Towner's request, Mr. Sammis first composed the familiar lines of the refrain:

> Trust and obey—for there's no other way
> To be happy in Jesus, but to trust and obey.

These lines became the capsule thought for the verses, which he then developed in the present five stanzas, detailing more fully the various areas of life that a believer must commit to the Lord, in order to be truly happy. The text with this tune first appeared in the collection, *Hymns Old and New*, published by the Revell Company, in 1887. It has been a favorite with God's people to the present time and has been translated into many foreign languages.

The author, John H. Sammis, was born on July 6, 1846, in Brooklyn, New York. At the age of twenty-three, he moved to Logansport, Indiana, where he became a successful business man and an active Christian layman. Later, he gave up his business interests to serve as a Y.M.C.A. secretary. Soon he felt called of God to enter the full-time Christian ministry. He attended McCormick and Lane Theological Seminaries, graduating from the latter, in 1881. Following his ordination to the Presbyterian denomination, Sammis pastored churches in Iowa, Indiana, Michigan, Minnesota, and Indiana. In 1901, John Sammis moved to California to become a faculty member of the Bible Institute of Los Angeles. Here he died on June 12, 1919, having completed a lifetime of fruitful Christian service.

The composer, Daniel Brink Towner, was one who exerted a strong influence upon evangelical church music, both with his own compositions as well as in the training of other church music leaders. In 1890, Dwight L. Moody founded the Moody Bible Institute in Chicago, Illinois, for the express purpose of training evangelists and song leaders to carry on the work he had begun. Three years later, Towner was personally chosen by Mr. Moody to become the first head of the Music Department at the school, a position he had until his death, in 1919. Daniel B. Towner is credited with more than 2,000 published songs, including such gospel favorites as "At Calvary" (No. 9), "Grace Greater Than Our Sin," "Saved by the Blood," "Nor Silver Nor Gold," "My Anchor Holds," "Anywhere With Jesus," and "Only a Sinner." In addition to his own gospel compositions, Mr. Towner was also associated with the publication of four-teen collections and hymnals as well as various textbooks on music theory and practice. As a teacher, he trained such notable musicians as Charles M. Alexander (See No. 99), Harry Dixon Loes, Homer Hammontree, H. E. Tovey, George S. Schuler, and many others. Daniel B. Towner's death occurred on October 3, 1919, no doubt as he would have desired it, while leading the music in an evangelistic meeting in Longwood, Missouri.

* * *

"Oh, the joy of trusting Jesus, trusting where we cannot trace;
Leaning hard upon His promise, proving His sufficient grace."
Katie V. Hall

93

Trusting Jesus

Edgar Page Stites, 1836-1921

Ira D. Sankey, 1840-1908

1. Sim - ply trust - ing ev - 'ry day, Trust-ing thru a storm-y way;
2. Bright-ly doth His Spir - it shine In - to this poor heart of mine;
3. Sing - ing if my way is clear, Pray-ing if the path be drear;
4. Trust-ing Him while life shall last, Trust-ing Him till earth be past;

E - ven when my faith is small, Trust-ing Je - sus— that is all.
While He leads I can-not fall, Trust-ing Je - sus— that is all.
If in dan - ger, for Him call, Trust-ing Je - sus— that is all.
Till with-in the jas - per wall, Trust-ing Je - sus— that is all.

CHORUS

Trust-ing as the mo-ments fly, Trust-ing as the days go by;

Trust-ing Him what-e'er be - fall; Trust-ing Je - sus— that is all.

293

Trusting Jesus

Author—Edgar Page Stites, 1836-1921
Composer—Ira D. Sankey, 1840-1908

Trust in the Lord, and do good; so shalt thou dwell in the land, and verily thou shalt be fed. Delight thyself also in the Lord; and He shall give thee the desires of thine heart. Commit thy way unto the Lord; trust also in Him, and He shall bring it to pass.

Psalm 37:3, 4, 5

Recently I read an article by a medical doctor who told of examining an increasing number of patients with various alleged symptoms, and of how he finally had to coin a new word when determining a diagnosis—"incopability." These were people who had no apparent physical malady but somehow were just unable to cope with the pace, pressures, and problems of contemporary life. Tragically this "incopability," in turn, often triggers a whole chain reaction of physical, emotional, and spiritual responses which can be devastating to our lives.

How important, then, that we as believers allow a simple gospel hymn with such a profound truth as this to minister to us daily:

> Simply trusting every day, trusting through a stormy way;
> Even when my faith is small, trusting Jesus—that is all.
> Singing if my way is clear, praying if the path be drear;
> If in danger, for Him call, trusting Jesus—that is all.

Also, we need to appropriate daily such promises of Scripture as Deuteronomy 33:25—"As thy days, so shall thy strength be." And, "No good thing does the Lord withhold from those who walk uprightly" Psalm 84:11.

Ira D. Sankey, the composer, relates the following incident regarding the birth of this hymn:

294

> The words of this hymn were handed to Mr. Moody in Chicago, in 1876, in the form of a newspaper clipping. He gave them to me, and asked me to write a tune for them. I assented, on condition that he should vouch for the doctrine taught in the verses, and he said he would.

The hymn was first published in Sankey's *Gospel Hymns* No. 2, published in 1876. It was widely used in the great Moody and Sankey evangelistic meetings in the ensuing year. This textually and musically simple expression of child-like trust in Jesus has met the daily spiritual needs of many of God's people to the present time.

The author, Edgar Page Stites, was for many years an obscure but active lay-worker in the Methodist Church of Cape May, New Jersey. One of his ancestors was John Howland, who came to America on the Mayflower. Stites was also a cousin of the gospel hymnwriter, Eliza E. Hewitt (See "More About Jesus," No. 57). Mr. Stites served in the Civil War and later for a time was a riverboat pilot. He also worked for a period as a Methodist home missionary in the Dakotas. Another of Edgar P. Stites' hymn texts that has enjoyed popularity to the present time is "Beulah Land." ("I've reached the land of corn and wine...." based on Isaiah 35:10.) Frequently Stites used the pseudonym Edgar Page on his hymns. He died on January 7, 1921, in the same town where he was born, Cape May, New Jersey.

The composer, Ira D. Sankey, is a name well-known to evangelical Christians. He has been called the "Father of Gospel Music" because of his many contributions to gospel hymnody during the latter quarter of the nineteenth century. Mr. Sankey has contributed the music to such favorites as "A Shelter in the Time of Storm" (No. 2), "Hiding in Thee" (*101 Hymn Stories*, No. 29), and "The Ninety and Nine" (*ibid.*, No. 91). In all, Mr. Sankey contributed his talents to the writing of more than eighty gospel songs and the compiling of more than ten, important, hymnal collections.

The following is a brief resume of Ira D. Sankey's life:

Born August 28, 1840, at Edinburg, Pennsylvania.

Converted to Christ, in 1856, in a revival meeting at King's Chapel.

Moved to Newcastle, Pennsylvania, in 1857. Here he joined the Methodist Episcopal Church. Shortly after, he was elected Sunday-school superintendent and also became leader of the choir.

In 1860, enlisted in the Union Army during the Civil War. Attained the rank of sergeant.

On September 9, 1863, married Fanny V. Edwards, daughter of the Honorable John Edwards, a member of the State Senate. They had two sons.

Following the war, he returned to Newcastle and assisted his father as a collector of internal revenue.

In 1867, was elected secretary, then president of the local Y.M.C.A.

In 1870, was sent as a delegate to the Y.M.C.A. conference at Indianapolis, Indiana, and there met D. L. Moody, who challenged him for full-time Christian service.

In 1871, moved to Chicago, Illinois, to begin a relationship with D. L. Moody that extended for the next thirty years.

From 1873-75, made an extended evangelistic tour of the British Isles.

In 1873, published his first collection of songs entitled *Sacred Songs and Solos*. Additional songs were added in subsequent editions until the 1903 publication contained twelve hundred songs. It is estimated that during the first fifty years these books sold more than eighty million copies.

In 1874, merged with Philip P. Bliss in publishing *Gospel Hymns*, Nos. 1-6, containing a total of 739 hymns. This series had an extraordinary influence on the gospel song movement.

From 1881-84, made a second, extended, evangelistic mission to the British Isles.

In 1885, was able to give (from the royalties of his books) a gift of $40,000 for building a new Y.M.C.A. in Newcastle, Pennsylvania.

In 1891-92, made a third visit to the British Isles. In 1898, made a visit to the Holy Land. In 1899, made a farewell trip to England.

On December 22, 1899, mourned D. L. Moody's death.

In 1903, experienced the loss of his eyesight.

August 13, 1908—home with his Lord.

*   *   *

"Today is the tomorrow we worried about yesterday."

"You may trust the Lord too little, but you can never trust Him too much."

Anonymous

THE TIME TO TRUST
"When is the time to trust?
Is it when all is calm, when waves the victor's palm,
And life is one glad psalm of joy and praise?
"Nay, but the time to trust is when the waves beat high,
When storm clouds fill the sky, and prayer is one long cry,
'O, help and save.'

"When is the time to trust? Is it when friends are true,
Is it when comforts woo, and in all we say and do,
We meet but praise?
"Nay, but the time to trust is when we stand alone,
And summer birds have flown, and every prop is gone,
All else but God!

"When is the time to trust? Is it some future day
When you have tried your way, and learned to trust and pray,
By bitter woe?
"Nay, but the time to trust is in this moment's need.
Poor broken, bruised reed. Poor troubled soul, make speed
To trust thy God!

"When is the time to trust? Is it when hopes beat high,
The sunshine guilds the sky, and joy and ecstasy
Fill all the heart?
"Nay, but the time to trust is when joy is fled,
When sorrow bows the head, and all is cold and dead,
All else but God."

Unknown

94 Turn Your Eyes Upon Jesus

Helen H. Lemmel, 1864-1961   Helen H. Lemmel, 1864-1961

1. O soul, are you wea-ry and trou-bled? No light in the
2. Thru death in-to life ev-er-last-ing He passed, and we
3. His word shall not fail you— He prom-ised; Be-lieve Him, and

dark-ness you see? There's light for a look at the Sav-ior, And
fol-low Him there; O-ver us sin no more hath do-min-ion— For
all will be well: Then go to a world that is dy-ing, His

CHORUS

life more a-bun-dant and free!
more than con-q'rors we are!   Turn your eyes up-on Je-sus,
per-fect sal-va-tion to tell!

297

Look full in His won-der-ful face, _____ And the things of
won-der-ful face,

earth will grow strange-ly dim In the light of His glo-ry and grace.

© Copyright 1922. Renewal 1950 by H. H. Lemmel. Assigned to Singspiration, Inc. All rights reserved. Used by permission.

Turn Your Eyes Upon Jesus

Author and Composer—Helen H. Lemmel, 1864-1961

> Looking unto Jesus the author and finisher of our faith; who for the joy that was set before Him endured the cross, despising the shame, and is set down at the right hand of the throne of God.   Hebrews 12:2

The Scriptures abound in teachings concerning the importance of living our lives with a focused attention on Christ—seeking only those values that have eternal worth. Consider several of these familiar verses:

> But seek ye first the kingdom of God, and His righteousness; and all these things shall be added unto you.   Matthew 6:33

> Look unto me, and be ye saved, all the ends of the earth: For I am God, and there is none else.   Isaiah 45:22

> If ye then be risen with Christ, seek those things which are above, where Christ sitteth on the right hand of God. Set your affection on things above, not on things on the earth. For ye are dead, and your life is hid with Christ in God.
>   Colossians 3:1-3

298

"Turn Your Eyes Upon Jesus" has become a familiar hymn, that has been widely used in Christian circles to challenge believers musically, with the necessity of making Christ the paramount priority in their lives, and then living each day with eternity's values in view. The author and composer of this hymn, Helen H. Lemmel, relates that one day, in 1918, a missionary friend gave her a tract entitled "Focused." The pamphlet contained these words: "So then, turn your eyes upon Him, look full into His face and you will find that the things of earth will acquire a strange new dimness."

These words made a deep impression upon Helen Lemmel. She could not dismiss them from her mind. She recalls this experience following the reading of that tract:

> Suddenly, as if commanded to stop and listen, I stood still, and singing in my soul and spirit was the chorus, with not one conscious moment of putting word to word to make rhyme, or note to note to make melody. The verses were written the same week, after the usual manner of composition, but none the less dictated by the Holy Spirit.

The hymn was first published, in 1918, in the form of a pamphlet in London, England. Four years later, it was included in a collection titled,

Glad Songs, a book containing sixty-seven songs by Mrs. Lemmel. This hymn became especially popular that same year at the Keswick Bible Conference in northern England, where it was first introduced. It first appeared in the United States, in 1924, in a song collection called, *Gospel Truth in Song*, published by Harry Clarke in Chicago, Illinois. Since that time, the song has been included in most evangelical hymnals and has been translated into many languages around the world.

Helen Howarth Lemmel was born on November 14, 1864, in Wardle, England. She was the daughter of a Wesleyan Methodist pastor, and she came to this country with her family at the age of twelve. Helen lived briefly in Mississippi before settling in Wisconsin. Soon she developed a reputation as a brilliant singer, even studying private voice in Germany for four years. She traveled widely throughout the midwest during the early 1900's, giving concerts in many churches. Later, Mrs. Lemmel taught voice at the Moody Bible Institute and then at the Bible Institute of Los Angeles. In 1961, Helen Lemmel settled in Seattle, Washington, where she remained active with Christian activities, as a member of the Ballard Baptist Church of that city, during the last days of her life.

In addition to being known as a brilliant singer and musician, Mrs. Lemmel was also widely recognized as a woman with remarkable literary ability. She wrote more than 500 hymns and poems. Mrs. Lemmel also authored a very successful book for children entitled, *Story of the Bible* and composed many children's musical pieces. She remained active for God in her musical and literary pursuits, until her home-going at the age of ninety-seven.

299

How easy it becomes even for those of us who profess to be faithful followers of Christ to get caught up in the "things of earth," so that our heavenly vision and values become blurred and dull. This often happens even when we are active in our Christian activities, we become so involved in merely doing things for God that we miss the real blessing of enjoying the personal fellowship of Christ Himself in our daily lives.

*   *   *

"I've seen the face of Jesus... He smiled in love on me;
It filled my heart with rapture, my soul with ecstasy.
The scars of deepest anguish... were lost in glory bright;
I've seen the face of Jesus... it was a wondrous sight!
Oh, glorious face of beauty, Oh gentle touch of care;
If here it is so blessed, what will it be up there?"
Selected

95

We Gather Together

KREMSER

Source Unknown
Trans. by Theodore Baker, 1851-1934

Netherlands Folk Melody, c. 1625
Arr. by Edward Kremser, 1838-1914

1. We gath-er to-geth-er to ask the Lord's bless-ing—He chas-tens and
2. Be-side us to guide us, our God with us join-ing, Or-dain-ing, main-
3. We all do ex-tol Thee, Thou lead-er tri-um-phant, And pray that Thou

has-tens His will to make known; The wick-ed op-press-ing now cease
tain-ing His king-dom di-vine; So from the be-gin-ning the fight
still our de-fend-er wilt be; Let Thy con-gre-ga-tion es-cape

from dis-tress-ing: Sing prais-es to His name— He for-gets not His own.
we were win-ning: Thou, Lord, wast at our side— all glo-ry be Thine.
trib-u-la-tion: Thy name be ev-er praised! O Lord, make us free! *

We Gather Together

Author—Unknown
English Translation—Theodore Baker, 1851-1934
Music—Netherlands Folk Melody
Arranged by Edward Kremser, 1838-1914
Tune Name—"Kremser"
Meter—12 11. 12 11.

Continue in prayer, and watch in the same with thanksgiving.   Colossians 4:2

No Thanksgiving Day service would be complete without the singing of this traditional Dutch hymn. Today, we sing this hymn as an expression of thanks to God as our defender and guide throughout the past year. The text was originally written by an anonymous author, at the end of the six-teenth century, to celebrate the Dutch freedom from the Spanish overlords, who had been driven from their land, and the freedom that was theirs, both politically from Spain and religiously from the Catholic Church. A number of Dutch nationalistic songs developed as a result of this patriotic emphasis. "We Gather Together" is generally considered to be the finest of these musical expressions. It was first published in Adrian Valerius' *Nederlandtsche Gedenckclanck*, in 1626, in Haarleem. For the next two centuries, the singing of this hymn was limited to the Dutch people. In 1877, it was discovered by Edward Kremser, a Viennese musician, who published it in his collection entitled *Sechs Altniederlanddische Volkslieder*. The English translation of this text was made by Theodore Baker, in 1894, and it appeared in *Dutch Folk Songs* (1917) compiled by Coenraad V. Bos.

"We Gather Together" must be understood and appreciated from its historical setting. For many years, Holland had been under the scourge of Spain, and in 1576, Antwerp was captured and sacked by the Spanish armies. Again, in 1585, it was captured by the Spanish and all of the Protestant citizens were exiled. Many other Dutch cities suffered similar fates. One of the revered leaders of this struggle against Spain was William the Silent, who eventually was murdered by a Catholic assassin. In 1625, his youngest son, Frederick Henry, Prince of Orange, assumed the leadership of the Union of Dutch Provinces. Under his able leadership for more than a quarter century, a great golden age of prosperity and rich post-reformation culture developed throughout Holland. Commerce was expanded around the world, and this was the period of great Dutch art, with such well-known painters as Rembrandt and Vermeer. In 1648, the Spanish endeavors to control Holland were finally destroyed beyond recovery.

One can readily see the references to these historical events throughout the hymn's text: "The wicked oppressing now cease from distressing," "so from the beginning the fight we were winning," as well as the concern, in the final stanza, that God will continue to defend—"and pray that Thou still our defender will be."

The tune, "Kremser," was named after the Viennese musician, who discovered and published this hymn after two centuries of neglect. The original melody is thought to be a folk song from the Netherlands. Edward Kremser was born on April 10, 1838, in Vienna, Austria, and died there on November 27, 1914. He was a noted choral director as well as the composer and publisher of numerous vocal and instrumental works.

The English translator of this text, Theodore Baker, was born in New York City on June 3, 1851. He was highly respected as a noted music researcher. His famous *Biographical Dictionary of Musicians*, first published in 1900, became an authoritative, reference book for all serious students of music. From 1892 to 1926, Baker served as literary editor for the G. Schirmer Music Company. Upon his retirement in 1926, Theodore Baker returned to Germany, where he had received his earlier musical training, and died in Dresden, Germany, on October 13, 1934.

96

Whatever He Wants for Me

Louis Paul Lehman, 1914-1986

Louis Paul Lehman, 1914-1986

1. Sur-ren-dered to the per-fect will of God,____ I dare not give Him less; Though
2. My plan must not op-pose His per-fect will,____ I want to live His thought; My

He should lead my steps from here a-broad,____ I want His will my life to bless.
words and deeds His pur-pose to ful-fill,____ For I am His, so dear-ly bought.

CHORUS

What-ev-er He wants for me____ His will, His will I must know;____ Wher-

ev-er He wants to send me____ His way, His way I must go.____ If He but

speaks I'll o-bey at His voice, I've al-read-y de-cid-ed His will is my choice;

What-ev-er He wants for me,____ His will, His will I must do.____
I must do.

302

© Copyright 1960, arr. © 1984 by Singspiration (ASCAP), Division of the Zondervan Corp. All rights reserved. Used by permission.

Whatever He Wants for Me

Author and Composer—Louis Paul Lehman, 1914-1986

If any man will do His will, he shall know of the doctrine, whether it be of God, or whether I speak of myself. John 7:17

This fine hymn on Christian commitment is from the heart and pen of one of the truly gifted and colorful evangelical preachers of our era, Louis Paul Lehman.

The life story of L. P. Lehman is most remarkable. He was born in Chicago, Illinois, on September 12, 1914. At the age of six, he accepted Christ as Savior at a Moody Memorial Church Sunday School class. At the age of nine, he began preaching, and at the age of twelve was already well-known as a boy preacher. The following year, he was authorized by the Probate Court of Ohio to perform marriages. At the age of fifteen, he established the Franklin Gospel Tabernacle in Franklin, Pennsylvania, where his father, L. P. Lehman, Sr., served as business manager and music director. Many of the well-known evangelists and preachers of that day such as Billy Sunday, Dr. J. C. Massee, and Dr. A. P. Gouthey often preached here. "Junior" Lehman's radio ministry began in Franklin over station WLBL of Oil City, Pennsylvania, on April 13, 1929. Throughout the next forty years, his distinctive high-pitched voice and creative programs were heard daily on radio stations around the world. In 1932, the Lehman family established the Wheeling Gospel Tabernacle in Wheeling, West Virginia, with a schedule of fourteen hours of radio programs each week.

On January 15, 1941, Louis Paul took time out from his busy schedule to marry Edna Davis, whose gifts and musical talents have contributed greatly to the many-faceted ministry of this man. The Lehmans had two daughters, both of whom presently reside in Kansas City.

303

Though Louis Paul Lehman never went beyond a formal eighth grade education, he has been recognized by two institutions and given honorary degrees. In 1952, he received a Doctor of Divinity degree from Bob Jones University and an L.L.D. degree from Biola College/Talbot Seminary, in 1954. His eloquent, yet powerful preaching has caused him to be in great demand in churches and Bible conferences around the country.

Dr. Lehman was one of the forty-two members of the original group which founded Youth for Christ International. In 1946, he accepted the pastorate of a new church, still unnamed and without facilities, which later became the Evangel Baptist Church of Portland, Oregon. Within five and one-half years this church had five hundred members, a large missionary program, and a permanent building in Portland. In February, 1952, Dr. Lehman assumed the pulpit of Calvary Undenominational Church in Grand Rapids, Michigan. Here his ministry in the pulpit and on radio took on new proportions. His radio program, "Bit of Heaven," became a major radio broadcast, and the church, founded by Dr. M. R. DeHaan, was soon filled with fifteen hundred people at each Sunday service. In 1964, Lehman resigned from the Calvary Church pulpit to pursue the radio ministry more fully. Soon, however, he accepted the pastorate of the Mennonite Brethren Church in Bakersfield, California, and still later, the Mennonite Brethren

Church in Fresno, California. While with these churches, Lehman became actively involved with the television ministry of the Mennonite denomination as well.

On January 1, 1984, following a recovery from heart failure, Louis Paul Lehman announced his retirement, after sixty years of preaching. However, when a call came from his former church in Grand Rapids, Michigan, to be a supply-interim pastor, he responded with old-time vigor, and presently, he is leading this church in a building project of five million dollars for Calvary's future facilities.

In addition to a life-time of preaching and broadcasting, Dr. Lehman has written a number of gospel songs. Several of these songs have been widely used. His prayer chorus, "God Bless Our Boys," was sung around the world during World War II. Several of his other popular songs include: "Wonderful Guest," "Christian Love," and "Jesus Is Worthy of Praise." Regarding the writing of "Whatever He Wants for Me," Dr. Lehman gives the following account:

> While I was pastor of the Evangel Baptist Church, Portland, Oregon, a missionary conference in the church stimulated unusual excitement about the will of God. The concept of knowing and doing God's will became a logical sequence. There was no way to know God's will without a commitment to do His will. That idea echoed again and again, until "Whatever He Wants for Me" was the natural outcome. I knew immediately that it contained the best line I'd ever written: "If He but speaks, I'll obey at His voice; I've already decided, His will is my choice."
>
> The song was sketched out without being ready for publication. There was a melody line. My wife, Edna, jotted down the harmony. The words had fallen into place. I used it to end a message or fill in a radio program. Then it shuffled off into dim echoes.
>
> A few years later, as pastor of Calvary Undenominational Church, Grand Rapids, Michigan, board members of Gospel Films became personal friends. This company was producing a sports-oriented, youth-aimed film. Tony Fontane was the featured personality and soloist. Tony was flying in to record the music for the production, and a composer had been engaged to write a brand-new song on the subject of commitment. The song did not arrive. Tony was on hand to record, and my wife was engaged to be Fontane's accompanist. But there wasn't any song.
>
> Gospel Films personnel asked, "Do you have something unpublished that would fit this idea of commitment?" I remembered that half-finished, unpublished manuscript. It had to be somewhere. It was—and somewhere looked good when we found it. The words were in place, the chords were fixed in concrete. Tony liked it. "Whatever He Wants for Me" was rushed into the scene of that film.

304

The song did not catapult into prominence, however. It got printed and circulated through a few gospel musicians. Then it was recorded by the Sixteen Singing Men. Suddenly, it caught a little fire. Now, more than thirty-five years after it was written, it appears in song books, choir octavos, and often on radio programs. I am grateful for its ministry—even if it did bloom a little late.

*   *   *

"The best things in life are not free. They cost the sacrifice of everything less than best."

L. P. Lehman

"Some live as though this life would never end and the next would never begin."

L. P. Lehman

"Today isn't won by old victories nor lost by old defeats."

L. P. Lehman

"You can't pour deep spirituality into a shallow life."

L. P. Lehman   305

"God's best is known by surrender, not struggle."

L. P. Lehman

"It requires no faith to look back and say, 'It was the Lord!' But to see the dim-shadowed figure on today's stormy sea and say, 'It is the Lord!' requires faith and courage."

L. P. Lehman

"Blessed are they who build a corner of eternity in the dust bins of time."

L. P. Lehman

97

When He Cometh

William O. Cushing, 1823-1902

George F. Root, 1820-1895

306

1. When He com - eth, when He com - eth To make up His jew - els,
2. He will gath - er, He will gath - er The gems for His king - dom,
3. Lit - tle chil - dren, lit - tle chil - dren Who love their Re - deem - er

All His jew - els, pre-cious jew - els, His loved and His own:
All the pure ones, all the bright ones, His loved and His own:
Are the jew - els, pre-cious jew - els, His loved and His own:

REFRAIN

Like the stars of the morn - ing, His bright crown a - dorn - ing,

They shall shine in their beau - ty— Bright gems for His crown.

When He Cometh

Author—William O. Cushing, 1823-1902
Composer—George F. Root, 1820-1895
Scripture Reference—Malachi 3:17

When Christ, who is our life, shall appear, then shall ye also appear with Him in glory.
Colossians 3:4

The "Jewels Song" has long been recognized as one of the most-popular, sacred songs ever written for children. The author, William O. Cushing, wrote the words in 1856, especially for the youngsters in his own Sunday school. He based the text on the verse from Malachi 3:17 which reads:

And they shall be mine, saith the Lord of hosts, in that day when I make up my jewels; and I will spare them, as a man spareth his own son that serveth him.

William Cushing wrote a large number of songs that found wide popularity in Sunday school collections as well as many others that found acceptance in Ira D. Sankey's respected collection, *Sacred Songs and Solos*. Several of these gospel hymns still in use today include: "Hiding in Thee" (*101 Hymn Stories*, No. 29), "Ring the Bells of Heaven" (*ibid.*, No. 77), "Under His Wings," "There'll Be No Dark Valley," and "Down in the Valley With My Savior I Would Go."

William Orcutt Cushing was born in Hingham, Massachusetts, on December 31, 1823. For more than twenty years, he was a successful pastor of Disciples of Christ churches. Following the death of his wife in 1870, he was forced to retire from the active ministry because of his own poor health, including a creeping paralysis and the loss of speech. In this time of despair, Cushing prayed earnestly, "Lord, give me something to do for Thee." His prayer was answered, and it seemed as though God gave him the unusual gift for writing catchy, Sunday school style texts. He worked closely with such gospel musicians as Ira Sankey, Robert Lowry, George F. Root, and others. Altogether, Cushing wrote more than 300 gospel hymn texts during his life. William Cushing was known as a most noble, sweet, spiritual Christian gentleman. It was often said that his life was an inspiration to all who came in contact with him, and to know him was to love him. His fruitful life and ministry came to an end on October 19, 1902, at Lisbon, New York.

George Frederick Root was born on August 30, 1820, in Sheffield, Massachusetts. As a young man, he became the organist at the historic, Park Street Church in Boston. Later, he studied music for a time under the noted Lowell Mason and soon became a respected music teacher himself. Root then moved to New York City and for a time taught at the New York Institute for the Blind, where Fanny Crosby was one of his pupils. In 1850, he spent a year studying music in Paris, France. On his return, he composed a cantata, *The Flower-Queen*, for which Fanny Crosby wrote the text. During the time of the Civil War, Root continued to write a number of secular and patriotic songs which became exceedingly popular. Yet despite this secular popularity, Mr. Root's main interest, throughout his life, was that of continuing the work begun by William Bradbury— writing simple Sunday school type of gospel songs, that individuals of all ages could sing with meaning and enthusiasm. Root was highly respected both as a musician and as a man with a gracious, engaging personality and high, spiritual convictions. In 1872, the University of Chicago honored him with the Doctor of Music degree in recognition of his many accomplishments. Mr. Root composed several hundred gospel songs and was associated with the publishing of approximately seventy-five collections in addition to many instruction books, cantatas, and individual pieces of sheet music with the firm, Root and Cady. Several of his songs still widely used today include: "Ring the Bells of Heaven!" (*101 Hymn Stories*, No. 77), "The Lord Is in His Holy Temple," and "Come to the Savior, Make No Delay."

George Root is said to have adapted the tune for the "Jewel Hymn" from a popular, post-civil war, secular melody called "Johnny Schmoker." William Cushing's text combined with George Root's music soon became popular on both sides of the Atlantic Ocean. The following account is given in the Brown and Butterworth book, *The Story of the Hymns and Tunes*:

> An English steamer was coming to Canada with a number of immigrants. One day the minister in that area of the boat asked, "What shall we sing? It must be something we all know, for nearly all the countries of Europe are gathered here." The one in charge answered, "Then it must be an American tune—try 'Jewels.'" There were a thousand people in the area, speaking several different tongues, but with one voice they sang in full chorus, "When He Cometh." The vessel landed at Quebec, and the immigrants filled two long trains of cars, one going east and the other to the Georgian Bay; and as they parted, each began to sing "When He Cometh." The tune made the hymn a common language.

308

This popular and influential, nineteenth-century musician died on August 6, 1895, at Bailey's Island, Maine.

* * *

"Children have more need of models than of critics."

Joubert

> "If there is anything that will endure
> The eye of God, because it still is pure,
> It is the spirit of a little child,
> Fresh from His hand, and therefore undefiled."
> R. H. Stoddard: *The Children's Prayer*

98 When the Roll Is Called Up Yonder

James M. Black, 1856-1938   James M. Black, 1856-1938

1. When the trum-pet of the Lord shall sound and time shall be no more, And the
2. On that bright and cloudless morning when the dead in Christ shall rise And the
3. Let us la-bor for the Mas-ter from the dawn till set-ting sun, Let us

morn-ing breaks e-ter-nal, bright and fair— When the saved of earth shall gath-er
glo-ry of His res-ur-rec-tion share— When His cho-sen ones shall gath-er
talk of all His won-drous love and care; Then when all of life is o-ver

o-ver on the oth-er shore, And the roll is called up yon-der—
to their home be-yond the skies, And the roll is called up yon-der—
and our work on earth is done, And the roll is called up yon-der—

CHORUS

I'll be there! When the roll is called up yon - der, When the
I'll be there! When the roll is called up yon-der I'll be there,
I'll be there!

roll is called up yon - der, When the roll
When the roll is called up yon-der I'll be there,   When the roll

is called up yon-der— When the roll is called up yon-der I'll be there!

309

When the Roll Is Called Up Yonder

Author and Composer—James M. Black, 1856-1938

> Behold, I show you a mystery; we shall not all sleep, but we shall all be changed, in a moment, in the twinkling of an eye, at the last trump; for the trumpet shall sound, and the dead shall be raised incorruptible, and we shall be changed.
>
> 1 Corinthians 15:51, 52

James Milton Black, author and composer of this "roll-call" hymn, was born at South Hill, New York, on August 19, 1856. He was a member of the Pine Street Methodist Church of Williamsport, Pennsylvania, from 1904 until his death at the age of eighty-two. Following an early, musical education in singing and organ playing, Black became a teacher of singing schools. He was also the editor of more than a dozen gospel songbooks, which were published by the Methodist Book Concerns and by the Hall Mack Company in Philadelphia. His most popular collection was a book entitled, *Songs of the Soul*, published in 1894. This book sold more than four-hundred thousand copies during its first two years of publication. "When the Roll Is Called Up Yonder" first appeared in that book, and soon the hymn became widely used in evangelistic endeavors, both in this country and in Great Britain.

310

Mr. Black was an active Methodist layman throughout his lifetime, being especially involved in the social concerns of his church and community as well as in the ministries of the Sunday school and youth work. He gives the following account of the writing of this hymn:

While a teacher in the Sunday school and president of a young people's society, I one day met a girl, fourteen years old, poorly clad and a child of a drunkard. She accepted my invitation to attend the Sunday school and join the young people's society. One evening at a consecration meeting, when members answered the roll call by repeating Scripture texts, she failed to respond. I spoke of what a sad thing it would be when our names are called from the Lamb's Book of Life, if one of us should be absent: And I said, "O God, when my own name is called up yonder, may I be there to respond." I longed for something suitable to sing just then, but I could find nothing in the books. We closed the service, and, on my way home I was still wishing that there might be a song that could be sung on such occasions. The thought came to me, "Why don't you make it?" I dismissed the idea, thinking that I could never write such a hymn. When I reached my home, my wife saw that I was deeply troubled and questioned me, but I made no reply. Then the words in the first stanza came to me in full. In fifteen minutes more, I had composed the other two verses. Going to the piano, I played the music just as it is found today in the hymnbooks, note for note, and I have never dared to change a single word or note of the music since.

When the Roll Is Called Up Yonder

The subsequent death of the girl from pneumonia, after an illness of just ten days, furnished the dramatic finale to this account and gives a poignancy to this "roll call" song. But through this experience, these words with their accompanying music were born; they have since found an important place in the pages of our hymnals and in the lives of God's people.

James Black was appointed to serve on the joint commission for the *Methodist Hymnal* of 1905. He was the only gospel song composer to serve on the commission, yet interestingly, not one of his own songs was included in that publication. In addition to his "roll call" hymn, several of his other gospel songs, still in use today, include "Where Jesus Is 'Tis Heaven There" and "Look to the Lamb of God."

Upon occasion, James Black could be a little testy and sarcastic, it seems. Here is a portion of a letter he wrote, in 1913, from his home in Williamsport, Pennsylvania, to a Robert Coleman, who had just requested permission to use the "roll call" song in a hymnal he was compiling. This was Black's rather interesting reply:

> Everybody else is raising the prices of the great songs and why should not I? It is the common consent of all people everywhere that "When the Roll is Called Up Yonder" is the greatest song that has ever been written for the last twenty-five years. I am of that opinion myself. It goes into more books than any other one gospel song in the English language. That tells the story. Hereafter, the price of that song shall be $25.00. Do you blame me?

311

Most students of hymnody would never state that this hymn text should ever be rated as a great, literary classic. Nor does the music have unusual interest. The entire song is harmonized with just four basic chords. The rhythm is really rather monotonous with its repetitive, dotted eighth and sixteenth figures throughout. Yet, like so much of our early gospel music, this hymn meets the spiritual needs of many people—it lifts the heart in praise, it strengthens the soul in prayer, and it provides hope for the future. In the final analysis, all we can say is thank God for simply-stated gospel songs that minister in a very heart-felt manner to the spiritual needs of people in each generation.

*   *   *

"He who thinks most of heaven will do most for earth."
Anonymous

"Heaven is a place prepared for those who are prepared for it."
Houston Times, All Church Press

Wonderful Grace of Jesus

Haldor Lillenas, 1885-1959   Haldor Lillenas, 1885-1959

1. Won-der-ful grace of Je - sus, Great-er than all my sin;
2. Won-der-ful grace of Je - sus, Reach-ing to all the lost,
3. Won-der-ful grace of Je - sus, Reach-ing the most de - filed,

How shall my tongue de - scribe it, Where shall its praise be - gin?
By it I have been par - doned, Saved to the ut - ter - most;
By its trans-form - ing pow - er Mak - ing him God's dear child,

Tak - ing a - way my bur - den, Set - ting my spir - it free,
Chains have been torn a - sun - der, Giv - ing me lib - er - ty,
Pur - chas - ing peace and heav - en For all e - ter - ni - ty—

312

For the won - der-ful grace of Je - sus reach - es me.
For the won - der-ful grace of Je - sus reach - es me.
And the won - der-ful grace of Je - sus reach - es me.

CHORUS

the match-less grace of Je - sus,
Won - der-ful the match-less grace of Je - sus, Deep-er than the

Wonderful Grace of Jesus

the roll - ing sea; Won - der - ful
might-y roll - ing sea; High- er than the moun-tain,

grace, all suf - fi - - - cient for
spark-ling like a foun - tain, All - suf - fi - cient grace for e - ven

me, for e - ven me; Broad- er than the scope of my trans -
me; trans -

313

gres - sions, Great-er far than all my sin and shame;
gres-sions, sing it! my sin and shame;

O mag - ni - fy the pre - cious name of Je - sus, Praise His name!

Copyright 1918. Renewal 1946 by Hope Publishing Co., Carol Stream, IL 60188. All rights reserved. Used by permission.

Wonderful Grace of Jesus

Author and Composer—Haldor Lillenas, 1885-1959

> For ye know the grace of our Lord Jesus Christ, that, though He was rich, yet for your sakes He became poor, that ye through His poverty might be rich.
>
> 2 Corinthians 8:9

"Wonderful Grace of Jesus" is certainly one of the most inspiring hymns in our hymnals, one that has been used effectively either as a choir number or by the entire congregation. In fact, seldom can a song leader ask any group for the choice of a favorite without someone in the congregation requesting this still popular hymn, written and composed, in 1918, by one of the important, twentieth-century hymnwriters in this country, Haldor Lillenas.

Haldor Lillenas was born November 19, 1885, on the Island of Stord, in the beautiful fjord country of Bergen, Norway. He immigrated to this country as a child and lived with his family in South Dakota for two years before settling in Asotria, Oregon. He was raised in the Lutheran Church and was confirmed at the age of fifteen. Through the ministry of the Peniel Mission in Portland, Oregon, however, he had a dramatic conversion experience, in 1906, and soon felt the call to preach the gospel and to write songs that would reach the hearts of people. Haldor attended Pasadena College in Los Angeles and then married Bertha Mae Wilson, a songwriter in her own right. Following their marriage, Mr. and Mrs. Lillenas became active in the leadership of Nazarene churches.

For the next several years, Mr. and Mrs. Lillenas traveled extensively throughout this country, conducting evangelistic meetings as well as furnishing songs and choir music for many of the foremost song leaders of that era, such as Charles Alexander and Homer Hammontree. During this period, Mr. Lillenas also served short pastorates in various Nazarene churches in California, Texas, Indiana, and Illinois. It was while pastoring the Church of the Nazarene at Auburn, Illinois, between 1916 and 1919, that Haldor Lillenas wrote "Wonderful Grace of Jesus." He has left the following account:

In 1917, Mrs. Lillenas and I built our first little home in the town of Olivet, Illinois. Upon its completion, we had scarcely any money left to furnish the little home. Having no piano at the time, and needing an instrument of some kind, I managed to find, at one of the neighbor's home, a little wheezy organ which I purchased for $5.00. With the aid of this instrument, a number of my songs were written which are now popular, including "Wonderful Grace of Jesus." It was sung by the great chorus, in 1918, at the Northfield, Massachusetts Bible Conference, being introduced for the first time by Homer Hammontree.

314

"Wonderful Grace of Jesus" was first published, in 1922, in the *Tabernacle Choir Book*, edited by R. J. Oliver and Lance Latham, for which Mr. Lillenas was paid the grand sum of $5.00 for a hymn which soon became popular world-wide. Although we generally sing this hymn with an inspirational, brisk tempo, Mr. Lillenas often complained that most congregations sang the hymn too fast. "A song should be performed in such a fashion that the words can be comfortably pronounced without undue haste," he often said.

In 1924, Haldor Lillenas founded the Lillenas Music Company in Indianapolis, Indiana, which was later merged with the Nazarene Publishing Company in 1930. Lillenas remained with this company as music editor for the next twenty years. Before his home-going on August 18, 1959 at Aspen, Colorado, he was recognized for his many accomplishments and awarded the honorary Doctor of Music degree from Olivet Nazarene College of Kankakee, Illinois.

Altogether, Haldor wrote approximately 4,000 gospel hymn texts and tunes. In addition to "Wonderful Grace of Jesus," these are some of his songs that are still widely used by Christian congregations: "The Bible Stands Like a Rock Undaunted," "It Is Glory Just to Walk With Him," "Jesus Has Lifted Me," "Peace, Peace, Wonderful Peace," and "My Wonderful Lord."

"Wonderful Grace of Jesus" was especially useful as an inspiring mass choir selection in the days of the great evangelistic crusades in the early years of this century. Charles Alexander, an historic name among song leaders, was one who could assemble and inspire a great mass choir, using this hymn, at one of the city-wide campaigns during that era.

Charles Alexander lived from 1867 to 1920 and is regarded as the forerunner of the present-day evangelistic song leader. He became recognized as the most picturesque, most attractive, and one of the most successful and best-loved "singing evangelists" ever known. Through his leadership, there developed the concept of the song leader as the master of ceremonies for the service as well as the leader of the music. It was Alexander who spoke of "warming up" the audience in order to get mass involvement in the service.

Through the years writers have been impressed with the thought of God's grace—the unmerited favor of an omnipotent God in providing redemption for lost mankind. And truly any sincere believer must also stand in awe and be as impressed as Haldor Lillenas was with the scope of God's grace—"deeper than the mighty rolling sea," "higher than the mountain," "greater far than all my sin and shame." How important it is that we realize with conviction, that it is grace and grace alone that assures our eternal relationship with God—nothing that we can do or feel—simply the personal appropriation of God's wonderful grace.

100 Worthy Is the Lamb

Don Wyrtzen, 1942-   Don Wyrtzen, 1942-

316

© Copyright 1973 by Singspiration, Division of the Zondervan Corporation. All rights reserved. Used by permission.

Worthy is the Lamb

Author and Composer—Don Wyrtzen, 1942-
Scripture Reference—Revelation 5:12

> Thou art worthy, O Lord, to receive glory and honor and power; for Thou has created all things, and for Thy pleasure they are and were created.   Revelation 4:11

This popular, contemporary hymn is based directly on the words of Scripture, a text that could well be the believers' theme throughout eternity:

> Worthy is the Lamb that was slain to receive power, and riches, and wisdom, and strength, and honor, and glory, and blessing.   Revelation 5:12

Don Wyrtzen, Director of Music Publications for Singspiration Music, recalls the events that led to the writing of this hymn:

> In 1970, I was in Mexico City assisting evangelist Luis Palau conduct a series of crusades. As the messages were in Spanish, I spent the time during the sermons writing new songs. One day I became particularly impressed with the great truth of Revelation 5:12, and thought how effective this verse could be, if only the proper music was used to enhance it. I thought about the music used in the secular song "The Impossible Dream" and decided that a similar musical style would work well with these words. "Worthy" was first used in a musical titled "Breakthrough," in which I collaborated with John E. Walvoord. In more recent times, I have worked with Phil and Lynne Brower in producing an Easter musical based on this hymn. God has used this song to bless and inspire His people during the past decade perhaps more than any other work I have been privileged to write, for which I will be eternally grateful to Him.

Donald John Wyrtzen was born on August 16, 1942, in Brooklyn, New York. He is the son of Jack Wyrtzen, well-known founder and director of Word of Life, International. From childhood, Don remembers a life of continuous exposure to outstanding Christian speakers and musicians through his father's ministry. Don's songwriting efforts began in his early teens. By the time he had finished high school, Don had already written a number of gospel choruses, which his father published in his *Word of Life* chorus books. In 1963, Don graduated from the Moody Bible Institute and two years later received a bachelor's degree in music from King's College. Desiring to be even better grounded in the Scriptures, Don Wyrtzen entered Dallas Theological Seminary and received his Th.M. degree in 1969. During the summers of 1968-1970, he also did graduate work in composition at North Texas State University. Throughout these years, Don was also involved in teaching music at the Dallas Bible College and the Dallas Theological Seminary and served as music director at the Northwest Presbyterian Church in Dallas, Texas.

It was during his seminary years that Don Wyrtzen became really serious about gospel songwriting. Several of his early successes were "Yesterday, Today and Tomorrow" and "The Day That I Met Jesus." In 1970, Don and his family moved to Grand Rapids, Michigan, to accept a position at Singspiration Music, Inc. as a writer and an editing assistant with John W. Peterson. In this capacity Don arranged, orchestrated, and conducted various John Peterson musicals and numerous sacred albums. Today, Don Wyrtzen is responsible for all of the music publications produced by Singspiration. Currently, Don has written or composed more than two hundred sacred songs, including contemporary favorites such as "Love Was When," "Our Sacrifice of Praise," "Unbounded Grace," and "Finally Home."

Mr. Wyrtzen states that his goal in writing gospel music has always been to set God's truth to music in simple, attractive form. Once a new title or phrase inspires his thinking, he then spends more time developing the words of the song than he does the music. Don further believes that music itself has no absolutes, only the connotation that people give it, so that any style of music can be potentially used in the worship and service of God. Wyrtzen believes that often the church confuses culture with Scripture and tradition with the Christian life. He cautions, however, that a director or performer must be very sensitive to the spiritual needs and cultural tastes of a congregation when deciding on the style of music to use, as it is very possible that a certain association that people may give a style of music may make that music inappropriate for the Christian ministry.

318

It is encouraging to realize, that in every generation, God raises up individuals such as Don Wyrtzen with the talent and spiritual convictions to communicate His eternal truths, through the appealing yet easily understood means of gospel hymnody.

> "Come, let us join our cheerful songs
> With angels round the throne;
> Ten thousand thousand are their tongues,
> But all their joys are one.
> 'Worthy the Lamb that died,' they cry,
> 'To be exalted thus.'
> 'Worthy is the Lamb,' our lips reply,
> 'For He was slain for us.'
> "The whole creation joins as one
> To bless the sacred Name
> Of Him that sits upon throne,
> And to adore the Lamb."
>
> Isaac Watts

101   Ye Must Be Born Again

William T. Sleeper, 1819-1904   George C. Stebbins, 1846-1945

1. A rul-er once came to Je-sus by night To ask Him the
2. Ye chil-dren of men, at-tend to the word So sol-emn-ly
3. O ye who would en-ter that glo-ri-ous rest And sing with the

way of sal-va-tion and light; The Mas-ter made an-swer in
ut-tered by Je-sus the Lord; And let not this mes-sage to
ran-somed the song of the blest, The life ev-er-last-ing if

words true and plain, "Ye must be born a-gain."
you be in vain, "Ye must be born a-gain."
ye would ob-tain, "Ye must be born a-gain."

CHORUS

"Ye must be born a-gain, Ye must be born a-gain; I ver-i-ly,

319

ver-i-ly say un-to thee, Ye must be born a-gain."

Ye Must Be Born Again

Author—William T. Sleeper, 1819-1904
Composer—George C. Stebbins, 1846-1945
Scripture Reference—John 3:3-7

> Jesus answered and said unto him, Verily, verily, I say unto thee, except a man be born again, he cannot see the kingdom of God.   John 3:3

The composer of this hymn, George C. Stebbins, relates in his *Memoirs and Reminiscences*, published in 1924, his recollection of the writing of this song in August, 1877, while he was assisting Dr. George F. Pentecost in an evangelistic crusade in Worcester, Massachusetts:

> During those meetings, one of the subjects preached upon was the New Birth. While presenting the truth, enforcing it by referring to various passages of Scripture, Dr. Pentecost quoted Our Lord's words to Nicodemus, "Verily, verily, I say unto you, ye must be born again." It occurred to me that by taking the line, "Ye must be born again," and by transferring the word "I" from the middle of the first line to the beginning, so it would read, "I verily, verily, say unto thee, ye must be born again," those passages would then fall into rhythmical form, and by the use of some repetitions could be made available for a musical setting, and also for a chorus to a hymn, if some suitable verses could be found...I spoke to Rev. William Sleeper, one of the pastors of the city who sometimes wrote hymns, of my impression and asked him if he would write me some verses on the subject. He acted at once upon my suggestion and soon after came to me with the hymn that bears his name. Before the meetings closed, a musical setting was made.

320

The author, William True Sleeper, was born on February 9, 1819, at Danbury, New Hampshire. Following his graduation from the Andover Theological Seminary, Mr. Sleeper was ordained as a Congregational minister, serving in home mission work in Worcester, Massachusetts, and later in the state of Maine, where he helped establish three churches. In 1883, Mr. Sleeper published a book of verse entitled *The Rejected King and Hymns of Jesus.*

The composer, George C. Stebbins, is one of the influential names in the development of gospel music. He contributed the music for several hundred hymn texts, including such other well-known favorites as: "Have Thine Own Way, Lord!" (No. 32), "Saved By Grace" (No. 76), "There Is a Green Hill Far Away" (*101 Hymn Stories,* No. 96) "Jesus, I Come;" "Take Time to Be Holy;" and "Savior, Breathe an Evening Blessing." George Stebbins was also involved in publishing numerous gospel song collections, including his contributions in editing several editions of Ira

Sankey's important *Gospel Hymns* series. Mr. Stebbins was known as one of the truly fine song leaders of his day. For a quarter of a century he led the music for the great Northfield Bible Conference, begun by D. L. Moody, and was the music director for several other large conferences such as the Christian Endeavor Conventions, which were held annually at the turn of the century.

"Ye Must Be Born Again" first appeared in *Gospel Hymns* No. 3, published in 1878. The writing of this song was the beginning of a long friendship between William Sleeper and George Stebbins. Several years later, these two collaborated in writing and composing another fine gospel hymn, "Jesus, I Come," first published in *Gospel Hymns* No.5, 1887. This hymn and "Ye Must Be Born Again" have been widely used for evangelistic purposes to the present time.

*   *   *

"Better never to have been born at all, than never to have been born again."
Unknown

"Before God can deliver us from ourselves, we must undeceive ourselves."
St. Augustine

SALVATION'S MESSAGE

"Salvation's message, ringing so clear is calling sinners,
   Its word to hear;
God's voice is calling to small and great;
   'Come to the Savior, ere its too late.'

"Sinner now hasten, God's Word believe, come to the Savior,
   New life receive;
Your sin He'll pardon, and set you free,
   Jesus is longing your Lord to be.

"Christ the dear Savior, offers His love, and He will give you,
   Grace from above;
He died on Calv'ry, sin to atone, do not reject Him,
   Make Him your own.

"Gladness in sorrow, peace in great strife, clamness in death
   And joy in this life;
A home in heaven where all is bliss, all this He'll give you,
   If you'll be His."
Wm. Skooglund

SELECTED BIBLIOGRAPHY

Bailey, Albert E. *The Gospel in Hymns*, New York: Charles Scribner's Sons, 1950.

Barrows, Cliff, ed. *Crusade Hymn Stories*. Chicago: Hope Publishing Co., 1967.

Benson, Louis F. *The English Hymn*. New York: George H. Doran Co., 1915. (Reprint-John Knox Co., 1962).

Blanchard, Kathleen. *Stories of Favorite Hymns*. Grand Rapids: Zondervan Publishing House, 1940.

Brown, Theron, and Butterworth, Hezekiah. *The Story of the Hymns and Tunes*. New York: George H. Doran Co., 1906.

Clark, W. Thorburn. *Stories of Fadeless Hymns*. Nashville: Broadman Press, 1949.

Davies, James P. *Sing With Understanding*. Chicago: Covenant Press, 1966.

Douglas, Charles W. *Church Music in History and Practice*. New York: Charles Scribner's Sons, 1937. Revised 1962 by Leonard Ellinwood.

Emurian, Ernest K. *Living Stories of Famous Hymns*. Boston: W. A. Wilde Co., 1955.

Erickson, J. Irving. *Twice-Born Hymns*. Chicago: Covenant Press, 1976.

Frost, Maurice. *Historical Companion to Hymns Ancient and Modern*. London: William Clowes and Sons, 1962.

Gabriel, C. H. *The Singers and Their Songs*. Winona Lake, Ind.: The Rodeheaver Co., 1915.

Hagedorn, Ivan H. *Stories of Great Hymn Writers*. Grand Rapids: Zondervan Publishing House, 1948.

Hustad, Donald P. *Hymns for the Living Church*. Carol Stream, Ill.: Hope Publishing Co., 1978.

Hustad, Donald P. *Dictionary-Handbook to Hymns for the Living Church*. Carol Stream, Ill.: Hope Publishing Co.

Hustad, Donald P. *Jubilate! Church Music in the Evangelical Tradition*. Carol Stream, Ill.: Hope Publishing Co.

Julian, John. *A Dictionary of Hymnology*. 2 volumes. New York: Charles Scribner's Sons, 1892. (Reprint 2 vols.) Grand Rapids: Kregel Publications, 1985.

Kerr, Phil. *Music in Evangelism and Stories of Famous Christian Songs*. Glendale, Calif.: Gospel Music Publishers, 1939.

Lillenas, Haldor. *Modern Gospel Song Stories*. Kansas City, Mo.: Lillenas Publishing Company, 1952.

Loewen, Alice. Moyer, Harold. Oyer, Mary. *Exploring the Mennonite Hymnal: Handbook*. Newton, Kans.: Faith and Life Press, 1983.

Marks, Harvey B. *The Rise and Growth of English Hymnody*. New York: Fleming H. Revell Company, 1938.

McCutchan, Robert G. *Hymn Tune Names, Their Sources and Significance*. New York: Abingdon Press, 1957.

McCutchan, Robert G. *Our Hymnody: A Manual of the Methodist Hymnal*, 2nd ed. New York and Nashville: Abingdon-Cokesbury Press, 1942.

Peterson, John W. *The Miracle Goes On*. Grand Rapids: Zondervan Publishing House, 1976.

Reynolds, William J. *Hymns of Our Faith, A Handbook for the Baptist Hymnal*. Nashville: Broadman Press, 1964.

Reynolds, William J. *Companion to the Baptist Hymnal*. Nashville: Broadman Press, 1976.

Reynolds, William J. and Price, M. *A Joyful Sound*. New York: Holt, Rinehart and Winston, 1978.

Routley, Erik. *Hymns Today and Tomorrow*. New York: Abingdon Press, 1964.

Routley, Erik. *Hymns and the Faith*. Grand Rapids: Wm. B. Eerdmans Publishing Co., 1968.

Rudin, Cecilia Margaret. *Stories of Hymns We Love*. Chicago: John Rudin and Co. Inc., 1945.

Ruffin, Bernard. *Fanny Crosby*. New York: United Church Press, 1976.

Ryden, Ernest Edwin. *The Story of Christian Hymnody*. Rock Island, Ill.: Augustana Press, 1959.

Sallee, James. *A History of Evangelistic Hymnody*. Grand Rapids: Baker Book House, 1978.

Sankey, Ira D. *My Life and the Story of the Gospel Hymns*. New York: Harper and Brothers Publishers, 1906.

Sanville, George W. *Forty Gospel Hymn Stories*. Winona Lake, Ind.: The Rodeheaver-Hall-Mack Company, 1943.

Sellers, E. O. *Evangelism in Sermon and Song*. Chicago: Moody Press, 1946.

Shea, George Beverly with Fred Bauer. *Songs That Lift the Heart*. Minneapolis: World Wide Publications.

Smith, Oswald J. *Oswald J. Smith's Hymn Stories*. Winona lake, Ind.: The Rodeheaver Company, 1963.

Stebbins, George C. *Reminiscences and Gospel Hymn Stories*. New York: George H. Doran Company, 1924.

Selected Bibliography

Sydnor, James R. *The Hymn and Congregational Singing*. Richmond: John Knox Press, 1960.

Thompson, Ronald W. *Who's Who of Hymn Writers*. London: Epworth Press, 1967.

Wake, Arthur N. *Companion to Hymnbook for Christian Worship*. St. Louis, Mo.: The Bethany Press, 1970.

INDEX OF AUTHORS, TRANSLATORS, COMPOSERS, TUNE NAMES

325

Index of Authors, Translators, Composers, Tune Names

Index of Authors, Translators, Composers, Tune Names

327

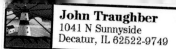

John Traughber
1041 N Sunnyside
Decatur, IL 62522-9749

An Ideal Companion Book!

Destined to be a daily
devotional classic . . .

by
Kenneth W. Osbeck

Author of:

101 Hymn Stories and
101 More Hymn Stories

An inspirational daily devotional based on 366 great hymns of the Christian faith. Each day's devotional highlights biblical truths drawn from true-to-life stories behind the writing of these well-known hymns of the faith. Each story includes a portion of the hymn itself, as well as suggested Scripture readings, meditations, and practical application.

Your personal or family devotional time will be enhanced by the challenging and inspiring thoughts contained in this thrilling collection of classical and contemporary hymn stories.

"... a must for both the home library and the church library. ... the ideal book for the church musician. ... It will make a great Christmas gift too."
—*The Church Music Report*

ISBN 0-8254-3425-4   384 pp.   paperback

Available from your local Christian bookstore, or

kregel
PUBLICATIONS

P.O. Box 2607, Grand Rapids, MI 49501